Counseling Multicultural and Diverse Populations: Strategies for Practitioners

FOURTH EDITION

Counseling Multicultural and Diverse Populations: Strategies for Practitioners

FOURTH EDITION

Written and Edited by

Nicholas A. Vacc, Susan B. DeVaney,
Johnston M. Brendel

Brunner-Routledge
NEW YORK AND HOVE

Published in 2003 by
Brunner-Routledge
29 West 35th Street
New York, NY 10001
www.brunner-routledge.com

Published in Great Britain by
Brunner-Routledge
27 Church Road
Hove, East Sussex
BN3 2FA
www.brunner-routledge.co.uk

Copyright © 2003 by Taylor & Francis Books, Inc.

Brunner-Routledge is an imprint of the Taylor & Francis Group.
Printed in the United States of America on acid-free paper.

10   9   8   7   6   5   4   3   2   1

Library of Congress Cataloging-in-Publication Data

Counseling multicultural and diverse populations : practical strategies
for counselors / edited by Nicholas A. Vacc, Susan Beck DeVaney,
Johnston M. Brendel.— 4th ed.
     p. ; cm.
Rev. ed. of: Experiencing and counseling multicultural and diverse
populations. 3rd ed. c1995.
   Includes bibliographical references and index.
   ISBN 1-58391-348-3 (hardcover : alk. paper)
   1. Social work with minorities—United States. 2.Minorities—Counseling of—
United States. [DNLM: 1. Counseling—methods—United States. 2. Cultural
Diversity—United States. 3. Ethnic Groups—United States. 4. Minority
Groups—United States. WM 55 C8537 2002] I. Vacc, Nicholas A. II.
DeVaney, Susan B., 1947– III. Brendel, Johnston M., 1961– IV.
Experiencing and counseling multicultural and diverse populations.

HV3176 .C68 2002
362.84′00973—dc21

                                                  2002153102

*To Nicholas Vacc, whose legacy of caring
and respect for all people continues
through his students and mentees, his writings,
and the organizations to which he devoted his energy.*

Contents

Counseling Multicultural and Diverse Populations: Strategies for Practitioners

FOURTH EDITION

CHAPTER 1

Introduction

Nicholas A. Vacc
Susan B. DeVaney
Johnston M. Brendel

Nicholas A. Vacc was the Joe Rosenthal Excellence Professor and past chairperson of the Department of Counseling and Educational Development at the University of North Carolina, Greensboro. He received his degrees from Western Reserve University, Syracuse University, and State University of New York. In former years he worked as a public school teacher and counselor, school psychologist, Veterans Administration counselor, and director of a university counselor center. During the course of his career he served as president of the Association for Assessment in Counseling; editor of *Measurement and Evaluation in Counseling and Development*; and president of Chi Sigma Iota, the international counseling honor society. He was instrumental in the development of the NBCC examination and the CACREP standards for professional preparation. Dr. Vacc had over 120 professional publications to his credit and was the recipient of many awards, including the Brooks Distinguished Mentor Award and the Sweeney Professional Leadership Award. He passed away in June, 2002.

Susan B. DeVaney, Ed.D., obtained her doctorate in counselor education from the University of North Carolina, Greensboro, in 1990 and worked in the field for twelve years. Before her retirement in 2002 she served as the counselor in residence at the Early Childhood Development Center at Texas A&M University–Corpus Christi, initiated the Family Place for

Counseling and Referral on the university campus, coordinated career and social skills programs for disadvantaged youth and their families, and incorporated service learning projects into her courses. She currently works as a freelance writer in North Carolina.

Johnston M. Brendel, Ed.D., obtained his doctorate in counselor education from the College of William and Mary in Virginia. He is an associate professor at Texas A&M University—Corpus Christi, and a former secondary school counselor. He works extensively with at-risk youth designing and evaluating effective programs that target this population. His research interests include adult development, cognitive development, and family involvement in schools.

SCOPE OF THE FOURTH EDITION

This book presents sixteen chapters devoted to thirteen special populations, designated by ethnicity, religion, physical characteristics, circumstance, or lifestyle. The authors of these chapters are counselors and counselor educators, and at least one author of each chapter, with the exception of "Counseling Incarcerated Clients," is also a member of the group under consideration. Our goal is to provide both a personal and an academic perspective on each population. In addition, we wish to provide information and insight into the diverse nature and commonly encountered strengths, barriers, difficulties, issues, and experiences of each population.

Published originally in 1980 as *Let Me Be Me: Special Populations and the Helping Professional*, the current edition represents a substantial transformation from its predecessors. The editors thought it important that we include populations with which today's counselors come in contact as well as groups associated with significant discrimination and misunderstanding. To achieve those ends, we have added chapters dealing with counseling Arab Americans, multiracial persons, incarcerated individuals, men, and women. We considered including other groups as well: religious groups such as conservative Christians, Jews, or Buddhists; persons united by poverty and dependence on government assistance; life stage groups such as adolescents; persons who are different in terms of their body size or shape. We struggled to be as inclusive as possible, but for reasons of space and thematic duplication, reluctantly left many important populations for others to describe. Using a similar rationale, we combined what were once separate chapters on Cuban Americans and Mexican Americans into a single chapter devoted to the American Hispanic population and incorporated material on single parents and women reentering the workplace into several other chapters. Finally, the chapter that once described the homosexual population now also includes bisexual, lesbian, transsexual, and transgendered persons and is entitled "Counseling Sexual Minority Persons." Although the fourth edition is by no means all-encompassing, we believe that the difficulties, experiences, and characteristics of the groups presented are representative of the multitude of divergent, unique, and ethnic subgroups in American society— these are truly *multicultural* and *diverse* populations.

In addition to the revised format, we are proud to introduce fifteen new authors who have worked diligently to present insights from their personal experience, demographics from the recent national census, and syntheses of current research. Each of these authors is a professional with both personal and scholarly experience with his or her selected population. Although we requested that the authors address common topics within their chapters (history, current counseling issues, career development, etc.), readers will find that the authors have distinct styles and viewpoints that sometimes vary substantially from those of their cocontributors. We believe that the unique quality of each chapter mirrors the uniqueness of the group it portrays. Readers may find themselves drawn to one or another chapter, much as they might be drawn to one group over another. We urge readers to use these reactions as an avenue to personal awareness of biases and preferences.

PURPOSE OF THE BOOK

The purpose of this book is to expose mental health practitioners such as counselors, psychologists, and social workers to the unique characteristics and social issues of representative American subgroups as a basis for understanding, assisting, and collaborating with members of these populations. We believe that the professional's struggle to acquire sufficient knowledge, awareness, and skill to work effectively with diverse populations is both ongoing and relative. It is ongoing in that one can never learn all there is to know about people from all ethnic groups, backgrounds, beliefs, and circumstances. It is relative in that helping transactions may be best judged in terms of their degree of effectiveness rather than the absolute correctness of the intervention. The process of becoming an effective helper begins with an openness to lifelong learning, self-examination, and supervised counseling practice. It is our hope that this book will contribute to these conditions. Assimilating information about groups and individuals whose racial, social, religious, and/or cultural backgrounds; sex; physical abilities; or language differ from those of mainstream society is a beginning. Adding to that an examination of one's own culture, biases, thoughts and beliefs, attitudes, and orientations deepens understanding through comparison. Stretching one's experience through interaction with diverse populations under the guidance of an experienced counselor supervisor taps the dimension of skill. In the hands of a receptive reader even a single book, such as this one, can produce grand results.

THE EDITORS' PHILOSOPHY

Our belief is that helping professionals can be instrumental in reducing the social and emotional barriers that prevent many members of America's subgroups from becoming secure citizens. To do this, helping professionals must make a concerted effort to approach their clientele with both care and understanding. Communicating with warmth, empathy, and authenticity are the core conditions for effective counseling—conditions relatively simple to describe but difficult to embrace and create when one faces the unknown or unfamiliar. Expanding one's knowledge base adds to those core conditions because knowing *that* makes situations more familiar and less uncertain. Hearing from members of a group different from one's own presents an opportunity to learn how others think, how they are products of their experience. It gives one knowledge of other cultures and creates a basis for awareness of one's own heritage.

Awareness of oneself and one's culture is as important as knowing about other cultures. As counselor educators, the editors have known many inexperienced master's students who, thinking that cultures are the property only of ethnic minority groups, have proclaimed, "I don't have a culture." The natural but naive understanding that what I experience is the norm and what others experience is not, forms a barrier to effective cross-cultural understanding. In addition, the phenomenon of assumed similarity, the belief that everyone is like me or should be like me, hinders accurate understanding of those who are different socially and culturally. We might ask ourselves, for example, is it truly possible that the Amish do not want television? That they choose to live without buttons and zippers in their clothing? Helpers with a sound cognitive knowledge of their clients' cultural background will more easily understand the source and reasons for behaviors that may appear odd or peculiar at times. Understanding one's heritage, belief system, values, and life assumptions requires honesty, openness, and continual self-examination. It is our hope that readers will use this book to hold their unique personal histories up to the mirror of our multicultural society.

In our view, knowledge and awareness are preconditions for good counseling. Positive counseling outcomes require a helper who embodies the core conditions, values the richness of human diversity, and looks deeply into self and others. Positive outcomes also require a helper with a broad knowledge base. One aspect of that knowledge is the acquisition of skills and a canny sense of when to apply them. Although skill development is ongoing and never ending, all students of counseling must make a beginning somewhere. We suggest that one point of beginning is engagement in the experiential activities at the end of each chapter in this book. Mustering the courage to come into contact with an unfamiliar group of people helps us to remember how it feels to be an outsider, how much we want to feel welcome, how awkward it is to make one's way in a new land. Engaging in conversation or discussion with people who speak another language, espouse a different system of thought, or seek a different result challenges us to step outside our comfort zones and stretch our interpersonal skills.

When functioning entirely within a congenial and familiar cultural situation, helpers tend to misapprehend and impose their personal values on the client. In many cases they do not recognize that they are doing so. In others, they hold their values so dear that they believe everyone should accept them. Imagine scenarios in which you might encounter the following familiar questions and statements, possibly similar to ones you have uttered yourself:

How can this woman continue to have more children when she can't support the ones she has?

How can that man expect societal acceptance when the Bible clearly states that homosexuality is a sin?

Of course we should search all dark, Arabic-looking people in airports; our national security is at stake.

If people come to live in this country they should learn to speak English.

As you read the subsequent chapters, you will gain appreciation for the fact that although all people desire acceptance, they also enjoy their uniqueness. In many cases they do not want to be mainstreamed, to develop middle-class values, or to lose their individuality and dignity. They prefer that their difficulties and differences be understood rather than interpreted and evaluated. Savvy counselors are not concerned with the *shoulds*. They are concerned with helping the individual navigate the storms of life. Part of their charge is to help people understand the price to be paid for being oneself, a major and lifelong challenge for all humanity. Without appreciation of the person, the group, and the culture, counselors are unlikely to recognize the level at which their clientele grapple with the problem of acceptance, to meet them at that level, and to facilitate improved individual functioning within the family, the subgroup, or society at large.

HISTORICAL AND POLITICAL INFLUENCES

We are all a product of our time and history. Entering into life in the 1960s, 1980s, or any decade in and of itself affects our perspectives on education, war, success, politics, morality, and human diversity. The social and political mood of the times directly affects national policy and opportunity for special groups. One of the editors, for example, grew up in a totally segregated society. Until she was in college she never attended a class or ate in a restaurant with anyone who was not Caucasian. Her only direct experience with different cultures came during vacation travel. Other, younger counselors may find this degree of segregation difficult to imagine but may have personal experience with court-ordered bussing, affirmative action, the Americans with Disabilities Act, the glass ceiling, or sexual harassment. Immigration and rapid shifts in demographics have fueled national debates on bilingual education, the rights of illegal aliens, and establishing English as the official national language.

Over the last fifteen years the counseling profession has promoted cultural awareness and, to a lesser degree, defined appropriate cross-cultural counseling practice. Counseling itself is a relatively new discipline, tracing its origins to the social reformers of the early twentieth century and solidifying as a profession in the 1960s and '70s. The study of counseling across cultures, a branch of the profession, is still in its infancy and enjoys a relatively small body of supportive research. Because the field is so new, definitions and principles are in the process of gaining acceptance. Scholars argue about the relative applicability and appropriateness of terms such as *cross-cultural, multicultural, transcultural,* and *diverse* populations. Is *disadvantaged, handicapped, at-risk, underserved, underorganized,* or *challenged* the best descriptor of a given group or individual? Are people with whom counselors work considered clients, consumers, or customers? Because there is wide disparity in the use of the language, the editors have left decisions regarding terminology to the chapter authors themselves.

Scholars also disagree about the assumptions basic to counseling and supporting groups and individuals in a given population. Again, the chapter authors are highly trained professionals and have their own assumptions, which may differ somewhat from those given below. Keeping this in mind, the editors nevertheless venture to supply some assumptions they have used in their research and publication, teaching, and counseling practice.

1. Individuals are products of their culture and experience and cannot be considered apart from the systems in which they participate.
2. People are individuals first and group members second.
3. Depending on the situation, the individual or the group may be the unit of consideration in counseling.
4. Accurate information is necessary as a foundation for providing services for the individual.
5. Self-awareness, including awareness of one's place within the subgroups and systems of which she or he is a member, is basic to becoming an effective counselor.

6. Counselor skill development occurs over time through a combination of training, experience, practice, and supervision.
7. Staffing of services by adequately trained professionals through preservice and in-service programs of preparation and skill development is essential to effective counseling practice.

Having supplied a summary of our rationale for creating *Counseling Multicultural and Diverse Populations: Strategies for Practitioners*, we would be remiss if we did not thank our mentors, teachers, clients, students, and collaborators of all ethnicities, backgrounds, and belief systems. We especially thank those who have presented arguments and placed barriers, challenges, and irritations in our paths. Without them we would not have traveled from the old to the new, from uninformed to better informed, from less to more skillful. We are grateful for the future obstacles that will move us off our current sticking spots and make us wiser and better counselors. Finally, we thank the readers of this book. The journey to human understanding and helpful interaction is a fascinating and difficult one, and we wish you well in your pursuit of effective practice with multicultural and diverse populations.

CHAPTER 2

Self-Awareness and Cultural Understanding

James Fuller

James O. Fuller is an associate professor of counseling and acting dean of the College of Graduate Studies at Indiana Wesleyan University. He is the director of the community counseling track at IWU. His interests are in the areas of school counseling, family counseling, and multicultural issues in counseling. Before his doctoral training, he was a school counselor in Seoul, Korea, at the Seoul Foreign School, an international school for expatriate children. He earned his B.A. in psychology at Asbury College, his M.Div. with an emphasis in counseling at Asbury Theological Seminary, and his Ph.D. at the University of North Carolina, Greensboro.

Dr. Fuller would like to add special thanks to Mindy Pierce, who assisted with editing and revising much of this chapter.

> Without willing it, I had gone from being ignorant of being ignorant to being aware of being aware.
> —Maya Angelou, *I Know Why the Caged Bird Sings*, p. 230

INTRODUCTION

When Socrates said, "know thyself," he was probably talking about a search to discover the world of one's inner self. This was, of course, the major thrust of the "find myself" decade of the '60s in the United States.

Little did Socrates know in his time, and little did we know in the '60s that "know thyself" would take a different slant for us in the twenty-first century. We need to understand ourselves in order to more adequately live and operate in a diverse society.

Counseling is an activity traditionally associated with a White, homogeneous, Western society (Sue, 1992). Anything attributed primarily to only one culture is monocultural or monoculturalism. In the United States some have used this concept to imply that a White, homogeneous, Western culture is "right" and superior to other cultures. I was fortunate to be able to live for one year in Honduras and twelve years in Seoul, South Korea. In both places, I was appalled and embarrassed at the apparently superior attitudes that Americans displayed. They were often loud and demanding of the nationals. Even if not intentional, the attitude communicated is one of self-focus and superiority. According to Sue, *ethnocentrism*, the attitude that one's own group (culture, society, etc.) is inherently superior to all others, formed the basis of our traditional theories of counseling and psychotherapy. In addition, ethnocentric attitudes defined what was normal and not normal in counseling and psychotherapy and created an atmosphere that nurtured the belief that differences were not to be tolerated. Many people have been comfortable, successful, and secure with this perspective—in particular, those people who created "the rules."

Much of the misunderstanding between the dominant American cultural group and people from other cultures is attributed to members of the dominant group who believe that everyone is like them or at least should be like them. Many in this group assume that "everyone shares our view of the world." People who tend to assume similarity also tend to lack the desire to understand persons who are socially or culturally different from themselves. Consciously or unconsciously, people who are guilty of assuming similarity do not usually want to change. Change, when it does occur, happens as a result of long-term immersion in cultures or groups different from one's own, or long-term contact with a person or persons different from one's self.

COUNSELOR AWARENESS

The need for counselors to be aware of their own cultures and population groups in order to more effectively serve people of diverse groups and cultures is a growing concern for all counselors in the United States, regardless of culture. Several demographically related reasons for this concern exist: increasing mobility, the growth of racial and ethnic minority groups, the recognition that society is comprised of diverse groups, the aging White American population, and the declining birth rate among White Americans.

The first of these reasons is the ever increasing mobility of the people of the world. The advent of telephones, television, airplanes, radios, computers, fax machines, E-mail, and other even newer technologies has rendered accessible even the remotest corners of the earth. Countries and peoples are not operating in isolation. Worldwide advances in technology promote interconnectedness and interdependence, thus demanding greater cultural awareness. During my last few years in Korea, I experienced a dramatic increase in the ability to communicate with family and business associates in other parts of the world. And the expense of trans-world communication decreased dramatically as well. Advancements in communications technology coupled with increased worldwide travel have certainly contributed to the sense of global interconnectedness.

Other reasons for counselors to be aware of their own cultures and population groups are related to the growth rates of minority groups and the concomitant recognition of diversity within the United States. The 2000 census indicates that White Americans' proportion of the total population in the United States dropped from 80.3% in 1990 to 75.1% in 2000 (U.S. Bureau of the Census, 2000). This fact, combined with the aging White American population, and the decline of White American birth rates are three striking indicators that a growing segment of the population may not accept or respond positively to traditional majority-based forms of counseling and therapy. We, as counselors, have a responsibility to become aware of our values, biases, stereotypes, and assumptions about human behavior as well as the population groups that comprise the United States. We must examine the worldviews we bring to the counseling encounter. Without this awareness and understanding as counselors, we may inadvertently fall into the trap of assumed similarity. Being unaware, unwilling to change, or unable to challenge our own assumptions promotes an ethnocentric point of view.

Whether unconscious or conscious, counselors who are not aware of their own cultural and ethnic heritage run the risk of imposing values on clients through group-learned assumptions or nonverbal behaviors. They will be limited in their treatment plans when working with diverse groups or different cultures. Insufficient understanding of the client's perspectives and a lack of open-mindedness to differences inhibit the counselor's ability to prepare a helpful treatment plan. Clients in cross-cultural settings often lack an understanding of certain issues within the new culture (e.g., communication, eye contact, gestures, expressions, etc.). In order to implement effective treatment plans, counselors must know the areas in which these cross-cultural clients tend to be uninformed or areas with which they may be unfamiliar. With respect to effective counseling of culturally different or diverse populations, counselors also need to know when to refer. Counselors who are unaware of their own heritage and cultural differences risk unintentionally offending clients and/or being offended by the client's behavior.

It is logical to assume that people are not intentionally unaware. We must first consider how we assimilate cultural characteristics without being aware that we possess them. In addition, it is essential to contemplate the process of becoming aware, first of our own culture or group, and then of other cultures or groups.

LEARNING A CULTURE

Cultural Encapsulation

People learn their cultures through *enculturation*, a process by which they acquire the skills necessary to function in a particular sociocultural system (Spradley & Phillips, 1972). An enculturated person "has incorporated the norms of a given culture with such thoroughness that the person exemplifies that culture" (Ward, 1984, p. 54). Becoming enculturated without personal cultural awareness can lead to *cultural encapsulation*. Encapsulation is defined metaphorically by Augsburger (1986) as "the natural tendency among humans to see the world as stretching only from horizon to horizon or to feel at one only with those between familiar boundaries. When such boundaries become—consciously or unconsciously—taken for granted and seen as givens, they function as if absolutized" (p. 22). Augsburger goes on to say that counselors are particularly susceptible to cultural encapsulation. Their sensitivity to communication patterns extends beyond the verbal and the tendency to interpret those patterns according to culturally bound assumptions. At the same time, these skills can be the same ones that aid culturally aware counselors in confronting and overcoming encapsulation.

Cultural encapsulation does not come about from a malicious desire to be ingrown and unaware but from a limited awareness of one's own culture and ethnicity, of other cultures and groups, and of significant differences among cultures. It usually develops as an unconscious attempt to simplify the confusion and contradiction presented by the overwhelming variety of experience found in the world. With regard to counselors, cultural encapsulation can result from four sources: (1) lack of exposure to diverse groups, whether by choice or by happenstance; (2) attaching little importance to noted cultural differences between themselves and their clients; (3) retaining the faulty conviction that certain methods of counseling and therapy are universally applicable; and (4) lack of willingness to explore and question their own beliefs, particularly with regard to stereotypes, biases, and assumptions.

The encapsulated individual rarely recognizes the process of cultural encapsulation. In their book on cross-cultural development, Munroe and Munroe (1975) suggest a helpful mental picture: analogous to the fish that does not notice the water in which it swims, humans remain unaware of the developing culture in which they live. In some ways, counselor training programs contribute to encapsulation by emphasizing traditional methods of counseling and therapy and by minimizing the importance of training counselors to recognize and respond to differences among groups (Augsburger, 1986). By unintentionally or intentionally avoiding these important topics and allowing ethnocentric thinking to persist, training programs implicitly teach cultural bias.

For counselors in a state of encapsulation, a certain sign of impending failure in the therapeutic relationship is the counselor's disregard of cultural difference. It is possibly even more dangerous for a counselor to be unaware that differences exist. In either case, in a world where counseling across cultures or diverse groups is an ever increasing necessity, neglecting to challenge one's assumptions will inevitably lead to an inability to communicate effectively across cultures.

Culture-Learning Model

There are three major ways in which we learn a culture. One is by *infusion*; that is, the unintentional gathering of cultural components and their assimilation into a working pattern of thinking and behavior. I spent most of my childhood in the deep South. By listening and observing relational interaction patterns, I learned, without formal training, that children always use "sir" and "ma'am" when addressing adults. I was somewhat dismayed when I attended college in the northern state of Kentucky that other regions of the United States did not observe those same practices. Similarly, a sense of the primacy of the group, a value held by much of the world, is naturally learned through association with the group, and not through formal education.

Next we learn our cultures intentionally, using more formal aspects of education. During this process our "second-nature" culture moves into consciousness. This cultural learning usually occurs in schools, at seminars and workshops, and through written or visual media. Much of what we have learned informally (e.g., "sir" and "ma'am" or primacy of the group) is reinforced in this setting. Although this form of culture learning requires more formal aspects of education, it is based on the unintentional learning of the first phase. The third method involves learning about cultures other than our own. This process employs aspects from the first two methods of culture learning. The formal elements of education can be a starting point for learning the technical aspects of other cultures, including customs, mores, traditions, and language. Finally, the unintentional aspect of learning again comes into play when we become more comfortable with the new culture, reaching the point where new information is infused rather than consciously added.

With the exception of physiological differences such as disabilities or neonatal drug dependency, most people enter the world in the same way. Newborn babies enter their culture with little or no cultural attachment; they share styles of behavior with other newborn babies, regardless of their cultural context. Gradually, through experience, they learn the culture into which they were born. They cry, smile, eat, crawl, walk, and talk in concert with cultural admonitions.

Within a very few years, babies are proficient enough to attend to their culturally appointed, necessary, and age-appropriate tasks. Through the process of learning, communicating, and incorporating—known as *assimilation*—children become a part of the culture in which they live, and the culture becomes a part of them. This is the process, which my culture-learning model labels as infusion, or being unintentional, that is representative of how all people learn their first culture. In this mode, culture learning is subtle and quiet. It is similar to learning to breathe: a natural and easy development, rather than a forced and difficult process. During this time of development, a person begins to notice within-culture differences. Logically, one would need to understand those in one's own culture who are different, but not significantly different, before attempting to cope with a second culture, which might present much more notable and significant differences. Therefore, within-culture understanding begins at the infusion stage.

The intentional method of learning culture involves school and other means of formal education. In this mode, people transition from the obscure stage of simply existing in a culture to a greater understanding and an increased mindfulness of the culture. This is the opportunity to think about and make explicit parts of one's culture that formerly have been blended and unconscious, to be able to know and understand one's cultural milieu.

Educational institutions contribute substantially to the intentional mode of culture learning. More specifically, schools offer an opportunity to study, examine, and discuss formal history as well as underlying cultural assumptions. These assumptions represent beliefs about government, interpersonal relations, geography, arts and literature, and politics. Although schools provide a primary avenue for implementing the intentional mode, teaching culture is not the primary focus of formal education. Instructors rarely make an intentional effort to teach values, assumptions, and biases; rather than incorporating it into the curriculum, culture learning naturally transpires when people interact. Coming together in an institution or organization or in ordinary, everyday interpersonal situations adds to the experience of culture learning. The unintentional mode, therefore, puts the activities, habits, and values of life into place, and the intentional mode allows for the identification, discussion, and evaluation of these aspects of life.

Learning another culture depends, to a great extent, upon how well an individual can understand his or her cultural roots, including biases, stereotypes, values, and communication patterns. An intensified awareness of one's own culture significantly improves one's interactions and ability to learn another culture. Contrary to what many people might think, learning another culture is different from learning one's own culture: there must be *intentionality*. Once a person is sufficiently enculturated in a first culture, second-culture learning comes about as a result of education. If an individual insufficiently learns his or her own culture, the differences encountered in another culture often generate frustrations rather than understandable differences to which he or she can adjust. I'll use language learning as an example. I once had a conversation with an American expatriate in Honduras. She had lived there for some years, but had not studied Spanish. She was perplexed to discover that the adjective often follows the noun in Spanish language construction. Because she had little understanding of the rudiments of English, understanding the grammatical structure of Spanish was beyond her comprehension. Her only response was a derisive "Why do they do it that way?" On the other hand, when one learns intentionally and sufficiently his or her own culture, that learning supplies a foundation for dealing with aspects of another culture.

One additional aspect of culture learning that may occur is enculturation to the second culture, learning a second culture to the same extent that the first culture is learned. Many people believe that this is not possible, rarely possible, or not preferred even if possible. In any case, enculturation into a second culture is a two-way operation—an individual must desire to become fully enculturated, and that individual also must be allowed by the culture to become fully enculturated. In most cases, one of these requirements is not met.

For the counselor, it is most important (1) to understand that each individual holds values, biases, stereotypes, and communication patterns that are molded by culture; (2) to recognize these values, biases, stereotypes, and communication patterns in himself or herself while at the same time understanding the process by which awareness happens; and (3) to recognize differences between his or her culture and other cultures in order to learn and understand the idiosyncratic nature of other cultures. In this way the counselor will be able to join with persons of other cultures for the purpose of counseling.

ACHIEVING SELF-AWARENESS

To the extent that the counselor and client bring their own personal cultures to counseling, any counseling relationship can be considered a cultural episode. Counselors should not only express interest in the facts about clients' cultures but also in how clients view their cultures. Cross-cultural counseling spotlights the cultural episode that occurs when aspects of the counselor's culture, the client's culture, and the counseling situation combine. From within this combination emerges the newly created, unique, and shared culture of the counseling experience.

Many counseling professionals believe that examining the client's culture greatly enhances the quality of the counseling process. Incorporated into this point of view is the attitude among some professionals that the counselor's background influences the counseling process in a direct way through the counselor's perceptions, expectations, understanding of the symptoms expressed, understanding of potential stressors, and awareness of available resources. Therefore, in order to effectively serve a client, the counselor should take his or her own cultural background into consideration, as well as the client's. The counselor should go beyond self-reference criteria and consider issues and problems in counseling from the client's cultural perspective. Sue, Arrendondo, and McDavis (1992) defined a culturally skilled counselor as one who is in the process of becoming personally aware of cultural assumptions, biases, stereotypes, and limitations.

CULTURAL DIFFERENCES

White Americans often have difficulty considering themselves members of a culture group. The depth of their own identification with "whiteness" or White Anglo-Saxon Protestant (WASP) traditions and values surprises many of that group. "Identification with the WASP culture is usually accepted by WASPs themselves as a matter of fact and without real awareness of the subtle influences on them or of how the culture might be viewed by non-WASPs" (Axelson, 1993, pp. 368–369). Informal classroom experiments conducted by Axelson asked college students, "Who are you?" WASP students answered, "American," "person," "adult," "man/woman," "job title," or some other general answer. Nonwhite students or White minority students answered with more ethnically related answers such as "Black," "Asian," or "Italian-American." Alternatively, when the White students were asked what they were not, they tended to answer with ethnically related answers.

VALUES

An essential aspect of self-awareness for counselors is the recognition that they cannot enter the counseling process value-free or value-neutral. If counselors enter with either of these two assumptions, they run the risk of coercing clients to make decisions or behave in ways that are consistent with their own (the counselors') values rather than the clients'. They also run the risk of making value judgments about clients and viewing clients as right or wrong, moral or immoral, instead of different.

The counselor's values also affect counseling goals. Counselors who say they have no goals will inadvertently impose their (unknown) goals on the client. Since counselors do assume some degree of authority in the counselor-client relationship, since counseling is not value-free, and since the values that are being transmitted are those that counselors learned in their background and training, clients may want to assume counselors' values or at least attribute more credence to them than they would in a noncounseling setting. Clients may reject help altogether due to the incongruence between the counselor's and client's value systems. In many cases, neither counselors nor clients will take responsibility for setting the goals for counseling. Accordingly, the results of counseling are tenuous. A well-stated axiom applies here: If you don't know where you're going, you'll end up somewhere else. The counselor's responsibilities include knowing his or her own values, knowing his or her goals for the counseling process, and refraining from imposing those values and goals on clients. "It is a demanding task to transcend the values, biases, and convictions that form our cultural contexts; it is far more difficult to recognize, own, and modify the cultural roots, depths, and patterns that shape our unconscious and automatic behavior" (Augsburger, 1986, p. 24).

Stereotypes

Stereotypes, personal theories of personality applied to others, consist of collected beliefs and perceptions about classes of individuals, groups, or objects (Axelson, 1993). Stereotypes differ from *prejudice*, which is defined by Axelson (1993) as "a preconceived judgment or opinion without just grounds or sufficient knowledge" (p. 155). When based on inaccurate information, stereotypes often resemble prejudice. Stereotypes, like prejudice, can be positive or negative. In a negative sense, they impede the counseling process by providing obstacles to viewing clients as individuals and hinder the creativity of the counselor by building a foundation for counseling that may or may not be accurate. Conversely, stereotypes can provide hypotheses useful in understanding individual clients. Counselors who become aware of the stereotypes they hold can then make those stereotypes work for them. This requires discovering the necessary information to make stereotypes more accurate. Culturally aware counselors will test their stereotypes by being aware of them, open to new experiences, receptive to new ideas, capable of looking at old facts in new ways, and willing to change old stereotypes if the hypotheses do not hold (Axelson, 1993).

COMMUNICATION DIFFERENCES

Learning another language provides the perfect opportunity to learn about one's own language. Likewise, a lack of understanding about one's own language severely hinders the process of learning a second language. These same principles apply to learning another culture: without knowledge of one's own culture, understanding another becomes more difficult.

Communication, including language, plays a major part in the counseling process. Communication barriers complicate and often hinder counseling in a cross-cultural or multicultural situation. Language barriers alone would be enough to impede the counseling process. My wife and I had many humorous experiences in Korea because of language misunderstanding. In Korean, the use of negatives is similar to a mathematical equation. If the question "Do you not want any more food?" is asked in English, a person who is sufficiently full will respond, "No." In Korean, they will say, "Yes," which affirms the negative question. "Yes, I do not want any more food." This was often confusing to Americans. But communication is much more than just language. Much communication can be designated "communication from the environment," based on selective perception of input. Our culture provides the major framework for making input selection. The process of selection involves a sort of "mental map" that serves as a filter through which input passes. Unintelligible or foreign information is filtered out, while other input passes through and becomes part of the communication and counseling process. Hoopes (1981) labeled this foreign input as "noise" in a cross-cultural communication situation. Noise represents obstacles to effective communication. For example, many Asians do not desire intense eye contact. Most counselor education programs in the United States teach that proficient counselors maintain eye contact. To the Asian client, this attempt may cause noise in the process. Culture also determines appropriate personal distances. Some cultures deem intimate relationships the only appropriate place for close proximity. In others, standing or sitting close is the norm. Counselors who sit close and lean toward the client may be inadvertently invading the client's personal space. In some instances clients' respect of the counselor's position or job title influences them to act or respond in certain culturally prescribed ways not necessarily helpful to the counseling process. For example, in cultures that revere the position of counselor, clients tend to respond as they believe the counselors want them to respond. None of these examples signals the certain death of the counseling relationship, but any of them can create an impediment to the process. When counselors are unaware of differences that are present in cross-cultural situations, the hindrances can accumulate and counseling can be less effective.

Operating in a culture different from our own offers few clues for decoding environmental communication messages. Language/communication difficulties comprise a major part of cultural adjustment for clients, and the counseling arena sometimes re-creates those difficulties. Counselors should identify their own "environmental communications" in order to better assist clients in handling their counseling issues, and possibly in handling communication issues in general from the dominant culture. If a client cannot resolve communication difficulties, reactions may range from mild discomfort to radical emotional dislocation that would render the client unable to function in that environment (Hoopes, 1981). When I first moved to Honduras, I desperately wanted to communicate with the nationals. Even though I studied Spanish diligently, I was convinced that I would never learn enough to be able to converse. The emotional dislocation and feeling of isolation became so intense that, during one period of time, I had dreams that everyone in Honduras could speak English. Fortunately, this was only a phase in my cross-cultural development, and before my time there was complete, I was speaking enough to be able to establish meaningful relationships with many Hondurans.

Much of the resolution of communication difficulties lies in developing an understanding of the cultural code of the dominant culture (Hoopes, 1981). *Cultural code* refers to the concept that everything within the range of human interaction has meaning. A culture's code includes interpretations of silence, smiles, touch, dress, taste in music, and so on. For the client, unfamiliarity with the dominant culture's code sometimes results in disorientation and culture shock (Hoopes, 1981). It is vital that counselors understand their own cultural code in order to work with clients without imposing their values, offending the client, being offended by the client, or misinterpreting clients' nonverbal behavior. In some cases, the counselor should ask the client's opinion about the physical arrangements that would provide the most comfortable environment. Awareness of cultural differences presents the counselor with an opportunity to empower the client to educate the counselor about his or her (the client's) culture, and to work on his or her counseling issues in an environment that is more conducive to client growth.

SUMMARY

This chapter dealt with the need for counselors to examine and be aware of their own cultures. This began with a discussion of the developing cultural makeup of the United States and continued with exploring how one's culture develops. The remainder of the chapter examined specific areas of cultural development, including the development of personal attitudes, biases, stereotypes, values, and communication patterns. The chapter also highlighted the dangers of not being aware of one's own culture from the standpoint of the quality of counselor-client relationships and the effectiveness of counseling interventions and treatment plans.

The following material presents activities that can be used for purposes of examination, discussion, and understanding of one's cultural and philosophical roots.

QUESTIONS FOR PERSONAL REFLECTION OR GROUP DISCUSSION

Cultural Self-Analysis

1. What factors do you believe define culture?
2. How would you define the elements of your culture?
3. Would you include national background, racial group, or membership in a diverse population group as important factors in determining culture?

Examination of your cultural heritage.

1. What is your national background, racial group, or membership in a diverse population or group?
2. What was your religious affiliation during your childhood?
3. What is your religious affiliation now?
4. What is your gender?
5. What is your age?
6. Based on your income and job, what is your current socioeconomic status?
7. In what geographic region were you reared?
8. In what geographic region do you currently reside?

Examination of your personal culture.

1. What is one thing you are proud of regarding your culture?
2. What is one thing that embarrasses you about your culture?
3. What is a trait, practice, or tradition that you admire about a culture other than your own?
4. Describe a time when you were hurt by someone's prejudice in words or action? Describe how you felt.
5. Describe a time you (intentionally or unintentionally) hurt someone because of your prejudice in words or action? Describe how you felt.
6. What is a stereotype, prejudice, or act of discrimination you learned in your youth?

7. What is a stereotype, prejudice, or act of discrimination you changed as you grew older? Why did you change?
8. Describe an incident regarding race relations that you recall from your work or school setting. How did you respond?
9. Thinking back on the events you describe in your answer to question 8, what would you do differently (if anything) if they were to occur now? Why?
10. Describe a time you saw an act of prejudice and did something about it?
11. Describe a time you saw an act of prejudice and did nothing about it?
12. In thinking back on the events you describe in your answers to questions 10 and 11, would you handle things differently now? Why?

Identifying your own ethnic/cultural origins.   Understanding one's own background (including how group membership affects biases, perceptions, behavioral habits, and assumptions) will enhance the counselor's understanding of the client population. This understanding enables the counselor to work more effectively and empathetically with persons of differing cultures, races, ethnicities, lifestyles, and religions. Use the following guidelines to begin exploring how your group membership has contributed to your psychological and cultural makeup.

1. Describe your affiliation with any particular subpopulation (i.e., a group that differs based on a feature or features that distinguish it from other groups).
2. What does it mean to you to be a member of this group? Who was significant in teaching or transmitting to you your subgroup identity? What impact does your identification with that group have on your present life?
3. Are there other groups that have features similar to those of your group? What are they and in what ways are they similar and different?
4. What is the most satisfying thing about being a member of your chosen subgroup? What is least satisfying?

5. What is the attitude of your subgroup concerning ways to approach personal or emotional problems? How would members of your group attempt to solve such problems?
6. How do you think members of your family would react if you were to seek the help of a professional counselor or therapist? How would they react if you were to ask them to participate in family counseling?

Another culture's worldviews.   After completing this exercise for your own culture or population group, repeat it with reference to the other population groups described in this book. By doing so, you may discover some of the hidden (or maybe not-so-hidden) differences between yourself and others—differences based on divergent worldviews and not on a "right" or "wrong" approach to the world.

Group Activities

Identifying cultural differences.   In a small group setting, recall a specific incident when you felt uncomfortable around a group of people who were different from you.

1. Describe the feelings you experienced.
2. What could have been done to make you feel more comfortable or more at ease (i.e., gestures, body language, activities, etc.)? How would you have responded?

A special event.   Special events are approached differently in different cultures and population groups. In your group, describe a special event from your childhood. Begin with the preparations that were made before the event, then describe what you remember about your involvement before the event, during the event, and after the event. Compare and contrast the behaviors, organization, meaning, and purposes of the event with others in your group who experienced a similar event in childhood.

If you cannot remember a special event from your childhood, describe the experience of someone else—a child, a sibling, a niece or nephew, neighbor, or friend.

What is your worldview?   Walsh and Middleton (1984) describe *worldview* as a perceptual framework through which a person sees the world. Worldviews impact our perspectives in at least eight general categories: family, the arts, environmental concerns, legal institutions, health care, education, politics, and religious institutions. In your group, briefly describe how you view each of these eight categories from the standpoint of your present cultural/population group context. For example, some people describe a family as a man and a woman, living together in a monogamous relationship, with children who are either biologically or legally (in the case of adoption) their own. Other people might add or subtract from these components when describing a family.

From your standpoint, describe and explain the general purpose(s) for:

1. The family.
2. The arts.
3. Environmental concerns.
4. Legal institutions.
5. Health care.
6. Education.
7. Politics.
8. Religious institutions.

REFERENCES

Angelou, M. (1969). *I know why the caged bird sings.* New York: Random House.

Augsburger, D.W. (1986). *Pastoral counseling across cultures.* Philadelphia: The West-minster Press.

Axelson, J.A. (1993). *Counseling and development in a multicultural society* (2nd Ed.). Monterey, CA: Brooks/Cole Publishing.

Hoopes, D.S. (1981). Intercultural communication concepts and the psychology of inter-cultural experience. In M.D. Pusch (Ed.), *Multicultural Education.* LaGrange Park, IL: Intercultural Press.

Munroe, R.L., & Munroe, R.M. (1975). *Cross-cultural human development.* Monterey, CA: Brooks/Cole.

Spradley, J.P., & Phillips, M. (1972). Culture and stress: A quantitative analysis. *American Anthropologist, 74,* 518–529.

Sue, D.W. (1992). The challenge of multiculturalism: The road less traveled. *American Counselor, 1,* 6–14.

Sue, D.W., Arrendondo, P., & McDavis, R.S. (1992, April). Multicultural counseling competencies and standards: A call to the profession. *Journal of Multicultural Counseling and Development,* 20(2), 64–68.

Thomas, K., & Althen, G. (1989). Counseling foreign students. In P.B. Pederson, J.G. Draguns, W.J. Lonner, & J.E. Trimble (Eds.), *Counseling across cultures* (pp. 205–241). Honolulu: University of Hawaii Press.

U.S. Bureau of the Census. (2000). *Statistical abstract.* Washington, DC: U.S. Government Printing Office.

Walsh , B.J. & Middleton, J.R. (1984). *The transforming vision.* Downers Grove, IL: InterVarsity Press.

Ward, T. (1984). *Living overseas.* New York: The Free Press.

CHAPTER 3

Counseling Native Americans

Michael Tlanusta Garrett

Michael Tlanusta Garrett, Eastern Band of Cherokee, is associate professor of counseling in the Department of Human Services at Western
Carolina University. He holds a Ph.D. in counseling and counselor education and a M.Ed. in counseling and development from the University of
North Carolina, Greensboro. His primary research areas deal with wellness, spirituality, acculturation, group techniques, counseling children
and adolescents, conflict resolution, date rape/sexual violence, play therapy, and cultural issues of counseling Native Americans. Michael has authored the book *Walking on the Wind: Cherokee Teachings for Harmony
and Balance* and coauthored the book *Medicine of the Cherokee: The Way
of Right Relationship*.

AWARENESS INDEX

Please test your knowledge by marking the following statements true or
false before proceeding to the text in this chapter. Compute your score
from the scoring guide at the end of the Awareness Index.

1. T F There is a difference socially and legally between people
that self-identify as Native versus those that are enrolled
tribal members.

2. T F Columbus was not the first one to explore "the new world"
or to have contact with the Native peoples of this continent.

3. T F From 1778 to 1871, there were 370 documented treaties negotiated between the U.S. government and Indian tribes.

4. T F Indian people were granted United States citizenship as soon as they were put on reservations.

5. T F All of the major tribes in the United States are located west of the Mississippi River.

6. T F Suicide rates are higher for Native Americans than any other group in the United States.

7. T F Approximately 50% of the Native American population resides in urban areas.

8. T F Native traditionalists worship multiple deities in their tribal spiritual traditions.

9. T F The eagle feather, in many Native traditions, serves as a sacred reminder that many things in this world are separate and opposite, and need to be kept that way.

10. T F Indian people are stoic and seldom laugh.

11. T F In the traditional style of Native communication, silence means that you lack confidence or that you are hiding something.

12. T F In Native traditions, speaking loudly and drawing a lot of attention to yourself is considered arrogant and boastful.

13. T F The one word that encompasses the essence of a traditional Native worldview is *relation*.

Scoring guide: **1.** T; **2.** T; **3.** T; **4.** F; **5.** F; **6.** T; **7.** T; **8.** F; **9.** F; **10.** F; **11.** F; **12.** T; **13.** T

DOWN BY THE RIVERSIDE

Some of my fondest memories of when I was still a little one go back to times spent with my grandfather, Oscar Rogers, who was Eastern Cherokee. We would spend time sitting on the rocks by the Oconaluftee River in Cherokee, North Carolina. "What do you see when you look into the water?" he would inquire, as he sat on a rock enjoying the afternoon sun. I would look closely to see the water rushing quickly downstream. My eyes would catch a glimpse of a fish, water beetles, flies touching the water, soaked wood floating along at the will of the water, rocks, and green plants.

"I see the water," I said. "What else do you see?" he asked. "Well, I see the fish," I answered, because there were little minnows swimming around in the water. "What else do you see?" he asked. "I see the rocks," I said. "What else do you see?" he asked again. My eyes began to water themselves as I stared intently, wanting so much to please my grandfather by seeing everything he saw.

"Ah, I see my reflection," I responded proudly. "That's good," he replied confidently. "What you see is your whole life ahead of you. Know that the Great One has a plan for you to be the keeper of everything you see with your eyes, 'cause every living thing is your brother and sister." "Even the rocks?" I questioned. "Yes, even the rocks," he answered, "because they have elements of Mother Earth and Father Sky, just as we do."

"Remember to give thanks every day for all things that make up the Universe," said my grandfather. "Always remember to walk the path of Good Medicine and see the good reflected in everything that occurs in life. Life is a lesson, and you must learn the lesson well to see your true reflection in the water."

—J.T. Garrett, Eastern Band of Cherokee (in Garrett, 1996b, p. 12)

THE PEOPLE

Native Americans consist of approximately 2.3 million self-identified people with a population that is steadily growing. Although this number represents only 1% of the total population of the United States (U.S. Bureau of the Census, 2001), Native people have been described as representing "fifty percent of the diversity" in our country (Hodgkinson, 1990, p. 1). Across the United States, there are more than 557 federally recognized and several hundred state recognized Native American nations (Russell, 1998). Given the wide-ranging diversity of this population, it is important to understand that the term *Native American* encompasses the vastness and essence of tribal traditions represented by hundreds of Indian nations. Navajo, Catawba, Shoshone, Lumbee, Cheyenne, Cherokee, Apache, Lakota, Seminole, Comanche, Pequot, Cree, Tuscarora, Paiute,

Creek, Pueblo, Shawnee, Hopi, Osage, Mohawk, Nez Perce, Seneca—these are but a handful of the hundreds of Indian nations that exist across the United States.

Native Americans have been described as a group of persons facing enormous problems, including unemployment rates that are three to eleven times greater than that of the general population, a median income half that of the majority population, high school drop-out rates exceeding 60% in many areas, arrest rates three times those for African Americans, and a rate of alcoholism double that of the general population (Heinrich, Corbine, & Thomas, 1990).

Fetal Alcohol Syndrome rates for Native people are thirty-three times higher than that of non-Native people. One in six Native adolescents has attempted suicide, a rate four times that of all other groups. Alcohol mortality is six times the rate for all other ethnic groups. Tuberculosis is 7.4 times greater than for non-Indians. Diabetes is 6.8 times greater than for non-Indians (Russell, 1998).

Only 52% of Native youth finish high school, and only 4% graduate from college; 75% of the Native workforce earns less than $7,000 per year, and 45% of Native people live below the poverty level. As for living conditions, 46% have no electricity; 54% have no indoor plumbing; 82% live without a telephone. Some of the possible challenges that Native people bring with them to the counseling process are evident (Russell, 1998).

Native Americans represent a wide-ranging diversity, illustrated, for example, by the fact that there are approximately 252 different Native American languages (Thomason, 1991). At the same time, a prevailing sense of "Indianness" based on common worldview and common history seems to bind Native Americans together as a people of many peoples (Herring, 1990; Thomason, 1991). Although acculturation plays a major factor in Native American worldview, there tends to be a high degree of psychological homogeneity, a certain degree of shared cultural standards and meanings, based on common core values that exist for traditional Native Americans across tribal groups (Garrett, 1999b).

Since approximately 50% of the Native American population resides in urban areas, the degree of traditionalism versus the degree of acculturation to mainstream American values and cultural standards for behavior is an important consideration in counseling Native people (Garrett & Garrett, 1994; Heinrich et al., 1990; Thomason, 1991). Native Americans come from different tribal groups with different customs, traditions, and beliefs; they live in a variety of settings including rural, urban, and reservation (Garrett & Garrett, 1994). Cherokees and Navajos are both Native Americans, but their regional cultures, climatic adaptations, and languages differ greatly. However, part of what they share in common is a strong sense of traditionalism based on basic cultural values and worldview (Herring, 1990; Thomason, 1991).

In order to better understand how to provide Native clients with culturally responsive services in the counseling process, we must enter the world of a Native client. The purpose of this chapter is not to offer information dealing with many of the specific problems/issues that are of particular concern for this population—such as poverty and high unemployment, alcoholism and substance abuse, teenage pregnancy, suicide rates, delinquency, diabetes and other health concerns—or even whether or not casinos and the gaming industry have beneficial or destructive consequences for tribes. The purpose of this chapter is to offer a comprehensive overview and understanding of this population by discussing (1) terminology, (2) historical context, (3) acculturation, (4) traditional Native values and worldview, (5) spirituality and wellness, (6) the symbolism of the eagle feather, (7) the use of humor, and (8) communication style, with implications and recommendations for practice related to counseling Native American clients.

WHO IS NATIVE AMERICAN: "HOW MUCH ARE YOU?"

The term *Native American* is often used to describe indigenous peoples of the Western Hemisphere in an effort to provide recognition—viewed by many as long overdue—of the unique history and status of these people as the first inhabitants of the American continent. The U.S. Bureau of Indian Affairs (1988) defines *Native American* in legal terms as a person who is an enrolled or registered member of a tribe or whose blood quantum is one-fourth or more genealogically derived from Native American ancestry. The U.S. Bureau of the Census (1991), meanwhile, relies on self-identification to determine who is a Native person. Oswalt (1988) points out, however, that "if a person is considered an Indian by other individuals in the community, he or she is legally an Indian . . . [in other words], if an individual is on the roll of a federally recognized Indian group, then he or she is an Indian; the degree of Indian blood is of no real consequence, although usually he or she has at least some Indian blood" (p. 5).

Among some of the terms used historically or currently to refer to Native people are *American Indian, Alaskan Native, Native person, Indian, First American, Amerindian, Amerind, First Nations person, Aboriginal person,* and *Indigenous person.* The term *Native American* or *Native* (and sometimes *Indian*) will be used here to refer generally to those Native people indigenous to the United States who self-identify as Native American and maintain cultural identification as a Native person through membership in a Native American tribe recognized by the state or federal government or through other tribal affiliation and community recognition.

SURVIVING "HISTORY": SPIRIT NEVER DIES

Many authors have described the deliberate attempts throughout U.S. history by mainstream American institutions such as government agencies, schools, and churches to destroy the Native American institutions of family, clan, and tribal structure, religious belief systems and practices, customs, and traditional way of life (Deloria, 1988; Heinrich et al., 1990; Locust, 1988; Reyhner & Eder, 1992). Deloria (1988) comments, "When questioned by an anthropologist about what the Indians called America before the White man came, an Indian said simply, Ours" (p. 166). Characterized by institutional racism and discrimination, dominant culture has a long history of opposition to Native cultures and the attempts to assimilate Native people, having a long-lasting effect on the cultures and Native people's way of life (Deloria, 1988; Locust, 1988).

It was not until 1924 that the U.S. government recognized the citizenship of Native Americans—no longer a threat to national expansion—through passage of the Citizenship Act (Deloria, 1988). In addition, Native Americans were not granted religious freedom until 1978 (I was eight years old) when the American Indian Religious Freedom Act was passed, overturning the Indian Religious Crimes Code of 1889 and guaranteeing Native people the constitutional right to exercise their traditional religious practices for the first time in a century (Deloria, 1988; Loftin, 1989). On a more personal note, every time I see a twenty-dollar bill, I am reminded of the betrayal of my tribe by the government back in 1838 when Andrew Jackson (depicted in all his glory on the bill) signed off on an illegal act forcing the removal of over sixteen thousand Cherokees from parts of North Carolina, South Carolina, Tennesseee, and Georgia to the Oklahoma territory (Garrett, 1998). In more recent times, massive efforts to "civilize" Native people through government-supported, religiously run boarding schools and the relocation programs of the 1950s have created a historical context of generational trauma and cultural discontinuity (Hirschfelder & Kreipe de Montano, 1993). These events have affected Native Americans psychologically, economically, and socially for generations. From both a historical and contemporary perspective, oppression is and continues to be a very real experience for Native people.

As counselors, we are trained professionals who encourage clients to tell their stories, make sense of their stories, and actively create their stories through intentional living. In working with minority clients, it is important to understand the influence of oppression on their experience, and to assess the extent to which the process of acculturation has affected the client's cultural identity (Lee, 2001, 2002; Robinson & Howard-Hamilton, 2000). In the following extract, a Navajo elder describes her first experience in boarding school, at age seven, over forty years ago, unable to speak any English and having never before left the reservation.

> It was the first time I've seen a brick building that was not a trading post. The ceilings were so high, and the rooms so big and empty. It was so cold. There was no warmth. Not as far as "brrr, I'm cold," but in a sense of emotional cold. Kind of an emptiness, when you're hanging onto your mom's skirt and trying hard not to cry. Then when you get up to your turn, she thumbprints the paper and she leaves and you watch her go out the big metal doors. The whole thing was cold. The doors were metal and they even had this big window with wires running through it. You watch your mama go down the sidewalk, actually it's the first time I seen a sidewalk, and you see her get into the truck and the truck starts moving and all the home smell goes with it. You see it all leaving.
>
> Then the woman takes you by the hand and takes you inside and the first thing they do is take down your bun. The first thing they do is cut off

your hair, and you been told your whole life that you never cut your hair
recklessly because that is your life. And that's the first thing them women
does is cut off your hair. And you see that long, black hair drop, and it's
like they take out your heart and they give you this cold thing that beats
inside. And now you're gonna be just like them. You're gonna be cold.
You're never gonna be happy or have that warm feeling and attitude towards life anymore. That's what it feels like, like taking your heart out
and putting in a cold river pebble.

When you go into the shower, you leave your squaw skirt and blouse
right there at the shower door. When you come out, it's gone. You don't
see it again. They cut your hair, now they take your squaw skirt. They
take from the beginning. When you first walk in there, they take everything that you're about. They jerk it away from you. They don't ask how
you feel about it. They never tell you anything. They never say what
they're gonna do, why they're doing it. They barely speak to you. They
take everything away from you. Then you think, mama must be whackers.
She wants me to be like them? Every time you don't know what they're
doing, they laugh at you. They yell at you. They jerk you around. It was
never what I wanted to be. I never wanted to be like them. But my mom
wanted me to be like them. As I got older, I found out that you don't have
to be like them. You can have a nice world and have everything that mama
wanted, but you don't have to be cold. (McLaughlin, 1994, pp. 47–48)

ACCULTURATION: CIRCLES WITH NO BEGINNINGS AND NO END

Although many of the core traditional values permeate the lives of Native
Americans across tribal groups (see Table 3.1, p. 50), Native Americans
are not a completely homogeneous group: they differ greatly in their level
of acceptance of and commitment to specific tribal values, beliefs, and
practices (Garrett & Garrett, 1996). Native individuals differ in terms of
their level of acculturation, geographic setting (urban, rural, or reservation), and socioeconomic status (Garrett & Garrett, 1994; Herring, 1996).
The following levels of acculturation, defined as "the cultural change that
occurs when two or more cultures are in persistent contact" (Garcia &
Ahler, 1992, p. 24), have been identified for Native Americans:

1. *Traditional:* May or may not speak English, but generally speak
   and think in their native language; hold only traditional values and

beliefs and practice only traditional tribal customs and methods of worship.

2. *Marginal:* May speak both the native language and English; may not, however, fully accept the cultural heritage and practices of their tribal group nor fully identify with mainstream cultural values and behaviors.

3. *Bicultural:* Generally accepted by dominant society and tribal society/nation; simultaneously able to know, accept, and practice both mainstream values/behaviors and the traditional values and beliefs of their cultural heritage.

4. *Assimilated:* Accepted by dominant society; embrace only mainstream cultural values, behaviors, and expectations.

5. *Pantraditional:* Assimilated Native Americans who have made a conscious choice to return to the "old ways." They are generally accepted by dominant society, but seek to embrace previously lost traditional cultural values, beliefs, and practices of their tribal heritage. Therefore, they may speak both English and their native tribal language. (Compiled from LaFromboise, Trimble, & Mohatt, 1990, p. 638.)

These five levels represent a continuum along which any given Native American individual may fall. Regardless of blood quantum, the most popular and most deceiving means of determining a person's "Indianness" and degree of traditionalism comes not only from ethnic heritage, but also from his or her life experiences and life choices (Garrett & Garrett, 1994).

NATIVE TRADITIONS: LIVING THE WAYS

Several authors have described common core values that characterize Native traditionalism across tribal nations (Heinrich et al., 1990; Herring, 1990; Little Soldier, 1992; Thomason, 1991). Some of these Native traditional values (see Table 3.1, p. 50) include the importance of community contribution, sharing, acceptance, cooperation, harmony and balance, noninterference, extended family, attention to nature, immediacy of time, awareness of the relationship, and a deep respect for elders (Dufrene, 1990; Garrett & Garrett, 1994, 1996; Garrett 1996b, 1998, 1999b; Heinrich et al., 1990;

Herring, 1990, 1999; Lake, 1991; Plank, 1994; Red Horse, 1997). All in all, these traditional values show the importance of honoring, through harmony and balance, what Native people believe to be a very sacred connection with the energy of life; this is the basis for a traditional Native worldview and spirituality across tribal nations.

The Tribe/Nation

Traditional Native people experience a unique relationship between themselves and the tribe. In a very real sense, Native American individuals are extensions of their tribal nation—socially, emotionally, historically, and politically. For many Indian people, cultural identity is rooted in tribal membership, community, and heritage. Many Native nations are matriarchal/matrilineal or matriarchal/patrilineal, but there are those that follow patriarchal/patrilineal ways too (or other variations of gender dominance and tracing of family heritage). This, in turn, affects not only communal and social structure and functioning, but also family/clan structure and functioning. The extended family (at least three generations) and tribal group take precedence over all else. The tribe is an interdependent system of people who perceive themselves as parts of the greater whole rather than a whole consisting of individual parts. Likewise, traditional Native people judge themselves and their actions according to whether or not they are benefiting the tribal community and its continued harmonious functioning.

In mainstream American society, worth and status are based on "what you do" or "what you have achieved." For Native Americans, "who you are is where you come from." Native Americans essentially believe that "if you know my family, clan, tribe, then you know me." As a result, traditional Native people might be likely to describe some aspect of their family or tribal heritage when asked to talk about themselves.

The Meaning of Family

It has been said that "about the most unfavorable moral judgement an Indian can pass on another person is to say 'he acts as if he didn't have any relatives'" (DuBray, 1985). Upon meeting for the first time, many Indian people ask, "Where do you come from? Who are your family? Who do you belong to? Who are your people?" The intent is to find out where they stand in relation to this new person, and what commonality exists. In fact, this is a simple way of building bridges, or recognizing bridges that already exist but are as yet unknown. Family may or may not consist of blood relatives. It is common practice in the Indian way, for instance, to claim another as a relative, thereby welcoming him or her as real family. From that point on, that person *is* a relative, and that is that. After all, family is a matter of blood as well as of spirit.

Wisdom Keepers

Native elders are the keepers of the sacred ways. They are protectors, mentors, teachers, and support-givers, regardless of their "social status." Native communities honor their Indian elders, the "Keepers of the Wisdom," for their lifetime's worth of knowledge and experience. Elders have always played an important part in the continuance of the tribal community by functioning in the role of parent, teacher, community leader, and spiritual guide (Garrett & Garrett, 1997). To refer to an elder as "Grandmother," "Grandfather," "Uncle," "Aunt," "old woman," or "old man" is to refer to a very special relationship that exists with that elder characterized by deep respect and admiration.

In the traditional way, the prevalence of cooperation and sharing in the spirit of community is essential for harmony and balance. It is not unusual for a Native child to be raised in several different households over time. This is generally not due to a lack of caring or responsibility, but because it is both an obligation and a pleasure to share in raising and caring for the children in one's family. Grandparents, aunts, uncles, and other members of the community are all responsible for the raising of children, and they take this responsibility very seriously.

In the traditional way, elders direct young children's attention outward to the things with which they coexist (trees, plants, rocks, animals, elements, the land) and to the meaning of these things. They show the children the true relationship that exists among all things and the ways in which to honor this relationship. In this way, children develop a heightened level of sensitivity for cyclical flow of life energy, and for the traditions of their people.

There is a very special kind of relationship based on mutual respect and caring between Indian elders and Indian children as one moves through the life Circle from "being cared for" to "caring for," as Red

Horse (1997) puts it. With an increase in age comes an increase in the sacred obligation to family, clan, and tribe. Native American elders pass down to the children the tradition that their life force carries the spirits of their ancestors. With such an emphasis on connectedness, Native traditions revere children, not only as ones who will carry on the wisdom and traditions, but also as "little people" who are still very close to the spirit world and from whom we have much to learn. Brendtro, Brokenleg, and Van Bockern (1990) relate a story shared with them by Eddie Belleroe, a Cree elder from Alberta, Canada:

> In a conversation with his aging grandfather, a young Indian man asked, "Grandfather, what is the purpose of life?" After a long time in thought, the old man looked up and said, "Grandson, children are the purpose of life. We were once children and someone cared for us, and now it is our time to care."

SPIRITUALITY AND WELLNESS: WALKING IN STEP

Different tribal languages have different words or ways of referring to the idea of honoring one's sense of connection, but the meaning is similar across nations in referring to the belief that human beings exist on Mother Earth to be helpers and protectors of life. In Native communities, it is not uncommon, as an example, to hear people use the term *caretaker.* From the perspective of a traditionalist, to see one's purpose as that of caretaker is to accept responsibility for the gift of life by taking good care of that gift, the gift of life that others have received, and the surrounding beauty of the world in which we live (Garrett & Wilbur, 1999). More or less, the essence of Native American spirituality is about "feeling" (Wilbur, 1999a, 1999b). The feeling of connection is something that is available to all of us, though it is experienced in different ways. Although there are differences between individuals and across nations, it is possible to generalize to some extent about a number of basic beliefs characterizing Native American traditionalism and spirituality. The following, adapted from Locust (1988, pp. 317–318), elaborates on a number of basic Native American spiritual and traditional beliefs.

1. There is a single higher power known as Creator, Great Creator, Great Spirit, or Great One, among other names (this being is some-

times referred to in gender form, but does not necessarily exist as one particular gender or another). There are also lesser beings known as spirit beings or spirit helpers.

2. Plants and animals, like humans, are part of the spirit world. The spirit world exists side by side with, and intermingles with, the physical world. Moreover, the spirit existed in the spirit world before it came into a physical body and will exist after the body dies.

3. Human beings are made up of a spirit, mind, and body. The mind, body, and spirit are all interconnected; therefore, illness affects the mind and spirit as well as the body.

4. Wellness is harmony in body, mind, and spirit; unwellness is disharmony in mind, body, and spirit.

5. Natural unwellness is caused by the violation of a sacred social or natural law of Creation (e.g., participating in a sacred ceremony while under the influence of alcohol or drugs, or having had sex within four days of the ceremony).

6. Unnatural unwellness is caused by conjuring (witchcraft) from those with destructive intentions.

7. Each of us is responsible for our own wellness by keeping ourselves attuned to self, relations, environment, and universe.

This list of beliefs crosses tribal boundaries, but is by no means comprehensive. It does, however, provide a great deal of insight into some of the assumptions that may be held by a "traditional" Native client. In American mainstream ideology, the purpose of life consists of "life, liberty, and the pursuit of happiness." From a traditional Native perspective, a corollary would be "life, love, and the pursuit of learning." Understanding Native spiritual traditions means understanding the direction of one's path as a caretaker moving to the rhythm of the sacred heartbeat. As Black Elk put it, "the good road and the road of difficulties, you have made me cross; and where they cross, the place is holy" (cited in Garrett, 1998, p. 85).

LESSONS OF THE EAGLE FEATHER: RULE OF OPPOSITES

Eagle feathers are considered sacred among Native Americans who make use of the feathers for a variety of purposes, including ceremonial healing and purification. Eagle Medicine represents a state of presence achieved through diligence, understanding, awareness, and a completion of "tests of initiation" such as the Vision Quest (Lake, 1991) or other demanding life experiences. Highly respected elder status is associated with Eagle Medicine and the power of connectedness and truth. It is through experience and patience that this Medicine is earned over a lifetime. There is an old anecdote that probably best illustrates the lessons of the eagle feather:

> Once while acting as a guide for a hunting expedition, an Indian had lost the way home. One of the men with him said, "You're lost, chief." The Indian guy replied, "I'm not lost, my tepee is lost."

The eagle feather, which represents duality, tells the story of life. It tells of the many dualities that exist in the Circle of Life, such as light and dark, male and female, substance and shadow, summer and winter, life and death, peace and war (Garrett & Barret, in press; Garrett & Myers, 1996). The eagle feather has both light and dark colors, dualities and opposites. Though one can make a choice to argue which of the colors is most beautiful or most valuable, the truth is that both colors come from the same feather, both are true, both are connected, and it takes both to fly (Garrett, 1991; Garrett & Garrett, 1996). The colors are opposite, but they are part of the same truth. The importance of the feather does not lie in which color is most beautiful, but in discovering the purpose of the feather. In other words, there is no such thing as keeping the mountains and getting rid of the valleys; they are one and the same, and they exist because of one another.

INDIAN HUMOR: LAUGHING IT UP

Contrary to the stereotypical belief that Indian people are solemn, stoic figures poised against a backdrop of tepees, tomahawks, and head-dresses, the fact is, Indian people love to laugh (Garrett & Garrett, 1994; Garrett, Garrett, Wilbur, et al., in press; Maples et al., 2001). Laughing is a critical part of the culture, especially around mealtime. It is amazing to watch the transformation that occurs when people come together around food and really begin to open up. In Indian country, mealtime is sometimes the worst time to try to eat because everyone is laughing, cutting up, sharing side-splitting stories, and teasing each other. Many tribal oral traditions emphasize important life lessons through the subtle humor expressed in the stories. Often it is the arrogant, manipulative, vain, clownlike figure of Rabbit, Possum, Coyote, or Raven that learns a hard lesson in humility, much to the amusement of others (Garrett & Garrett, 1996; Garrett, 1998; Herring, 1994). Laughter plays a very important role in the continued survival of the tribal communities. After all, laughter relieves stress and creates an atmosphere of sharing and connectedness. As George Good Striker, Blackfoot elder, puts it, "Humor is the WD-40 of healing" (cited in Garrett, 1998, p. 137).

IMPLICATIONS FOR PRACTICE

Who Is Indian

As a counselor, Native or non-Native, respect for individual Native clients means finding out from which tribe that client comes, and possibly whether that person is directly affiliated with that tribe (federal, state, and/or community recognition). It is not our job as counselors to pass judgment on who is Indian and who is not. More specifically, don't ask a Native client how much Indian they are, or relate personal stories of Indian heritage in your family as a way of connecting with that client. That is a quick way to lose a Native person's receptivity and trust. If a client says he or she is Indian, then we must assume that they are. It is another way of better understanding that client without having to get into the painful (and sometimes irrelevant) politics of categorization. More important, a client's self-identification can give us insight into that person's perception of his or her experience and place in the world.

History

Given the historical and political context, the underlying issue in terms of counseling Native clients is trust versus mistrust. The question to ask yourself as a counselor of a Native American is, "What can I do to create and maintain trust with my client?" By educating yourself about the history of tribes from which clients come, you can better understand the impact of institutional racism and acculturation, as well as the meaning of the Native American experience for any given client.

Acculturation

When working with an Native client, it is important to get a sense of that person's level of acculturation by informally assessing (1) values (traditional, marginal, bicultural, assimilated, pantraditional); (2) geographic origin/residence (reservation, rural, urban); and (3) tribal affiliation (tribal structure, customs, beliefs). (For further discussion of formal and informal assessment of Native American acculturation, see Garrett & Pichette, 2000.) Both verbal and nonverbal cues will give counselors a good sense of a Native American client's level of acculturation (Garrett & Garrett, 1994). If questions remain, it is important to pose them in a respectful, unobtrusive way. Following are some examples of general leads intended to respectfully elicit important culturally relevant information.

- Where do you come from?
- Tell me about your family.
- What tribe/nation are you? Tell me a little bit about that.
- Tell me about you as a person, culturally and spiritually.
- Tell me how you identify yourself culturally.
- Tell me how your culture/spirituality plays into how you live your life.
- Tell me about your life as you see it, past, present, or future.

Counselors must avoid making assumptions about the cultural identity of Native American clients without gathering further information. For example, one cannot assume that because a person "looks Indian" he or she is traditional in his or her cultural and spiritual ways, or that because a person "does not look Indian" he or she is not traditional. In order to better understand the essence of traditional Native culture, though, it is important to explore the meaning of the core values and beliefs that characterize what it means to be Native for any given client.

Traditions

In contrast to many of the traditional Native values and beliefs discussed herein, mainstream American values tend to emphasize self-promotion, saving for the future, domination of others, accomplishment, competition and aggression, individualism and the nuclear family, mastery over nature, a time orientation toward living for the future, a preference for scientific explanations, time-consciousness, winning, and reverence of youth (Garrett, 1995, 1999a, 1999b). For Native people, there is great potential for cultural conflicts due to differing values within the context of the larger society. Therefore, exploration of cultural conflicts may be a viable goal for counseling. Native clients can be encouraged to talk about the meaning of family, clan, or tribe to them as a way of exploring worldview, especially in light of intergenerational differences or the effects of oppression or presenting issues.

Spirituality

Having a general understanding of Native American spirituality does not prepare one to participate in or conduct Native ceremonies as part of the counseling process (Matheson, 1996). That is the responsibility of those who are trained as Native Medicine persons, who can, however, serve as important resources to counselors working with Native clients. Native spirituality manifests in many different forms, such as traditional tribal ways, Christian traditions, or the teachings of the Native American church. With a client who seems to have more traditional values and beliefs, it may be particularly helpful to suggest that family or a Medicine person participate in the process to support the client as he or she moves through important personal transitions and subsequent personal cleansing.

Eagle Feather

For many Native clients, the understanding and reconciliation of discordant opposites is an essential therapeutic goal in achieving harmony and balance among the four directions—mind, body, spirit, and natural environment. An understanding of the rule of opposites is essential for working with Native American clients who may be experiencing dissonance in their lives but who may perceive that dissonance in a way that is much different from how a member of the cultural majority might be expected to experience those same issues. Asking the right questions, being open to what we do not readily perceive, bridges the gap between what we see and what really exists. When we understand that everything has meaning and purpose, our goal in counseling becomes helping Native clients to discover their purpose, to examine their assumptions, to seek an awareness of universal and personal truths, and to make choices that allow them to exist in a state of harmony and balance within the Circle of Life.

Humor

Humor is an important Native coping mechanism. Humor should be used only if the client invites it, meaning that the client trusts the counselor enough to connect on that level. What in one situation can be humor between two people, in another can be interpreted as ridicule or wearing a mask. Counselors working with Native clients should exercise caution when using humor, but definitely should not overlook it as a powerful therapeutic technique. Indian humor serves the purpose of reaffirming and enhancing the sense of connectedness as part of family, clan, and tribe. To the extent that it can serve that purpose in the counseling relationship, all the better.

Communication Style

Once the counselor has some general information concerning the client's cultural background and spiritual ways, he or she will have a better understanding of what may or may not be considered appropriate with and for the client. The following recommendations (Garrett & Pichette, 2000; Garrett, 1999b) are intended as culturally responsive ways for working with a traditional Native client:

1. *Greeting:* For traditional Native Americans, a gentle handshake is the proper way of greeting. Sometimes, just a word of greeting or head nod is sufficient. To use a firm handshake can be interpreted as an aggressive show of power and a personal insult. It may be important to follow, rather than lead, the client.
2. *Hospitality:* Given the traditional emphasis on generosity, kindness, and "gifting" as a way of honoring the relation, hospitality is an important part of Native American life. Therefore, it is helpful to be able to offer the Native client a beverage or snack as a sign of

good relation. In the traditional way, to not offer hospitality to a visitor or guest is to bring shame on oneself and one's family.

3. *Silence:* In the traditional way, when two people meet, very little may be said between them during the initial moments of the encounter. Quiet time at the beginning of a session is an appropriate way of transitioning into the therapeutic process by giving both counselor and client a chance to orient themselves to the situation, get in touch with themselves, and experience the presence of the other person. This brief time (perhaps a couple of minutes or so) can be nonverbal, noninteractive time that allows the client to be at ease. This is an important show of respect, understanding, and patience.

4. *Space:* Taking care to respect physical space is an extension of the principle that one need not always fill relational space with words. In Native tradition, both the physical form and the space between the physical is sacred. In counseling, it is important to respect the physical space of the client by not sitting too close, and not sitting directly across from the client, which allows scrutiny of the other. A more comfortable arrangement, traditionally, is sitting side by side, with the chairs at an angle to each other. The burning of sage, cedar, or sweetgrass (a method of spatial cleansing known as "smudging") should be done only at the request or with permission of the Native client.

5. *Eye contact:* Native American clients with traditional values (and possibly those who are marginal or bicultural) may tend to avert their eyes as a sign of respect. To subtly match this level of eye contact is respectful and shows an understanding of the client's way of being. The eyes are considered to be the pathway to the spirit; therefore to consistently look someone in the eye is to show a level of entitlement or aggression. It is good to glance at someone every once in a while, but listening, in the traditional way, is something that happens with the ears and the heart.

6. *Intention:* One of the biggest issues with many Indian clients in the counseling relationship is trust. This should come as no surprise given the history of broken promises and exploitation survived by many tribal nations. Typically, an Indian client will "read" the

counselor's nonverbal cues fairly quickly in order to determine whether the counselor is someone to be trusted or not. Counselors can focus on honoring the mental space between counselor and client by seeking to offer respect and humility in the counseling process. Acceptance by the counselor means not trying to control or influence the client, which would be considered "bad Medicine."

7. *Collaboration:* In counseling, more traditional clients may welcome the counselor's helpful suggestions or alternatives—and may even expect them. From a traditional perspective, respect for choice is important, but healing is a collaborative process. Offer suggestions without offering directions. There is a difference between encouraging and pushing. With traditional Native American clients, actions will always speak louder than words.

COUNSELING RECOMMENDATIONS

In addition to contemporary counseling interventions and treatment modalities, counselors can incorporate tribally specific interventions as appropriate to meet the cultural/spiritual/personal/career needs of specific Native clients. As a major part of collaboration with Native clients in the counseling process, the following (Garrett & Carroll, 2000) are offered as practical recommendations.

1. *Sociodemographics:* Native clients can reconnect with a sense of purpose by finding ways to combat the high rates of unemployment, inadequate housing, low educational levels, poverty-level incomes, and isolated living conditions. Participation in community-wide volunteer programs to help those in need has proven to be a successful part of healing for many Indian people.

2. *Physiology:* Native people should be encouraged to get regular physical checkups and blood tests (e.g., blood sugar).

3. *Historical context:* A critical component of counseling could include a psychoeducational piece or dialogue. This could provide systemic insight for some Native clients concerning many of the historical factors such as exploitation of Native people through discrimination, assimilation through boarding schools and relocation programs, and disruption of traditional cultural and familial pat-

terns. Discussions of this nature might be helpful to Native clients in exploring their own level of cultural identity development.

4. *Acculturation and identity:* Native clients can be assisted with exploration of personal cultural identity and career issues by focusing on the cultural themes of belonging, mastery, independence, and generosity, utilizing the following general questions for each of the four respective areas: (1) Where do you belong? (2) What are you good at and what do you enjoy doing? (3) What are your sources of strength, and what limits you? (4) What do you have to offer or contribute?

5. *Isolation and social connections:* Participation in social events such as family gatherings and powwows allows Native clients to experience social cohesion and social interaction in their communities. Some Native clients can benefit from a sense of reconnection with community and traditional roles. This has been accomplished through the revival of tribal ceremonies and practices (e.g., talking circles, sweat lodges, powwows, peyote meetings), reestablishing a sense of belonging and communal meaningfulness for Native people who might consider "returning to the old ways" as an integral part of modern life.

6. *Generational splits:* Native clients of all ages can benefit from acting as or learning from elders serving as role models and teachers for young people. This too has become more commonly practiced by tribal nations across the country in therapeutic programs and schools.

7. *Coping mechanisms:* Native clients can learn better methods of dealing with stress, boredom, powerlessness, and the sense of emptiness associated with acculturation and identity confusion. Consultation with or participation of a Medicine person (i.e., a traditional Native healer) may prove very helpful.

8. *Noninterference:* Avoidance behavior of family and community members can be addressed with Native clients as well as with family and community members to the extent that it may be destructive. Attneave's (1969, 1985) Network Therapy has been very effective with Indian clients as a way of working with an individual in family and community context.

CONCLUSION: CIRCLES RIPPLING

Somewhere even now, a young child sits by the riverside with a grandfather or grandmother, looking at the water and at him- or herself, one and the same. The elder and the child sit together, honoring Mother Earth and all that she has to offer us, honoring life and its constant motion. The elder and the child sit together, one and the same. Stories will be told, and many generations will hear their words flow alongside the trickling of the river's water. Someday, the little boy or girl may earn his or her first eagle feather, and in doing so, he or she may earn the responsibility and the joy of looking at the surface of the river's water and seeing the true reflection of his or her own grandchild looking back.

EXPERIENTIAL ACTIVITIES

Following are but a few suggestions for individual and group experiential activities to increase knowledge, awareness, and skills with for working with Native clients.

Individual Activities
1. Read novels, poetry, short stories, historical accounts, and biographies of Native people or written by Native authors (see www.nativeauthors.com for examples).
2. Investigate sources listed in this chapter for further information on particular issues or interventions (e.g., Appleton & Dykeman, 1996; Ashby, Gilchrist, & Miramontez, 1987; Brendtro et al., 1990; Colmant & Merta, 1999; Four Worlds Development Project, 1984; Garrett, 2001; Garrett & Garrett, 1996; Garrett, 1998; Garrett & Carroll, 2000; Garrett & Crutchfield, 1997; Garrett & Garrett, in press; Garrett, Garrett, & Brotherton, 2001; Garrett & Osborne, 1995; Heinrich et al., 1990; Herring, 1999; LaFromboise & Rowe, 1983; LaFromboise et al., 1990; Lake, 1991; Roberts-Wilbur et al., in press; Thomason, 1991; Vick, Smith, & Iron Rope Herrera, 1998).
3. Read current professional journal articles dealing with Native issues.

4. Read current Native periodicals such as *Native Peoples Magazine* (www.nativepeoples.com), *Indian Country Today* (www.indian country.com), *Whispering Wind Magazine, The Indian Trader, News from Indian Country, Arizona Native Scene, Four Winds Trading Company, National Museum of the American Indian, Native American Times* (www.okit.com), or tribally specific periodicals (i.e., newspapers, magazines, or any other material published by a particular tribe).

5. Listen to some Native music: powwow, traditional chant, flute, contemporary, rock, rap, chicken scratch, blues, or country (check out www.nativeamericanmusic.com, www.amdest.com/az/Scottsdale/db/CRVideo.html, and www.silverwave.com).

6. Watch some movies dealing with Native issues, especially those directed by, produced by, or starring Native people.

7. Check out current informational Native Web sites, such as www.nativepeoples.com, www.nativeamericanonline.com, www.native web.org, or others, as well as Web sites for specific tribes.

8. Learn more about Native social, economic, educational, and political organizations, such as the American Indian Movement, First Nations Development Institute, Morningstar Institute, American Indian College Fund, American Indian Science and Engineering Society, Native American Public Broadcasting Consortium, and Native American Rights Fund (www.narf.org).

9. Research and learn more about current legal issues facing specific tribes.

10. Research and learn more about current health issues facing Native people.

Group Activities

1. Attend powwows, cultural demonstrations, art exhibits, or other Native gatherings or festivities as appropriate and available.

2. Attend the museums and/or arts and crafts cooperatives of particular tribes, or find information about these on the Web.

3. Find out about local Native organizations or resources and meet with their members.

4. Meet and talk with willing Native people of any age.

Table 3.1 Comparison of Cultural Values and Expectations (Garrett & Pichette, 2000)

Traditional Native American	Contemporary Mainstream American
Harmony with nature	Power over nature
Cooperation	Competition
Group needs more important than individual needs	Personal goals considered important
Privacy and noninterference; try to control self, not others	Need to control and affect others
Self-discipline both in body and mind	Self-expression and self-disclosure
Participation after observation (only when certain of ability)	Trial-and-error learning; new skills practiced until they are mastered
Explanation according to nature	Scientific explanation for everything
Reliance on extended family	Reliance on experts
Emotional relationships valued	Concerned mostly with facts
Patience encouraged (allow others to go first)	Aggressive and competitive
Humility	Fame and recognition; winning
Win once, but let others win also	Win first prize all the time
Follow the old ways	Climb the ladder of success; importance of progress and change
Discipline distributed among many; no one person takes blame	Blame one person at cost to others
Physical punishment rare	Physical punishment accepted
Present-time focus	Future-time focus
Time is always with us	Clock-watching
Present goals considered important; future accepted as it comes	Plan for future and how to get ahead
Encourage sharing freely and keeping only enough to satisfy present needs	Private property; encourage acquisition of material comfort and saving for the future
Speak softly, at a slower rate	Speak louder and faster
Avoid singling out the listener	Address listener directly (by name)
Interject less	Interrupt frequently
Use fewer "encouraging signs" ("uh-huh," head nodding)	Use verbal encouragement
Delayed response to auditory messages	Immediate response
Nonverbal communication	Verbal skills highly prized

REFERENCES

Appleton, V.E., & Dykeman, C. (1996). Using art in group counseling with Native American youth. *Journal for Specialists in Group Work, 24,* 224–231.

Ashby, M.R., Gilchrist, L.D., & Miramontez, A. (1987). Group treatment for sexually abused American Indian adolescents. *Social Work with Groups, 10,* 21–32.

Attneave, C.L. (1969). Therapy in tribal settings and urban network intervention. *Family Process, 8,* 192–210.

Attneave, C.L. (1985). Practical counseling with American Indian and Alaska Native clients. In P. Pedersen (Ed.), *Handbook of cross-cultural counseling and therapy* (pp. 135–140). Westport, CT: Greenwood.

Brendtro, L.K., Brokenleg, M., & Van Bockern, S. (1990). *Reclaiming youth at risk: Our hope for the future.* Bloomington, IN: National Education Service.

Colmant, S.A., & Merta, R.J. (1999). Using the sweat lodge ceremony as group therapy for Navajo youth. *Journal for Specialists in Group Work, 24,* 55–73.

Deloria, V., Jr. (1988). *Custer died for your sins: An Indian manifesto.* Norman: University of Oklahoma Press.

DuBray, W.H. (1985). American Indian values: Critical factor in casework. *Social Casework: The Journal of Contemporary Social Work, 66,* 30–37.

Dufrene, P.M. (1990). Exploring Native American symbolism. *Journal of Multicultural and Cross-Cultural Research in Art Education, 8,* 38–50.

Four Worlds Development Project. (1984). *The sacred tree: Reflections on Native American spirituality.* Wilmot, WI: Lotus Light.

Garcia, R.L., & Ahler, J.G. (1992). Indian education: Assumptions, ideologies, strategies. In J. Reyhner (Ed.), *Teaching American Indian students* (pp. 13–32). Norman, OK: University of Oklahoma Press.

Garrett, J.T. (1991). Where the medicine wheel meets medical science. In S. McFadden (Ed.), *Profiles in wisdom: Native elders speak about the earth* (pp. 167–179). Santa Fe, NM: Bear and Company.

Garrett, J.T. (2001). *Meditations with the Cherokee: Prayers, songs, and stories of healing and harmony.* Rochester, VT: Bear and Company.

Garrett, J.T., & Garrett, M.T. (1994). The path of good medicine: Understanding and counseling Native Americans. *Journal of Multicultural Counseling and Development, 22* (3), 134–144.

Garrett, J.T., & Garrett, M.T. (1996). *Medicine of the Cherokee: The way of right relationship.* Santa Fe, NM: Bear and Company.

Garrett, M.T. (1995). Between two worlds: Cultural discontinuity in the dropout of Native American youth. *School Counselor, 42,* 186–195.

Garrett, M.T. (1996). Reflection by the riverside: The traditional education of Native American children. *Journal of Humanistic Education and Development, 35* (1), 12–28.

Garrett, M.T. (1998). *Walking on the wind: Cherokee teachings for harmony and balance.* Santa Fe, NM: Bear and Company.

Garrett, M.T. (1999a). Soaring on the wings of the eagle: Wellness of Native American high school students. *Professional School Counseling, 3,* 57–64.

Garrett, M.T. (1999b). Understanding the "Medicine" of Native American traditional values: An integrative review. *Counseling and Values, 43,* 84–98.

Garrett, M.T., & Barret, R.L. (In press). Two-spirit: Counseling Native American sexual minority people. *Journal of Multicultural Counseling and Development.*

Garrett, M.T., & Carroll, J. (2000). Mending the broken circle: Treatment and prevention of substance abuse among Native Americans. *Journal of Counseling and Development, 78,* 379–388.

Garrett, M.T., & Crutchfield, L.B. (1997). Moving full circle: A unity model of group work with children. *Journal for Specialists in Group Work, 22,* 175–188.

Garrett, M.T., & Garrett, J.T. (1997). Counseling Native American elders. *Directions in Rehabilitation Counseling: Therapeutic Strategies with the Older Adult, 3,* 3–18.

Garrett, M.T., & Garrett, J.T. (In press). Ayeli: Centering technique based on Cherokee spiritual traditions. *Counseling and Values.*

Garrett, M.T., Garrett, J.T., & Brotherton, D. (2001). Inner circle/outer circle: Native American group technique. *Journal for Specialists in Group Work, 26,* 17–30.

Garrett, M.T., Garrett, J.T., Wilbur, M., Roberts-Wilbur, J., & Torres-Rivera, E. (In press). Native American humor as spiritual tradition: Implications for counseling. *Journal of Multicultural Counseling and Development.*

Garrett, M.T., & Myers, J.E. (1996). The rule of opposites: A paradigm for counseling Native Americans. *Journal of Multicultural Counseling and Development, 24,* 89–104.

Garrett, M.T., & Osborne, W.L. (1995). The Native American sweat lodge as metaphor for group work. *Journal for Specialists in Group Work, 20,* 33–39.

Garrett, M.T., & Pichette, E.F. (2000). Red as an apple: Native American acculturation and counseling with or without reservation. *Journal of Counseling and Development, 78,* 3–13.

Garrett, M.T., & Wilbur, M.P. (1999). Does the worm live in the ground? Reflections on Native American spirituality. *Journal of Multicultural Counseling and Development, 27,* 193–206.

Heinrich, R.K., Corbine, J.L., & Thomas, K.R. (1990). Counseling Native Americans. *Journal of Counseling and Development, 69,* 128–133.

Herring, R.D. (1990). Understanding Native American values: Process and content concerns for counselors. *Counseling and Values, 34,* 134–137.

Herring, R.D. (1994). The clown or contrary figure as a counseling intervention strategy with Native American Indian clients. *Journal of Multicultural Counseling and Development, 22* (3), 153–164.

Herring, R.D. (1996). Synergetic counseling and Native American Indian students. *Journal of Counseling and Development, 74* (6), 542–547.

Herring, R.D. (1999). *Counseling with Native American Indians and Alaska Natives: Strategies for helping professionals.* Thousand Oaks, CA: Sage.

Hirschfelder, A., & Kreipe de Montano, M. (1993). *The Native American almanac: A portrait of Native America today.* New York: Macmillan.

Hodgkinson, H.L. (1990). *The demographics of American Indians: One percent of the people; fifty percent of the diversity.* Washington, DC: Institute for Educational Leadership.

LaFromboise, T.D., & Rowe, W. (1983). Skills training for bicultural competence: Rationale and application. *Journal of Counseling Psychology, 30,* 589–595.

LaFromboise, T.D., Trimble, J.E., & Mohatt, G.V. (1990). Counseling intervention and American Indian tradition: An integrative approach. *Counseling Psychologist, 18* (4), 628–654.

Lake, M.G. (1991). *Native healer: Initiation into an ancient art.* Wheaton, IL: Quest Books.

Lee, C.C. (2001). Defining and responding to racial and ethnic diversity. In D.C. Locke, J.E. Myers, & E.L. Herr (Eds.), *The handbook of counseling* (pp. 581–588). Thousand Oaks, CA: Sage.

Lee, C.C. (Ed.). (2002). *Multicultural issues in counseling: New approaches to diversity* (3rd ed.). Alexandria, VA: American Counseling Association.

Little Soldier, L. (1992). Building optimum learning environments for Navajo students. *Childhood Education, 68* (3), 145–148.

Locust, C. (1988). Wounding the spirit: Discrimination and traditional American Indian belief systems. *Harvard Educational Review, 58* (3), 315–330.

Loftin, J.D. (1989). Anglo-American jurisprudence and the Native American tribal quest for religious freedom. *American Indian Culture and Research Journal, 13*(1), 1–52.

Maples, M.F., Dupey, P., Torres-Rivera, E., Phan, L.T., Vereen, L., & Garrett, M.T. (2001). Ethnic diversity and the use of humor in counseling: Appropriate or inappropriate? *Journal of Counseling and Development, 79,* 53–60.

Matheson, L. (1996). Valuing spirituality among Native American populations. *Counseling and Values, 41,* 51–58.

McLaughlin, D. (1994). Critical literacy for Navajo and other American Indian learners. *Journal of American Indian Education, 33* (3), 47–59.

Oswalt, W.H. (1988). *This land was theirs: A study of North American Indians* (4th ed.). Mountain View, CA: Mayfield.

Plank, G.A. (1994). What silence means for educators of American Indian children. *Journal of American Indian Education, 34* (1), 3–19.

Red Horse, J.G. (1997). Traditional American Indian family systems. *Families, Systems, and Health, 15,* 243–250.

Reyhner, J., & Eder, J. (1992). A history of Indian education. In J. Reyhner (Ed.), *Teaching American Indian students* (pp. 33–58). Norman, OK: University of Oklahoma Press.

Roberts-Wilbur, J., Wilbur, M., Garrett, M.T., & Yuhas, M. (In press). Talking circles: Listen or your tongue will make you deaf. *Journal for Specialists in Group Work.*

Robinson, T.L., & Howard-Hamilton, M.F. (2000). *The convergence of race, ethnicity, and gender: Multiple identities in counseling.* Upper Saddle River, NJ: Merrill.

Russell, G. (1998). *American Indian facts of life: A profile of today's tribes and reservations.* Phoenix, AZ: Russell.

Thomason, T.C. (1991). Counseling Native Americans: An introduction for non–Native American counselors. *Journal of Counseling and Development, 69* (4), 321–327.

U.S. Bureau of the Census. (2001). *2000 census counts of American Indians, Eskimos, or Aleuts and American Indian and Alaska Native areas*. Washington, DC: U.S. Bureau of the Census.

Vick, R.D., Sr., Smith, L.M., & Iron Rope Herrera, C. (1998). The healing circle: An alternative path to alcoholism recovery. *Counseling and Values, 42,* 132–141.

Wilbur, M.P. (1999a). The rivers of a wounded heart. *Journal of Counseling and Development, 77,* 47–50.

Wilbur, M.P. (1999b). Finding balance in the winds. *Journal for Specialists in Group Work, 24,* 342–353.

CHAPTER 4

African Americans: A Remarkable People

Karen Westbrooks

Karen Westbrooks, Ph.D., is professor of family therapy in the Department of Counseling and Student Affairs at Western Kentucky University and past president of the Kentucky Association for Marriage and Family Therapy. She has published three books and has made numerous contributions to publications for youth and families. Prior to her career as an academic, Dr. Westbrooks spent ten years working in the trenches of St. Louis with a diverse population of clients, including homeless families, troubled youth, the terminally ill, and abused women and children.

AWARENESS INDEX

Please test your knowledge by marking the following statements true or false before proceeding to the text in this chapter. Compute your score from the scoring guide at the end of the Awareness Index.

1. T F All races of people have already achieved the same levels of respect and regard in our society.

2. T F There is a widely held assumption that African Americans can understand or explain both past and present race-based experiences.

3. T F Racial horrors are a thing of the past.

4. T F A conflict for many African Americans is a conflict between freedom and bondage.

5. T F Not being able to speak in real and honest ways without
worrying about the reactions of others is a form of
bondage.

6. T F Relegating a focus of counseling to merely a set of "behaviors or choices" can sometimes minimize and disregard the multidimensionality of client lives.

7. T F An essential problem in having only a race-based identification is that such identification is often accompanied
by socially inherited beliefs.

8. T F A purposeful life demands resilience that is formed from
an intelligent combination of grace and strength.

9. T F Being greatly passionate, thoroughly proud, fully alive,
and filled with purpose creates peaceful and joyful interactions with different-race others.

10. T F Awareness makes you competent to counsel.

Scoring guide: **1.** F; **2.** T; **3.** F; **4.** T; **5.** T; **6.** T; **7.** T; **8.** T; **9.** F; **10.** F

CASE STUDY: A TRUE STORY

Gina Wolfe was a beautiful African American baby girl and would remain
an African American throughout her life. She was truly beautiful in spirit
and enormously gifted with intellect, creativity, energy, and generosity.
Gina was consistently functioning several notches higher than her grade
level in all academic areas, but her wise mother decided that Gina would
never skip grades; instead, she would remain in the same grade as her
same age peers. The lesson for Gina, thought her mom, is to grow in emotional maturity. Labels such as "gifted" and "talented" became commonplace descriptors for Gina throughout her elementary and secondary
school years.

When going to a predominantly White university, Gina realized that
her gifted and talented status had changed to that of "Black student." Was
she no longer gifted and talented? Gina noticed that her grades dropped

to mostly Bs. Was Gina no longer exceptional? At the beginning of one particular class period, Gina saw that her research paper was on top of a stack of papers that a professor would be returning to students. Gina noted that the professor reviewed her paper briefly (for what looked to be a second or third time), then began to teach the contents of her paper during the class period! She knew in her heart of hearts that she had earned an A on that paper. With anticipation Gina ran back to her residence hall to read all the wonderful comments that she knew her paper contained. What she saw instead was a B− and no comments. Gina had not only worked hard on her own research, she had also stayed up long hours helping Pourani, her classmate and roommate, write and edit a research paper for the same class. Pourani received an A+. Perplexed, Gina waited patiently to talk to the professor during the next class period. "I thought you would be happy. That's the highest grade I have ever given a Black student," said the professor. With tearful eyes and an overwhelming feeling of disbelief and disgust, Gina walked away quietly and took a seat in the front of the class.

In graduate school, Gina could not escape being counted as merely a Black graduate student. Furthermore, where was everybody? Where were the many other talented African American students from Gina's undergraduate years? Surely there were African Americans who were now in graduate school. Gina had known many such undergraduates. Where was the guy who walked around campus with his lips pressed down on a pipe telling everyone that he was practicing being a professor? Where was the incredible artist who was majoring in architecture? Where was the profoundly brilliant pre-med student? Where was the savvy journalism student who could write in forty-five minutes a compelling and documented piece of work that it took his student peers four to five days to compose?

Whatever

"Whatever" has become commonplace for the apathy that sometimes accompanies stories like Gina's. Perhaps it may be possible to read this entire chapter and walk away untouched. If so, that would be quite a pity indeed. Awareness and skills needed to counsel African Americans are not elusive or complicated or beyond the learning curve. In fact, they are more basic than one might imagine. Although Locke (1990), Parham (1989), and Harvey (2001) advocate culture-specific approaches, Sue, Arrendondo, and McDavis (1992) profess in the Multicultural Counseling Competencies that "all of counseling is cross-cultural and counseling is culture-bound." This author defines culture-bound, in part, to mean the values, beliefs, and experiences that direct us or touch us.

So What?

You might remember that what may have been revolutionary to the professor was disgusting to Gina. With tearful eyes she took a seat in the front of the class. What aspect of Gina's response seemed to grab you? Was it the tearful eyes? Was it the fact that she did not ask, "Why would you factor race into my grade?" Was it quietly walking away? Was it taking a seat in the front of the class? Was it the clash of perceptions between Gina and the professor? If the tearful eyes stirred you, this is a beginning. If you noticed that Gina did not ask about the professor's bigotry, this is a beginning too. If you did not consider Gina to be "avoiding conflict," perhaps you were open to her strategy of "subtle confrontation." When Gina quietly walked away she did not retreat. Instead, she took a seat in the front of the class. Gina was not powerless. Her nonverbal behavior was saying that she would not be bullied to the back of the class or discouraged from being an active participant in the class. She would sit front and center. Did Gina have an issue? Yes. Did the professor have an issue? Yes. Gina's issue of being minimized and needing to figure out what to do about it is connected with the professor's issues of race and ability.

When she submitted a more than solid paper, the professor did two things: (1) he taught her ideas to the class; (2) he reassessed his views of Black students, and in a "revolutionary move" gave her "the highest grade" he had ever given a Black student.

Gina's story is one that is familiar to many African Americans. It is a story of being dismissed, disempowered, and disregarded—all actions of racism and oppression. In turn, Gina responded with actions of resilience and strength that demonstrate presence, pride, persistence, and power (Westbrooks & Starks, 2001). African Americans as a whole are a strong, vital, intelligent people. An author, athlete, leader, rapper, professor, if

African American, is often defined as Black author, Black athlete, Black leader, Black rapper, Black professor. What would happen if we were Black *and some*—say, spirited, determined, persevering, battle-ready, dream-filled, faith-filled, freedom-filled, wise, trustworthy, gifted, outstanding, responsive, competitive, proud, resilient, strategic, hopeful, remarkable?

Perhaps Michael Jordan came the closest to transcending the color scope, as he is often known as a "great basketball player, a six-time NBA champion." We are just as filled with greatness, aliveness, and joy as we are despair, pain, and sorrow. It is particularly difficult to pinpoint when we simply became African American and nothing more. Unfortunately, *nothing more* is all too often implicitly registered in the brains of folks and often implicitly and explicitly acted out in interactions with African American persons. The essential problem in only a race-based identification of African Americans is that such a race identification is often accompanied by socially inherited beliefs. In the case above, Gina had beliefs of herself that the professor did not have.

Learning to cope effectively with a continuous onslaught of "dissing" is not an easy task for anyone. Strength and grace must be intelligently combined to form the kind of resilience that is necessary for a purposeful life. According to Stevens (2000), honesty and courage are needed to challenge unethical behavior in others and wisdom to recognize our own deficiencies. Would you consider an onslaught of "dissing" a client unethical? Would you consider a lack of awareness a deficiency?

A conflict for many African Americans is a conflict between freedom and bondage. Freedom involves a desire to engage in the reality of our true lives. That life involves family, interests, strengths, abilities, worries, wishes, and goals. Bondage, on the other hand, involves a constant battle between imposed, boxed-in identities of our public lives (employee, citizen, student) and more relaxed identities of our private lives (family member, friend). It is more often in our private lives that we are free to be "a Black person." This means that many characteristics of African Americans that involve being greatly passionate, thoroughly proud, and fully alive, when manifest publicly, tend to "scare" some people. When African Americans passionately speak out in the public arena it is more often viewed as militancy and disruption. While at a national conference, an

African American male shared his experience of being a faculty member: "If I fully express my anger and disagreement with a decision, I'm viewed as out of control. I'm not out of control. I'm angry." In my own experience as a faculty member, I remember being stopped cold when a senior faculty member publicly commented, "You're on an emotional binge." Any further contributions I made at the meeting that day were immediately and thoroughly dismissed.

Many African Americans toil in silence rather than subject themselves to the judgments of others who might blame them for their "condition" of pain, suffering, or disconnect. Durodoye (1999) speaks of a tiredness attached to her experience as a counselor educator:

> I am sometimes fatigued as I go about choosing the manner in which I relate to those ethnically dissimilar to me. This fatigue derives from trying to estimate how much of any emotion or behavior it might be safe to display in various situations, so as not to be perceived as a threat to the preconceived notions of some people. *I have laughed, smiled, and grinned all in the name of making others comfortable. I have remained speechless and impotent in situations in which the only appropriate reaction was speaking out.* There have been times that I have felt like a fly caught up in a spider's web of mental shame and castigation for falling into this internally oppressive trap. . . . Each time I relate an incident, I sometimes believe that I run the risk of having the story minimized. (p. 47)

Like some of the women presented in the research of Ward and Westbrooks (2000), the statement above reflects "not speaking" and in effect a belief that "if you can't hear me, you don't have to deal with me. If I don't say anything, I don't have to deal with you." Not being able to speak in real and honest ways without worrying about the reactions of others is a form of bondage. Such bondage involves a feeling of being trapped or stuck, isolation, grief, confusion, and despair.

A place where the bondage experienced by many is discussed and called by name is the church. With needed doses of inspiration and strength, spirited warriors known as granddaddies, grandmamas, mamas, daddies, uncles, aunts, sisters, brothers, daughters, and sons week after week march back into unfriendly territory. In the words of James Weldon Johnson in the Negro National Anthem, "Lift Every Voice and Sing,"

Stony the road we trod, bitter the chastening rod
Felt in the days when hope unborn had died
Yet with a steady beat, have not our weary feet
Come to the place for which our fathers sighed?

LEARNING ABOUT AFRICAN AMERICANS

Just as Ivey and Ivey (1999) designed *Intentional Interviewing and Counseling* to "demystify" the helping process, I designed this chapter to demystify the process of understanding African Americans. According to Durodoye (1999), "both novice and seasoned counselors think about how we are taught to actively listen but seem to forget this basic skill when the issue deals with an ethnic (person) and color parity in the United States" (p. 47).

This chapter intends to help you listen by using the words *our*, *we*, and *us* to involve you more personally in a deeply personal heritage. Because we are all connected, who *we* are as a people influences and impacts all of humanity—including *you*.

Who We Are

When reviewing information from the 2000 U.S. census data, the most updated information on African Americans was from 1999. According to the 1999 data, there are 34,658,000 African Americans living in the United States. This means we comprise 12.6% of the total 274,596,000 persons in America. Close to 5 million African Americans (15%) live at or below the poverty level; 12 million (35%) earn between 101% and 200% of the maximum poverty-level income. The median income for all African Americans is $22,491 (U.S. Bureau of the Census, 1998). Those who speak of the growing Black middle class refer to merely .5% whose income is between $40,000 and $79,999. Although many are familiar with Michael Jordan, Bill Cosby, Colin Powell, and Oprah Winfrey, these African Americans have incomes more exorbitant than many Americans will see in two or three lifetimes.

If there were more African Americans with a college education would the facts be different? The U.S. census offers 1999 data on the relationship of income level and educational attainment for the Black population.

For those with a minimum of a bachelor's degree, the findings were strikingly inconsistent. Slightly over 10% of degreed persons had incomes over $50,000. Another 10% had incomes between $1 and $14,999. This is not a typo. Be hopeful, however: slightly over 30% of degreed African Americans have incomes between $25,000 and $49,999, and another 30% of degreed African Americans have incomes between $15,000 and $29,999. The data set did not provide clarity on the actual percentage of African Americans who were earning $25,000 to $29,000. Those who labor to attain the "education key" to a bright future may stand at many doors before they are able to unlock even one.

Our Past and Present

This section will respond to the questions: What have been our themes? How have we been stuck? What do we need to move on? A complete set of encyclopedias could not contain a truly comprehensive account of events and people who have played key roles in the history of our people in this country. As James Weldon Johnson wrote in the Negro National Anthem, "Lift Every Voice and Sing:"

> We have come, over a way that with tears has been watered
> We have come, treading our path through the blood of the slaughtered
> Out of the gloomy past, till now we stand at last,
> Where the white gleam of our bright star is cast

Being stuck and moving on: The link.   African Americans have a history filled with perseverance and pain, strength and hope. This joint presentation of past and present is intended to tell the story between the lines. The most often told story of our beginnings in the United States is the story of "strange fruit." Strange fruit hung on trees with blood on the leaves and blood at the root. We hung for the sun to rot, the bugs to swarm, the rain to drench, the crows to pluck, and the wind to sweep the foul order of human carcass over fields and plantations. The unknown songwriter of "Strange Fruit" embraced with shocking truth the ugly reality of a horror that is still too difficult for many people to wrap their minds around. To consider strange fruit as merely a sin of "ancestors" is extremely short-sighted and dismissive: the "inheritance" is very much a present-day reality. Given the reaction of horror, fear, pain, and anger across the country on what is now known as 9/11/2001, the Day of Terror, the Attack on America, it can be surmised that few Americans had ever known true horror. Sadly, experiencing inherited and present-day horror is a continuing reality for African Americans, even after the Emancipation Proclamation of 1863. As an already horrified people, we continued to experience lynching, murder, slaughter, rape, bloodshed, house burning, and the theft of our land, all of which were "lawful acts of hate," yet we moved forward anyway. Generations upon generations were desecrated, dismissed, and ignored, yet we found sanctity, presence, and voice.

A little-known fact is that some African Americans were here (in the United States) years before slavery. The first Africans to settle in the United States arrived in South Carolina in 1526. (This was before North America was "discovered" by the Europeans.) In fact, twenty-six of the first forty-six settlers of what became Los Angeles were of African descent (Cosby, 2002). In addition, African American genius contributed greatly to the civilized world with the inventions of the traffic light (Garrett A. Morgan), clock (Benjamin Banneker), filament in light bulbs (Lewis Latimer), long-distance phone calling (Granvillie T. Woods), and a method of mass producing shoes (Jan Matzeliger) to name a few (Grevious, 1993). Had you, for example, always thought that Thomas Edison invented the light in the light bulb? In truth, there were many African Americans who had been minimized and dismissed long before Gina Wolfe.

Our contributions are truly phenomenal when you consider three hundred years of being denied a formal education in this country. Even by the mid-twentieth century there were countless colleges and universities that did not admit Black students no matter how brilliant they may have been. I currently teach at a university that did not have "Black graduates" until after the desegregation ruling of *Brown v. Board of Education* (1954), a case that Thurgood Marshall craftily executed and won. Just as "Black students" and "Black faculty," are still foreign to many predominantly White institutions, the university culture is also foreign to many "Black students," "Black faculty" and "Black families." Helping our sons and daughters prepare for and negotiate a foreign sociopolitical climate is quite difficult.

Bondage can be seen in narrow venues of opportunity, and education, economics, and ownership of property, as well as in the social, emotional, and psychological realms of living. Of the fourteen types of bondages that Sherrer and Garlock (1994) present in their discussion for guiding women out of bondage, I will address seven and discuss their application to a historical bondage of African American women and men in general. They are:

- anger;
- doubt and unbelief;
- fear;
- grief and disappointment;
- unforgiveness;
- rejection and shame; and
- generational influences. (p. 11)

Like Weingarten (2000), I believe that the African philosophy of *ubuntu,* the emphasis of which is on the self in community, in contrast to the Western emphasis on the individual, may be a better fit for understanding African Americans. Understanding African Americans, then, means listening to what we are saying about "others" in our world and gaining an appreciation for such relationships. African Americans who have experienced incredible discrimination, minimization, and injustice are likely to have many issues around anger, doubt, fear, grief, unforgiveness, rejection, and generational influences. Our anger is often expected to be accompanied by violence—a stereotype that continues to do us harm because the stereotype is believed to be accurate. In truth, the word *violence* comes from the Latin root *vis*, which means life force. When the life force is suppressed, the flip side of love can become manifest (Moore, 1992).

When Gina's abilities were minimized, her life force was suppressed. She got angry. She feared what would happen if she openly confronted the professor's racism. She inwardly grieved not being viewed as gifted and talented. She carried unforgiveness because of the unexplainable rejection of her true ability. However, she gave tribute to generations of resilience and courage by sitting in the front of the class anyway.

Generational issues involve what we remember and pass on about how to interact with others. Doubt takes the form of mistrust. Grief takes the form of despair. Unforgiveness takes the form of an unexplainable burden. Doubt, grief, and unforgiveness cannot and do not exist independently. These dynamics exist in relationship. A serious scholar and clinician must ask, "What are the clues in this counselor-client relationship that would suggest that this client has no sound reasons to trust me, to have hope in my helping abilities, or to hold me in regard?" According to Westbrooks and Starks (2001), another question to always consider in the interview process is "What does the client think will happen or fear will happen?" Such questions can also be applied to the counseling process.

Anger regarding our conflicted status in a free country is enough to be enraged about. Pre–civil rights Jim Crow laws governed where people could take a drink of water, eat, and relieve themselves. Pre–affirmative action, many qualified candidates for law schools, medical schools, and doctoral programs were not admitted because a race-based "quota" was not yet the law. In the 1980s and '90s many qualified candidates for positions in academe or corporate America were not given jobs because the race-based quota had already been filled. This means that many young, gifted African American persons were running into a brick wall at the very beginning of their professional careers. No empirical data is available to substantiate the above claims, as no intelligent employer would boldly admit that their institution or company flagrantly involved themselves in such practices. At this juncture a reader may distrust our stories and minimize our experiences. Ironically, a reader who disregards what has so far been written actively substantiates my point about being dismissed.

What makes anger, doubt, fear, grief, unforgiveness, rejection, and generational influences apply to centuries of African American life? Recall that experiencing horror was a non-self-imposed reality for African Americans before and after the Emancipation Proclamation. Thus a variety of bondages and freedoms link yesterday and today. For African Americans, "what happened" is not just history, but a deeply personal chain of experiences that affects our triumph and resolve. Despair can reflect what is happening in relationships and applies to social contexts as immediate as marriage and family and as broad as community. Again, despair is grief transfigured. If we accept that grief is a form of bondage and that the church is a major player in "setting the captives free," then it is a message of freedom that quenches the thirst of those yearning to live freely. Again, I quote Johnson's "Lift Every Voice and Sing":

> God of our weary years, God of our silent tears
> Thou Who has brought us thus far on the way
> Thou Who hast by Thy might, led us into the light
> Keep us forever in the path we pray

Triumphs: Selective surrender.   Battle-weary from emotional, social, psychological, educational, economic, and political bondages, we walk forward, always preparing ourselves for the next assault to our integrity and strength. It is too much to surrender all and it is also too much to surrender not at all, so our hope in triumph is selective surrender. Surrendering all would mean that we allow our lives to be defeated by injustice and controlled by oppressive forces such as racism, sexism, ageism, or able-ism that tend to define how we might be treated. In other words, being on the receiving end of these "isms" is not only a hard road, but also an ultimate test of being the ruler of our own spirits. In not surrendering, our militant stance might mean that we join Malcolm X and pay a price figuratively similar to the one he paid. While Martin Luther King in his nonviolent approach was also assassinated, today we have a holiday for King, but no holiday for Malcolm X. In other words, we have found that a militant stance is not only self-destructive but also officially unrecognized. Surrendering all or surrendering nothing would both mean that we allow our lives to be defeated by oppressive forces.

There is of course a great deal of middle ground between being militant and being nonviolent. So what do we do? In an effort to free ourselves from political, economic, educational, psychological, social, and emotional bondage, we try to choose wisely what freedoms are worth the fight. "You may be deprived of many things in this life, but you should never simply surrender your self-respect." This has been a mantra in African American families for centuries. Respect carries enormous importance in a vast history of being on the receiving end of flagrant disrespect. Respect includes a regard for relationships, needs, goals, history, power, value, and opportunity (Westbrooks, 1995).

Strengths: Standing firm. Given a mere glimpse of our issues and our triumphs, what remains extraordinarily real is the fact that we are still standing. How can that be? After centuries of bondage and struggle, praying and breaking loose, how can a people still have strength? While there are a variety of means to be strong, for some African Americans a meaningful sense of presence, pride, pertinence, and power can be derived through spiritual life (Westbrooks & Starks, 2001). To truly appreciate what it means to stand strong would mean to recognize that at some point instead of being defeated by forces that tend to dismiss, disrespect, disregard, and disempower, we summon the power to transcend (Westbrooks & Starks, 2001). It is indeed even more important to recognize spirituality as a healthy, powerful, and humane way of living. Recent perspectives recognize spirituality as a form of functional diversity (Westbrooks, 1997).

Boyd-Franklin (1989) identifies the major strengths of African American clients as extended family support, centrality of spirituality or religion, adaptability of family roles, high value placed on children, informal adoption, cultural loyalty, high priority on education (strong work orientation), and strong women. Our men, our resolve, and our resilience are also key strengths and it is about time that they are recognized as such. As the old saying goes, you don't help someone be good by telling them how bad they are. Were not W.E.B. DuBois, Frederick Douglas, Thurgood Marshall, and Martin Luther King men? Our men *and* our women are keys to our resolve, resilience, and our voice as a people.

ENHANCING COUNSELOR EFFECTIVENESS

Needed Awareness

1. Hear us.
2. Consider emotion, motivation, behavior, pain, perseverance, issues, triumphs, and strengths.
3. Understand the relevance of personal history to the presenting issue.
4. Get a sense of whether *we* think you "get it."
5. Yield to our authority to define, name, and lead.

To hear us by necessity means validating our experience as legitimate in the full complexity of its layers. The emotional, mental, social, psychological, and physical toll involved in being both bound and free can be enormous. Ongoing challenges, struggles, and, yes, horrors are enough to make a life difficult at best and possibly dangerous. Therefore, our perseverance, triumphs, and strengths have come through "the refiner's fire" and are not only worthy of notice, but also worthy of pride and celebration.

Finally, yielding to client authority to define, name, and lead is standard practice (Cormier & Hackney, 1999; Ivey & Ivey, 1999; Ivey, Ivey, & Simek-Morgan, 1997; Lee & Richardson, 1991), even though many counselors continue to impose their own worldviews on clients. To demonstrate the point, Holcomb-McCoy & Myers (1999) reported in their empirical study that "most training strategies focus on 'knowing that' (i.e., knowledge) cultural differences exist rather than 'knowing how' (i.e., skills) to conduct effective counseling sessions with diverse clients."

Sue and Sue (1990) note a problem with the fact that some counselors see the sole focus of the session as individualistic rather than contextual—that is, counselors view the client's problems as "residing within the individual rather than society" (p. 72). This point is further emphasized by Leung (1995), who notes that current models of career development and counseling do not take into consideration the effects of social and economic barriers, such as economic hardship, immigration disruption, and racial discrimination, on career behavior. The models usually assume an individualistic and self-actualizing perspective regarding career behavior and choices.

In my 1995 book, I refer to families' responses to the community as external systems interactions. For African Americans, it is truly difficult "to hide." We will be noticed no matter what. We will be noticed in our neighborhoods, in the workplace, at church, and so on. For this reason, we are always conscious of how we respond "to the outside world." At best, we gird ourselves with self-respect, patience, and hope.

CONCLUSION

Complex issues around anger, doubt, fear, grief, unforgiveness, rejection, and generational influences are consistent factors in African American life regardless of the person, circumstance or set of relationships. At all levels of African American life there is bondage and freedom that is complicated by "attacks" on the life force. Attacks involve dismissing, disempowering, disregarding, and disrespecting (Westbrooks & Starks, 2001) on the one hand and stereotyping and boxing-in on the other hand. When asked to contribute a chapter to this book, I found myself feeling conflicted. With an ability to write on any number of topics, including counseling foundations and techniques, I was invited specifically to write the chapter on African Americans. Was I surprised? I experienced a familiar battle between a boxed-in racial identity and an identity as a counselor educator. To bring resolve to my own struggle, I surmised that being African American could not and should not in itself be "enough" to be a credible contributor. Surely it is necessary to be African American *and some*—say, a thoughtful teacher, a conscientious writer, a serious scholar. As I gird myself with self-respect, patience, and hope, I trust that you will do the same.

EXPERIENTIAL ACTIVITIES

These exercises are intended to take you to the crossroads of experience and awareness. The first is a focus on other. The second is a focus on self. (God bless you on your journey.)

1. You land at a predominately White university where Gina, Jr., is an undergraduate. She enters a counseling center as one of your clients. She tells you, "I was gifted and talented throughout elementary school, middle school, and high school. I don't understand why I'm getting mostly Bs and Cs. I've made one A– all semester, and that was after getting 100% on all three organic chemistry lab assignments. My organic chemistry teacher asked me how I am able to do so well. I'm not sure what he was getting at. This place is getting on my nerves." What are you hearing Gina say in this statement? Is it about the grades? What is the presenting issue? Is it simple or complex? If you wanted to "hear" Gina, what would you ask? To consider her emotion, motivation, behavior, pain, perseverance, issues, triumphs, and strengths, what would you do? What would Gina's personal history have to do with the presenting issue?

How would she know that you "got her"? How could you help Gina define and name her experience? What could you do to lead her through that experience once it had a name?

2. Consider the complexity of your own life and the ways in which you, too, have experienced bondage and freedom given your age, race, gender, class, and ethnicity. Is your experience simple or complex? If you wanted to truly listen to yourself, what questions would you contemplate? To consider your emotion, motivation, behavior, pain, perseverance, issues, triumphs, and strengths, what would you do? What would your personal history have to do with some of the primary issues in your life? How would you know that you "got *you*"? How would you define and name your own life experience? What significant differences and similarities do you foresee between you and your future clients?

REFERENCES

Boyd-Franklin, N. (1989). *Black families in therapy: A multisystems approach*. New York: Guilford.

Cormier, S., & Hackney, H. (1999). *Counseling strategies and interventions*. (5th ed.). Boston: Allyn and Bacon.

Cosby, B. (2002). Invitation to Schomburg Society. Available at: www.schomburgcenter. org.

Durodoye, B. (1999). On the receiving end. *Journal of Counseling and Development, 77 (1)*, 45–47.

Grevious, S.C. (1993). *Multicultural activities for primary children*. New York: Center for Applied Research.

Harvey, A.R. (2001). Individual and family intervention skills with African Americans: An Africentric approach. In R. Fong & S. Furuto (Eds.) *Culturally competent practice: Skills, interventions, and evaluations*. Boston: Allyn and Bacon.

Holcomb-McCoy, C.C., & Myers, J.E. (1999). Multicultural competence and counselor training: A national survey. *Journal of Counseling and Development, 77* (3), 294–302.

Ivey, A.E., & Ivey, M.B. (1999). *Intentional interviewing and counseling: Facilitating client development in a multicultural society* (4th ed.). Pacific Grove, CA: Brooks/Cole.

Ivey, A.E., Ivey, M.B., & Simek-Morgan, L. (1997). *Counseling and psychotherapy: A multicultural perspective* (4th ed.). Boston: Allyn and Bacon.

Lee, C.C., & Richardson, B.L. (1991). Promise and pitfalls of multicultural counseling. In C.C. Lee & B.L. Richardson (Eds.), *Multicultural issues in counseling: New approaches to diversity*. Alexandria, VA: American Counseling Association.

Locke, D.C. (1990). A not so provincial view of multicultural counseling. *Counselor Education and Supervision, 30*, 18–25.

Moore, T. (1992). *Care of the soul*. New York: Harper Perennial.

Parham, T.A. (1989). Cycles of psychological nigrescence. *Counseling Psychologist, 17*, 187–226.

Sherrer, Q., & Garlock, R. (1994). *A woman's guide to breaking bondages*. Ann Arbor, MI: Vine Books.

Stevens, P. (2000). The ethics of being ethical. *The Family Journal, 8* (2), 177–178.

Sue, D.W., Arrendondo, P., & McDavis, R.J. (1992). Multicultural counseling competencies: A call to the profession. *Journal of Counseling and Development, 70*, 477–486.

Sue, D.W., & Sue, D. (1990). *Counseling the culturally different*. New York: Wiley.

U.S. Bureau of the Census (1998). What we earn: Detailed tables for occupied units with Black householder. Available at: www.census.gov/hhes/www/housing/ahs/97cdtchrt/tab5–12.html.

U.S. Bureau of the Census (1999). Relationship of income level and educational attainment for the Black population. Available at: www/thuban.com/census/graphs/bincedu 1.gif.

Ward, C., & Westbrooks, K. (2000). *Oral histories and analyses of nontraditional women students: A study of unconventional strengths*. Lewiston, NY: Edwin Mellen Press.

Weingarten, K. (2000). Witnessing, wonder, and hope. *Family Process, 39* (4), 389–402.

Westbrooks, K. (1995). *Functional low-income families: Activating strengths*. New York: Vantage.

Westbrooks, K. (1997). Spirituality as a form of functional diversity: Activating unconventional strengths. *Journal of Family Social Work, 2* (A), 77–87.

Westbrooks, K., & Starks, S. (2001). Strengths perspective inherent in cultural empowerment: A tool for assessment with African American individuals and families. In R. Fong & S. Furuto (Eds.), *Culturally competent practice: Skills, interventions, and evaluations*. Boston: Allyn and Bacon.

CHAPTER 5

Counseling Asian Americans

Catherine Y. Chang

Catherine Y. Chang, Ph.D., was born in Daegu, Korea, and immigrated to the United States with her parents and two siblings at the age of four. Currently, she is an assistant professor at Georgia State University. Previously, she was an assistant professor in the Counseling Program at Clemson University. She received her doctorate in counselor education from the University of North Carolina, Greensboro. Her areas of interest include multicultural counseling and supervision, Asian and Korean concerns, and multicultural issues in assessment.

AWARENESS INDEX

Please test your knowledge by marking the following statements true or false before proceeding to the text in this chapter. Compute your score from the scoring guide at the end of the Awareness Index.

1. T F According to the 2000 census, Asian Americans make up approximately 4% of the total U.S. population.

2. T F Confucianism is the predominant system of thought among many Asian cultures.

3. T F Asian Americans are a homogenous group.

4. T F Asians are a very emotionally expressive cultural group.

5. T F Virtually all Asian Americans have a history that includes immigration to this country.

6. T F Generally, Asian Americans prefer a counseling style that is structured and directive.

7. T F Asian Americans utilize mental health counseling more readily than the general public.

8. T F Asian American clients are more likely to seek help for academic and vocational issues than for personal ones.

9. T F Counselors who do not understand Asian culture may misdiagnose Asian American clients.

10. T F Asian Americans are the "model minority."

Scoring guide: **1.** T; **2.** T; **3.** F; **4.** F; **5.** T; **6.** T; **7.** F; **8.** T; **9.** T; **10.** F

INTRODUCTION

Asian and Pacific Islanders were the fastest growing race group in the United States during the 1980s. This trend continued in the 1990s with an average annual growth rate of 4.5% (O'Hare & Felt, 1991; U.S. Department of Commerce, 1995). In 1980 there were 3.7 million Asian and Pacific Islanders in the United States, but by 1990 that number had doubled to 7.4 million (U.S. Department of Commerce, 1993). According to the 2000 census, approximately 11.9 million Asians represent a little over 4% of the total population (Grieco & Cassidy, 2001). The dramatic increase resulted from increased immigration from China, India, Korea, and the Philippines following the adoption of the Immigration and Nationality Act of 1965 (U.S. Department of Commerce, 1993). Immigration to the United States accounted for much of the growth (approximately 86%) in the Asian population. The remaining growth was due to national increases by births minus deaths (U.S. Department of Commerce, 1995). By 2050, it is anticipated that Asian Americans will comprise 10 percent of the total population (LEAP & UCLA Asian American Studies Center, 1993). A brief history of the Asian immigration will be discussed later in this chapter.

Asian Americans are a heterogeneous population, which includes groups who differ in their language, culture, religious affiliations, and recency of immigration. Over twenty-nine distinct subgroups of this population are recognized, including persons of Chinese, Japanese, Filipino, Vietnamese, Laotian, Cambodian, Thai, and Korean cultures (Moy, 1992). Sandhu (1997) reports more than forty disparate cultural groups in this population. Sue and Sue (1999) broadly classify Asian and Pacific Islander Americans into three major categories: Asian Americans, which include Asian Indians, Chinese, Filipinos, Japanese, and Koreans; Southeast Asians, including Cambodians, Laotians, and Vietnamese; and Pacific Islanders, including Hawaiian, Guamanians, and Somoans.

Although this population is increasing, our understanding of these individuals and groups remains limited (Nah, 1993). One reason for this is the extreme diversity within and between subgroups of the total population (Alva, 1993; Chang & Myers, 1997). In fact, Asian Americans are described as the most diverse of America's major minority groups (Kim & Chun, 1994; O'Hare & Felt, 1991). Much of the literature overlooks the diversity within the Asian American population, describing Asian Americans as a monolithic group rather than a heterogeneous group with a wide range of within-group differences (Alva, 1993; Berg & Miller, 1992; Hardy, 1989; Kwon, 1995). Each Asian group has distinct traditions, customs, religions, and languages, and unique life circumstances resulting from recency of immigration (Iwamasa, 1996; Moy, 1992). However, important commonalities also exist among Asian American cultures, including group and family values, communication and emotional expression, time orientation, the myth of the "model minority," and educational pressures. These commonalities will be discussed following two case studies that illustrate typical experiences encountered by many Asian Americans.

CASE EXAMPLES

Jon

Jon is a nineteen-year-old Korean American who immigrated to the United States with his parents and younger sister when he was eight years old and she was four years old. Jon is a freshman at an elite university.

His parents sent him to college with instructions that he study hard and make good grades so that he will become a doctor and take care of his parents when they grow older. Overall, Jon enjoys being away at college. This is the farthest he's been from home and the longest time he's spent without seeing his family. Even though Jon has made some friends and gets along well with his roommate, he misses his family and feels lonely and depressed.

Contrary to the stereotypical view of Asian students excelling in math and the sciences, Jon struggles in his biology and chemistry classes while excelling in his English and history classes. He knows that he must do well in his science classes in order to be admitted to medical school, and he must go to medical school in order to make his parents proud. Jon suffers from headaches and stomach aches. He has difficulty sleeping and feels "nervous" much of the time. After several visits to the health clinic, the medical doctor makes an appointment for Jon to visit the counseling center. Jon does not understand why he needs to see a counselor but promises the doctor he will attend the first meeting.

Li Na

Li Na had always stayed at home and taken care of her two small children. Her husband was a dentist and the sole financial provider for the family. After immigrating to the United States, Li Na's husband accepted a job managing a convenience store because he could not obtain licensure as a dentist without returning to school. His income allows the family only a marginal existence. After much discussion and debate, they decided that Li Na would seek employment outside the home.

The following year, their daughter's school counselor referred the family to counseling. Li Na is experiencing depression over the constant fights with her husband and children. Li Na enjoys the new sense of independence from working outside the home but feels torn between working and maintaining the home. Both Li Na and her husband work outside the home, but she continues to have sole responsibility for the cooking and housework, and is the primary caregiver to their children. To further complicate matters, Li Na's parents-in-law moved in with them three months ago. Although Li Na opposes these living arrangements, her husband feels it is his duty as eldest son to care for his aging parents.

Group and Family Values

Confucianism, which is a system of social and ethical philosophy based on the teachings of Confucius and his followers, provides the foundation for the behavior pattern and structure of the family and community in many Asian cultures. Family is a central pillar of Confucianism. An Asian's identity stems from his or her family and group; therefore, the whole family feels disgrace or pride collectively when one member does something shameful or worthy of praise (Kitano & Maki, 1996). Studies indicate that Asians place a greater emphasis on the group than on the individual, while Americans from a Western background tend to emphasize the individual more than the group (Hirayama & Hirayama, 1984). The Asian socialization pattern is one of interdependence rather than independence (Chang & Myers, 1997). This emphasis on group and family values can explain Jon's feelings of loneliness and depression at being separated from his family.

Confucian ethics emphasize order and hierarchical relationships, where authority is centralized and responsibility, leadership, and patriarchy are at the top of the hierarchy (Berg & Jaya, 1993; Hamilton, 1996; Kim & Chun, 1994; Sue, 1998). In this patriarchal role structure, women play a passive, subservient role. They teach their children at an early age to respect authority and value harmonious interpersonal relationships (Chang & Myers, 1997). Well-defined and interdependent roles emphasized in Asian culture help promote strong group and family commitment and cohesiveness (Chung, 1992). By contrast, Euro-Americans come from an egalitarian environment with a decentralized social structure and value the individual over the family (Moy, 1992).

Filial piety, the concept of respecting and caring for one's parents, also plays an important role in all aspects of traditional Asian family life (Sung, 1995; Youn & Song, 1991). Filial obligation dictates that children will provide for their parents physically, financially, and socio-psychologically. Filial piety ensures harmony and order in the family and, by extension, in society (Hyun, 2001). The cases of both Jon and Lin Na demonstrate the importance of filial piety. Jon feels obligated to do well in school in order to bring pride to his family, and Li Na's husband feels obligated to care for his aging parents despite the difficulties in his own nuclear family. Filial piety may be in conflict with Euro-American emphasis on the nuclear family, primary allegiance to the spouse (Sue, 1998), and individual goals and desires.

Communication and Emotional Expression

Apparent in the communication pattern of Asians are the traditional values of interpersonal harmony, deference, and respect for authority figures. A restrained, rather than expressive pattern of communication maintains interpersonal harmony. In order to avoid confrontation and situations that may bring shame to others, Asians prefer to use silence and more subtle or indirect forms of communication (Lee & Cynn, 1991). Asian culture views silence as promoting harmony and politeness, and many Asians may regard spoken words suspiciously (Franks, 2000). In general, Asians value high-context communication, in which meaning derives from the context of the communication, in contrast to Euro-Americans, who tend to value low-context communication, with its emphasis on clarity and explicitness (Yook & Albert, 1998).

Time Orientation

Whereas American attitudes toward time require either implicit or explicit scheduling, Asian cultures do not view time as strictly; they are satisfied with general guidelines or plans and believe that everything has its own time. Many Americans schedule their time intensively, separating objectives into different periods with immediate, short-term, and long-term goals. In the macroculture, overtime is rewarded and lateness and failure to keep commitments within a certain time frame are penalized. In contrast, Asians view time collectively. Time belongs not only to the individual but also to others: the family, organizations, community, and nature. There is a process orientation to time that views time as springing from the self rather than from an external source (Chung, 1992).

Myth of the "Model Minority"

Asian Americans also face the common stereotype of the "model minority" that perpetuates the perception of a single, monolithic group that is socially well adjusted and consistently successful in scholastic and economic achievement (Gould, 1988). The term *model minority* evokes images of a supernormal group that enjoys extraordinary success in American society. Contrary to this myth, Asian Americans experience economic hardships, violence, and prejudice and racial discrimination (Chang & Myers, 1997). Atkinson, Morten, and Sue (1998) outline three detrimental functions of the model minority stereotype. First, by portraying the image that one minority group has "made it" in United States society, it reaffirms the belief that with hard work any group can succeed, and thus blames the victims if they do not succeed. The myth also creates conflicts and antagonisms among Asian Americans, the "privileged group," and other minority groups. Finally, the myth allows institutions and policymakers to consider Asian Americans as ineligible for special programs and policies.

Educational Pressures

Many Asian American cultures greatly value academic achievement and education. Related to this emphasis, many parents expect their children to continue their education beyond high school and college, and actively participate in ACT/SAT plans and preparation and the decision to go to college (Asakawa & Csikszentmihalyi, 2000). Because academic achievement brings honor to the family and is synonymous with prestige for the family (Smith, 1996), many Asian American children feel driven and controlled by parental pressures and guilt (Yagi & Oh, 1995). This emphasis on academic pressure can lead to achievement anxiety and desperation when students lack academic ability (Lee & Cynn, 1991). Jon, like many Asian children, feels great pressure to do well in school and bring pride to his parents as well as to use his education to later take care of his parents. Jon's academic pressure may be the root cause of his headaches and stomach aches.

A HISTORICAL OVERVIEW

Immigration contributed greatly to the growth of the Asian population after the passage of the Immigration and Nationality Act of 1965; however, the immigration rate and history has varied among the different Asian groups (U.S. Department of Commerce, 1993). The first significant wave of Asian immigrants was the Chinese, who arrived on the West

Coast as cheap laborers to work in the gold mines and on the railroads (Cao & Novas, 1996). With the completion of the Union-Pacific-Central railroad in 1869 and a decline in many businesses, the Chinese became targets for discrimination, resulting in the Chinese Exclusion act of 1882. This act suspended immigration of Chinese laborers and made Chinese immigrants who were born in China ineligible for American citizenship. This policy was not repealed until 1943 (Axelson, 1999).

The Japanese followed the first wave of Chinese immigrants in the 1890s, also as laborers for the railroads, canneries, and gold mines. Because many of the Japanese immigrants were from the farming class, they worked unwanted land or found work as agricultural laborers. Their success in agriculture made them economic competitors and the target of violence and harassment (Sue & Sue, 1999). The harassment culminated with the passing of the Alien Land Law in 1913, which forbade aliens to own land. The number of Japanese immigrants declined as a result of the Gentlemen's Agreement of 1908, when Japan began restricting immigration to the United States (Axelson, 1999). The Immigration Act of 1924, which denied admission to the United States of all persons ineligible for citizenship, further restricted immigration from Asian countries (Kim, 1978).

The next wave of Asian immigrants occurred as a result of the Immigration and Nationality Act of 1965, which ended discriminatory provisions of citizenship eligibility based on national origins and replaced individual national quotas with annual limits for persons from countries outside the Western Hemisphere. This group consisted mainly of immigrants from China, India, Korea, and the Philippines (U.S. Department of Commerce, 1993). Both Jon and Li Na represent immigrants from this third wave of immigration.

Immigration continues to contribute to the growth of the Asian population for several reasons. The current immigration policy emphasizes family reunification, and with the growing number of Asian Americans presently in the United States the number of Asian individuals eligible for entry under the family reunification has increased (O'Hare & Felt, 1991). In 1990 the yearly quota of immigrants allowed to enter the United States increased, allowing a great number of Asians entry into the United States. Finally, immigration laws give preference to individuals who have work skills needed by American business (i.e., technical and professional expertise), which also promotes immigration from Asia (O'Hare & Felt, 1991).

CURRENT ISSUES

Asian Americans encounter certain difficulties associated with their minority and immigration status, thus putting them at risk for certain mental health issues. Issues that affect the mental heath of Asian Americans will be discussed in this section.

Barriers to Mental Health Services

Despite the fact that many Asian Americans are at risk for certain mental health issues, they are less likely than the general public to utilize social and mental health resources and are more likely to terminate counseling prematurely (Choi & Wynne, 2000). Some Asian Americans are reluctant to seek assistance due to language and cultural barriers, while others simply are unaware of community resources (Thomas, 2000). Other proposed explanations for these findings relate to values, acculturation, problems inherent in the mental health system, and counselor bias (Atkinson & Gim, 1989; Atkinson & Matsushita, 1991).

The emotional and verbal expression emphasized in Western-style psychotherapy may be contrary to the Asian cultural value of emotional restraint and internalization of individual problems. Talking to a professional about one's personal problems directly reflects on the entire family and brings shame to the family name. Open discussions of personal feelings and issues violate traditional cultural norms. Many Asians believe that mental health can and should be obtained by exercising willpower and avoiding bad thoughts (Atkinson & Gim, 1989). Because of the stigma associated with mental distress, Asian Americans are more likely to present somatic complaints when expressing emotional distress and social problems. Based on this concept, a counselor might hypothesize that Jon's headaches and stomach aches are somatic representations of an emotional problem. In addition, personal and cultural backgrounds of the therapists, lack of knowledge regarding the unique concerns of Asian American clients, and insufficient training programs contribute to biased perceptions of Asian American clients and impede the counseling process and outcome (Leong, 1986).

Academic and Career Issues

Although Asian Americans may underutilize mental health services, some studies indicate that they are more likely to overutilize academic and vocational counseling services (Morrissey, 1997). Because Asian American cultures value educational achievement, conflicts between students' goals and their parents' expectations may arise. Vocational counseling may be more acceptable than seeking counseling for personal and emotional problems (Morrissey, 1997). Counselors should be sensitive to Asian American clients seeking vocational counseling because under the surface of vocational concerns may be personal and emotional issues.

Cultural Conflicts

Immigrants face the process of acculturation, which is the "process of adapting to and adopting a new culture" (Atkinson & Matsushita, 1991, p. 474). This process creates demands that may conflict with their native cultural system, thus causing cultural conflicts, which may lead to mental health problems (Atkinson & Gim, 1989; Atkinson & Matsushita, 1991; Berry, 1997). Because this process changes over time and across generations, interpersonal difficulties may arise as parents and children, and men and women, acculturate differently (Chang & Myers, 1997; Nah, 1993).

Relations between Asian American parents and children become strained as parents and children adapt to the new culture differently. Immigrant parents struggling to adjust to the new culture have less time for their children. Asian American children, with their exposure to school, tend to adopt American values of independence and autonomy more quickly than their traditional Asian parents do. Children also acquire the English language more quickly than their parents do. This difference in acculturation rate and language acquisition can lead to cultural conflicts as parents struggle to maintain traditional Asian values and children struggle with identity issues (Chang & Myers, 1997; Lee & Cynn, 1991).

Just as parents and children acculturate at different rates, so do men and women. Marital difficulties may arise as Asian American women seek employment for the first time and are exposed to Western ideologies (Nah, 1993; True, 1990). Along with employment, Asian American women find new economic independence, which gives them power and teaches them assertiveness. Li Na represents a typical Asian American woman who has found independence and a sense of power with employment outside of the house. Asian American men ingrained with the male-dominated cultural influence of Confucianism may feel threatened and resistant to change and adaptation (Nah, 1993).

Effects of Immigration

Virtually all Asian Americans have a history that includes immigration to this country. Upon arrival, immigrants typically experience a significant decline in social economic status. Asian immigrants accept low-paying, unskilled positions because the United States does not recognize professional degrees obtained in their home country. Asian women who have never worked outside the home enter the labor market while simultaneously maintaining their responsibilities at home (Chang & Myers, 1997). The emotional strain related to the immigration process can lead to feelings of depression, low self-esteem, problems with significant relationships, readjustment to a new culture, somatic complaints, and isolation (Gould, 1988). The case of Li Na demonstrates how economic strain can lead to additional emotional and interpersonal distress. Studies indicate that immigrants are likely to experience stresses related to minority status, prejudice and discrimination, changes in employment, communication difficulties, identity confusion, and differences in customs (Shin, Berkson, & Crittenden, 2000).

SUGGESTIONS FOR ENHANCING COUNSELOR EFFECTIVENESS

Although specific cultural knowledge is important in understanding and helping the counselor working with Asian American clients, the counselor must be careful not to apply cultural information in a stereotypical manner. Counselors must remember that "the basic skills of an effective therapist remain the same: listening to what the client communicates; respecting the client's perspective and experience; formulating treatment goals that take into account clients' level of functioning, their resources, and their environment; and pacing" (Root, 1998, p. 224). To become a culturally sensitive and effective counselor, one must consider the cultural context of the information and adapt one's skills accordingly.

Communication Differences

As stated earlier, Asian Americans and Western-trained counselors may differ in communication styles. Asians typically value emotional restraint and silence while counselors from a European American background may value more direct language and expression and may devalue silence. For these counselors, silence may be conceptualized as a sign of avoidance, anger, or discomfort (Franks, 2000).

Self-disclosure can also be a communication obstacle. Asian American clients may prefer discussing events or factual information or analyzing problems related to people in general to discussing feelings. Self-disclosure may be considered a violation of the private self and the family (Yu, 1999). Furthermore, Asian American clients may nod in agreement even when they do not understand or agree with what is being said out of respect for authority figures (Chang & Myers, 1997). Asian American clients may also express more dependence on the counselor due to their respect for authority (Chan & Leong, 1994). In considering counseling with Jon or Li Na, the counselor will need to consider their communication styles as well as the counselor's communication style and how that may impact the counseling relationship.

Role of the Counselor

In order to work effectively with Asian American clients, counselors need to examine their own biases and sensitivity, and then recognize that many Asian American clients may be unfamiliar with traditional "talk therapy." The counselor must consider treatment strategies that are culturally appropriate (Chang & Myers, 1997; Moy, 1992). Counselors must interact in a culturally meaningful way in order to gain credibility and decrease client anxiety. Because Asian Americans may have difficulties with unstructured counseling processes and be reluctant to express their emotions (Atkinson & Matsushita, 1991; Leong, 1986), counselors should consider utilizing a more directive, paternalistic, and authoritarian style (Chang & Myers, 1997).

Moy (1992) suggests that counselors adopt a "teacher-expert" role (i.e., active, directive, and structured) in order to effectively establish rapport and trust with Asian American clients. By educating the client about the therapeutic process, the counselor assists in reducing client anxiety and ensures that the client develops more realistic expectations of treatment outcome. Counselors who assume a clear leadership role and provide guidance and direction will be more effective than counselors who assume a democratic approach (Chan & Leong, 1994).

Assessment Issues

When working with Asian American clients, it is important to consider the cultural and ethnic background of clients and how these factors influence the assessment process. Failure to consider these factors coupled with clinical bias and institutional racism may lead to invalid assumptions and misdiagnoses (Soloman, 1992). For example, a counselor may miss the signs of depression in an Asian American client by assuming that their withdrawn and submissive behaviors are "normal" within the Asian culture. Counselors also may overlook or minimize existing mental health concerns by misinterpreting culturally determined responses such as self-control, lack of verbal expression, or body posture (Chang & Myers, 1997).

Counselors can minimize their invalid assumptions and misdiagnoses by conducting a thorough assessment. Huang (1994) recommends an integrative, ethnocultural assessment that includes questions regarding four domains: individual, family, school, and peers. Specific areas of inquiry include generational status or immigration history, acculturation level, and salience of ethnicity. As in any assessment process, the counselor must consider both the macro (general) and the micro (culture-specific) view. Thus, although culture-specific information and cultural issues are important, counselors must be aware that cultural issues are not always the central or the presenting issue with all clients of Asian heritage (Chang

& Myers, 1997). Neither Jon's nor Li Na's specific ethnic background is identified in the case study. In order to conduct a thorough assessment, however, it is imperative that the counselor assess the salience of ethnic identity to the client, as suggested by Huang (1994).

Counseling Strategies

In considering counseling strategies for working effectively with Asian American clients, it is important to remember that Asian American clients may exhibit help-seeking behaviors different from those of White Americans. Asian American clients are more likely to seek assistance from family members, friends, church groups, and/or religious leaders (Chin, 1998; Shin et al., 2000; Yeh & Wang, 2000). If Asian Americans do seek assistance from mental health professionals, it is typically as a last resort; thus, they may enter counseling in a more disturbed state than non-Asian clients (Okazaki, 2000). Because many Asian cultures emphasize a holistic perspective, which does not separate body and mind and the stigmatization of mental illness, they are more likely to express psychological distress in the form of somatic illness (Chin, 1998; Moy, 1992).

With the importance that family plays in many Asian American cultures, counseling strategies that recognize the role of the family and focus on solving problems within the family are often effective with Asian American clients (Bae & Kung, 2000; Morrissey, 1997; Shin et al., 2000). Counselors should be cognizant and respectful of the existing hierarchical role structure within the family rather than attempting to change that family system too quickly. Showing respect for the hierarchical role structure may include addressing the father first, or, if the father is not present, encouraging the mother to consult with her husband before making any commitments. The counselor also may want to interview the parents and children separately. This will allow parents an opportunity to discuss adult issues without losing parental authority and allow children to discuss issues they feel uncomfortable discussing in their parents' presence (Song, 1999).

Some authors recommend solution-focused therapy as an effective treatment modality for working with Asian American clients (Berg & Miller, 1992; Morrissey, 1997). Solution-focused therapy, with its focus on the present tense and problem solving, is congruent with Asian American expectations about counseling and provides a quick solution to problems. Berg and Miller (1992) suggest utilizing exception questions (e.g., Describe a time when you are not depressed), miracle questions (e.g., If a miracle happened last night and your problem was solved, how would you know? What would be different?), coping questions (e.g., Despite all that is happening in your life, how are you able to cope each day?), and scaling questions (e.g., On a scale of zero to ten, how depressed are you today?) as means to assist Asian American clients restore their dignity and sense of competence.

In conclusion, counselors working with Asian American clients should incorporate counseling strategies that include an educational/ informational approach; a structured setting; a family-focused versus an individual-focused approach; respect for the client's communication style; a directive, active style; and consideration of somatic complaints.

CONCLUDING REMARKS

This chapter has provided a general description of the Asian American population, emphasizing the commonalities among all Asian cultures and a brief history of Asian immigration. These commonalities include group and family values, communication and emotional expression, time orientation, the myth of the model minority and educational pressures. Also presented were discussions of current mental health issues and suggestions for enhancing counselor effectiveness. Issues that affect the mental health of Asian Americans include barriers to mental health services, academic and career issues, and effects of immigration. Counselors working with Asian American clients should consider communication differences, the role of the counselor, assessment issues, and specific counseling strategies.

Finally, counselors should consider these words of caution: Asian Americans are a heterogeneous group. Understanding the cultural knowledge and values that many Asian Americans share is important, but counselors must be careful not to overgeneralize cultural knowledge and values. Instead, counselors must seek to understand the specific background of each client. Specific cultural information is helpful in identifying possible areas for cultural conflicts and mental health issues but should

not replace sound clinical judgment and recognition of individual uniqueness and consideration of the client's country of origin, generation status,
language, ethnic group, and other individual factors.

EXPERIENTIAL ACTIVITIES

Questions for Reflection

Review the case studies and discuss the following questions:

1. What issues would you consider in working with each case?
2. What cultural conflicts did you see?
3. What additional information would you want from each person?
4. How would you assess and treat the person(s) in the case study?
5. What interventions would be most effective with each of the cases?
6. What cultural biases or cultural conflicts would you have in working with each case?

Classroom Activities

1. Watch the film *The Joy Luck Club* (dir. Wang, 1993) and discuss
   the following questions: What were your reactions to the movie?
   What traditional Asian and non-Asian values did you see in the
   movie? Identify the themes of the movie. Identify any cultural conflicts presented in the film. What were the most important differences between the mothers, who were born and lived in China, and
   their American-born daughters? What can you take from this movie
   to assist in your work with Asian American clients?
2. Break up into groups of four or five students and discuss the following issues: There has been some debate related to the "model
   minority" stereotype. What are your thoughts on this issue? Do you
   believe that Asian Americans are the model minority? What evidence do you have that supports or defies this stereotype? How
   might this stereotype either help or hinder Asian Americans?
3. Discuss your own communication style and how it compares with
   the communication style of some Asian Americans. How will your
   communication style either help or hinder your work with Asian
   American clients?

Individual Activities

1. Make a list of stereotypes about Asian Americans. (You do not have to believe in these stereotypes.) Where do you think these stereotypes originated? How are they perpetuated? How might these stereotypes affect interaction?
2. Attend an Asian cultural event in your community. How do your observations compare to earlier beliefs and perceptions about this population? What have you learned about yourself and Asian Americans as a result of this experience?

REFERENCES

Alva, S.A. (1993). Differential patterns of achievement among Asian-American adolescents. *Journal of Youth and Adolescence, 22,* 407–423.

Asakawa, K., & Csikszentmihalyi, M. (2000). Feelings of connectedness and internalization of values in Asian American adolescents. *Journal of Youth and Adolescence, 29,* 121–145.

Atkinson, D.R., & Gim, R.H. (1989). Asian-American cultural identity and attitudes toward mental health services. *Journal of Counseling Psychology, 36,* 209–212.

Atkinson, D.R., & Matsushita, Y.J. (1991). Japanese-American acculturation, gender, and willingness to seek counseling. *Journal of Multicultural Counseling and Development, 23,* 473–478.

Atkinson, D.R., Morten, G., & Sue, D.W. (Eds.). (1998). *Counseling American minorities.* (5th Ed.). Boston: McGraw-Hill.

Axelson, J.A. (1999). *Counseling the development in a multicultural society.* (3rd Ed.). Pacific Grove, CA: Brooks & Cole.

Bae, S.W., & Kung, W.W.M. (2000). Family intervention for Asian Americans with a schizophrenic patient in the family. *American Journal of Orthopsychiatry, 70,* 532–541.

Berg, I.K., & Jaya, A. (1993). Different and same: Family therapy with Asian-American families. *Journal of Marital and Family Therapy, 19,* 31–38.

Berg, I.K., & Miller, S.D. (1992). Working with Asian American clients: One person at a time. *Families in Society: The Journal of Contemporary Human Services, 73* (6), 356–363.

Berry, J.W. (1997). Immigration, acculturation, and adaptation. *Applied Psychology: An International Review, 46,* 5–34.

Cao, L., & Novas, H. (1996). *Everything you need to know about Asian American history.* New York: Plume.

Chan, S., & Leong, C. W. (1994). Chinese families in transition: Cultural conflicts and adjustment problems. *Journal of Social Distress and the Homeless, 3,* 263–281.

Chang, C.Y., & Myers, J.E. (1997). Understanding and counseling Korean Americans: Implications for training. *Counselor Education and Supervision, 37,* 35–49.

Chin, J.L. (1998). Mental health services and treatment. In L.C. Lee & N.W.S. Zane (Eds.), *Handbook of Asian American psychology* (pp. 485–504). Thousand Oaks, CA: Sage.

Choi, K.H., & Wynne, M.E. (2000). Providing services to Asian Americans with developmental disabilities and their families: Mainstream service providers' perspective. *Community Mental Health Journal, 36,* 589–595.

Chung, D.K. (1992). Asian cultural commonalities: A comparison with mainstream American culture. In S.M. Furoto, R. Biswas, D.K. Chung, K. Murase, & F. Ross-Sheriff (Eds.), *Social work practice with Asian Americans* (pp. 27–44). Newbury Park, CA: Sage.

Franks, P.H. (2000). *Silence/listening and intercultural differences.* Paper presented at the annual meeting of the International Listening Association. Virginia Beach, VA.

Gould, K.H. (1988). Asian and Pacific Islanders: Myth and reality. *Social Work, 33,* 143–147.

Grieco, E.M., & Cassidy, R.C. (2001). *Overview of race and Hispanic origin: Census 2000 brief.* Washington, DC: U.S. Department of Commerce.

Hamilton, B. (1996). Ethnicity and the family life cycle: The Chinese-American family. *Family Therapy, 23* (3), 199–212.

Hardy, K.V. (1989). The theoretical myth of sameness: A critical issue in family therapy training and treatment. *Journal of Psychotherapy and the Family, 6,* 17–33.

Hirayama, H., & Hirayama, K.K. (1984). Individuality versus group identity: A comparison between Japan and the United States. *Journal of International and Comparative Social Welfare, 2,* 11–28.

Huang, L.N. (1994). An integrative approach to clinical assessment and intervention with Asian-American adolescents. *Journal of Clinical Child Psychology, 23,* 21–31.

Hyun, K.J. (2001). Sociocultural change and traditional values: Confucian values among Koreans and Korean Americans. *International Journal of Intercultural Relations, 25,* 203–229.

Iwamasa, G.Y. (1996). Acculturation of Asian American university students. *Assessment, 3,* 99–102.

Kim, B.C. (1978). *The Asian Americans: Changing patterns, changing needs.* Urbana, IL: AKCS/Publication Services.

Kim, U., & Chun, M.B.J. (1994). Educational "success" of Asian Americans: An indigenous perspective. *Journal of Applied Developmental Psychology, 15,* 329–343.

Kitano, H.H.L., & Maki, M.T. (1996). Continuity, change, and diversity: Counseling Asian Americans. In P.B. Pedersen, J.G. Draguns, W.J. Lonner, & J.E. Trimble (Eds.), *Counseling across cultures* (4th ed.; pp. 124–145.). Thousand Oaks, CA: Sage.

Kwon, P. (1995). Application of social cognition principles to treatment recommendations for ethnic minority clients: The case of Asian Americans. *Clinical Psychological Review, 15,* 613–529.

LEAP and UCLA Asian American Studies Center. (1993). *The state of Asian Pacific America: Policy issues to the year 2020.* Los Angeles: Author.

Lee, J.C., & Cynn, V.E.H. (1991). Issues in counseling 1.5 generation Korean Americans. In C.C. Lee & B.L. Richardson (Eds.), *Multicultural issues in counseling: New approaches to diversity* (pp. 127–140). Alexandria, VA: American Association for Counseling and Development.

Leong, F.T.L. (1986). Counseling and psychotherapy with Asian-Americans: Review of the literature. *Journal of Counseling Psychology, 33,* 196–206.

Morrissey, M. (1997, October). The invisible minority: Counseling Asian Americans. *Counseling Today,* pp. 1, 21–22.

Moy, S. (1992). A culturally sensitive, psychoeducational model for understanding and treating Asian-American clients. *Journal of Psychology and Christianity, 11,* 358–367.

Nah, K.H. (1993). Perceived problems and service delivery for Korean immigrants. *Social Work, 38,* 289–296.

O'Hare, W.P., & Felt, J.C. (1991). *Asian Americans: America's fastest growing minority group.* Washington, DC: Population Reference Bureau.

Okazaki, S. (2000). Treatment delay among Asian-American patients with severe mental illness. *American Journal of Orthopsychiatry, 70,* 58–64.

Root, M.P.P. (1998). Facilitating psychotherapy with Asian American clients. In D.R. Atkinson, G. Morten, & D.W. Sue (Eds.), *Counseling American minorities* (5th ed.; pp. 214–234). Boston: McGraw-Hill.

Sandhu, D.S. (1997). Psychocultural profiles of Asian and Pacific Islander Americans: Implications for counseling and psychotherapy. *Journal of Multicultural Counseling and Development, 25,* 7–22.

Shin, J.Y., Berkson, G., & Crittenden, K. (2000). Informal and professional support for solving psychological problems among Korean-speaking immigrants. *Journal of Multicultural Counseling and Development, 28,* 144–159.

Smith, S.E. (1996). Willingness of Korean-American elementary school children to participate with counselors in a developmental guidance program. *Early Child Development and Care, 125,* 85–94.

Soloman, A. (1992). Clinical diagnosis among diverse populations: A multicultural perspective. *Families in Society: The Journal of Contemporary Human Services, 73,* 371–377.

Song, S.J. (1999). Using solution-focused therapy with Korean families. In K.S. Ng (Ed.), *Counseling Asian families from systems perspective* (pp. 127–141). Alexandria, VA: American Counseling Association.

Sue, D. (1998). The interplay of sociocultural factors on the psychological development of Asians in American. In D.R. Atkinson, G. Morten, & D.W. Sue (Eds.), *Counseling American minorities* (5th ed.; pp. 205–213). Boston: McGraw-Hill.

Sue, D.W., & Sue, D. (1999). *Counseling the culturally different: Theory and practice* (3rd ed.). New York: John Wiley & Sons.

Sung, K. (1995). Measures and dimensions of filial piety in Korea. *The Gerontologist, 35,* 240–247.

Thomas, E.K. (2000). Domestic violence in the African-American and Asian-American communities: A comparative analysis of two racial/ethnic minority cultures and implications for mental health service provision for women of color. *Psychology: A Journal of Human Behavior, 37,* 32–43.

True, R.H. (1990). Psychotherapeutic issues with Asian American women. *Sex Roles, 22,* 477–486.

U.S. Department of Commerce. (1993). *We the Americans: Asians.* Washington, DC: U.S. Government Printing Office.

U.S. Department of Commerce. (1995). *Statistical brief: The nation's Asian and Pacific Islander Population.* Washington, DC: Author.

Wang, W. (Dir), & Wang, W., Tan, A., Bass, R., & Markay, P. (Prod.). (1993). *The joy luck club.* (Videotape; available from Hollywood Pictures.)

Wagi, D.T., & Oh, M.Y. (1995). Counseling Asian American students. In C.C. Lee (Ed.), *Counseling for diversity: A guide for school counselors and related professionals* (pp. 61–83). Boston: Allyn and Bacon.

Yeh, C., & Wang, Y.W. (2000). Asian American coping attitudes, sources, and practices: Implications for indigenous counseling strategies. *Journal of College Student Development, 41* (1), 94–103.

Yook, E.L., & Albert, R.D. (1998). Perceptions of the appropriateness of negotiation in educational settings: A cross-cultural comparison among Koreans and Americans. *Communication Education, 47,* 18–29.

Youn, G., & Song, D. (1991). Aging Koreans' perceived conflicts in relationships with their offspring as a function of age, gender, cohabitation status, and marital status. *Journal of Social Psychology, 132,* 299–305.

Yu, M.M. (1999). Multimodal assessment of Asian families. In K.S. Ng (Ed.), *Counseling Asian families from a systems perspective* (pp. 15–26). Alexandria, VA: American Counseling Association.

CHAPTER 6

Counseling Hispanic Americans

Johnston M. Brendel
Christina M. Sustaeta

Johnston M. Brendel, L.P.C., Ed.D., is an associate professor at Texas A&M University–Corpus Christi, a Hispanic-Serving Institution in south Texas. He has worked extensively with Hispanic at-risk youth designing and evaluating effective programs that target this population and advising on retention issues in higher education.

Christina M. Sustaeta, M.S., completed graduate school at Texas A&M University–Corpus Christi in 1996. Her clinical experience has included working with Hispanic families of blind children, Hispanic teenage mothers, and Hispanic at-risk youth. She lived in Spain for eighteen months and is currently working with youth in south Texas.

AWARENESS INDEX

Please test your knowledge by marking the following statements true or false before proceeding to the text in this chapter. Compute your score from the scoring guide at the end of the Awareness Index.

1. T F *Machismo* is a negative term used to define sexist and male chauvinistic behavior.

2. T F Traditional Hispanic families are patriarchal.

3. T F There is tremendous diversity among different Hispanic groups.

4. T F The term *Hispanic* has been used for approximately one hundred years to describe people of Mexican, Puerto Rican, and Cuban heritage.

5. T F Cubans have the greatest economic power of any of the Latino ethnic groups.

6. T F A significant percentage of Hispanic eighth graders have repeated one grade.

7. T F Traditional Hispanic women are expected to be sentimental, gentle, intuitive, impulsive, docile, submissive, and dependent.

8. T F Many Hispanics live in communities that are riddled with social problems such as crime, drugs, rape, and AIDS.

9. T F Counselors should be prepared to collaborate with folk healers when working with this group.

10. T F Hispanic clients should be urged to speak in English during counseling sessions.

Scoring guide: **1.** F; **2.** T; **3.** T; **4.** F; **5.** T; **6.** F; **7.** T; **8.** T; **9.** T; **10.** F

INTRODUCTION

Hispanics are a broad and varied population made up of 20 Spanish-speaking countries and two with the native tongue of Portuguese (Portugal and Brazil): in North America, Mexico; in Central America, Belize, Guatemala, El Salvador, Honduras, Nicaragua, Costa Rica, and Panama; in South America, Columbia, Venezuela, Ecuador, Peru, Bolivia, Chile, Argentina, Uruguay, Paraguay, and Brazil; the Carribean Islands, Puerto Rico, and Cuba, and the European countries of Spain and Portugal (Flores, 2000). Given their worldwide presence, there is naturally a tremendous diversity among these groups, with the only common element being their native languages. It is paramount for counselors, teachers, and others to avoid generalizations or assumptions and to treat Hispanics as a heterogeneous group containing unique individuals.

According to the U.S. Bureau of the Census (2000), the Hispanic population increased from 22.4 million people in 1990 to 35.3 million in 2000. Currently the group constitutes more than 12% of the U.S. population. Nationally, the Hispanic population grew nearly 58% during the 1990s, catching up to Black non-Hispanics and also signaling swift social and political change in this country (Cohn, 2001). In 2000, Mexicans were 58.5% of all Hispanics (down from 60.4% in 1990), Puerto Ricans were 9.6% (down from 12.2%), Cubans were 3.5% (down from 4.7%), and the remaining 28.4% were of other Hispanic origins (up from 22.8%) (U.S. Bureau of the Census, 2000). The majority of the increase in the Hispanic population in recent years can be attributed to immigration (Zambrana, Silva-Palacios, & Powell, 1992). The immigrant experience can be vastly different depending on legal status, and many recent immigrants are undocumented (Schick & Schick, 1991). Most Hispanic American families have lived in the United States for generations. They are U.S. citizens born of U.S. citizens. Some Hispanics trace their roots to the Louisiana Purchase in 1803 and the concomitant acquisition of the territory that is modern-day California, New Mexico, and Louisiana. Others became citizens with the annexation of Texas. Economic and political turmoil in Cuba, Mexico, and many Latin American countries resulted in several waves of immigration to the United States during the twentieth century. Just as citizens of Irish, Japanese, German, or African descent had ancestors who arrived in this country in the 1700s, 1800s, or early 1900s, so citizens with the name Ramos, Molina, Salinas, or Martinez may or may not speak the language of their forefathers, celebrate ethnic customs, or personally relate to current immigration issues.

The ascension of Hispanic peoples in terms of their increasing social and economic influence is evident in many facets of today's society. Food products, such as tortillas, guacamole, packaged corn chips, and many varieties of salsa and picante sauce, virtually unavailable a decade ago, are now mainstays of the American diet. In fact, salsa now outsells ketchup. No town is without its Mexican restaurant, and beverages such as tequila and margaritas have newfound popularity. Contemporary cultural icons include musical artists Jennifer Lopez, Gloria Estefan, and

Ricky Martin; sports figures like Sammy Sosa and Roberto Clemente; popular Hispanic characters on Sesame Street and weekly television dramas; and the Quincieñera Barbie Doll. Walt Disney Studios recently promoted the cartoon film *El Dorado*, and most geographic areas claim at least one exclusively Spanish radio channel and television stations such as Telemundo and Univision.

Highly visible political figures in President George W. Bush's cabinet bear witness to the growing political influence of the group. President Bush speaks Spanish and has been an advocate for favorable free trade with Mexico. Hopeful political candidates solicit the Hispanic vote by conducting political debates in Spanish and dispensing bilingual campaign literature.

Data on the Hispanic community are sometimes confusing because Hispanics may be of any race. In the 2000 census, nearly 17 million Hispanics described themselves as White, while nearly 15 million checked "some other race" (U.S. Bureau of the Census, 2000). More than 6 million declined to identify the country where their ancestors were born. Experts disagree on the reason for this lack of disclosure. Some attribute it to confusion over the census form; others believe that increasing assimilation has resulted in many Hispanics no longer identifying with a home country but viewing themselves as U.S. residents (Cohn, 2001). The census reported the Hispanic population as relatively young, with a median age of 25.9 years compared with the median age of 35.3 for the overall population. More than three-quarters live in the south and the west, with three million, or almost 10%, living in Los Angeles County. This chapter will focus on the three largest groups of Hispanics in the United States: Mexican, Puerto Rican, and Cuban.

Correct Terminology: Hispanics or Latinos?

The term *Hispanic* is not widely accepted by many Spanish-speaking immigrants. An obvious reasons is that the letter *h* is silent in Spanish, so when the word *Hispanic* is used, it seems like a mispronunciation of *Hispania*. *Hispania* is the root of the word *España*. There are several divergent views on the origin of this word, both dating back to the time of the Phoenicians. Some believe it is a derivation of the word *Ispan*, meaning the land of the Andalucian sun god *Is*. Others believe it is attributed to the word *Ishpan*, which literally means nightfall, and figuratively means land of the nightfall, or where the sun sets. Historically, modern-day Spain was believed to be the westernmost landmass (Flores, 2000).

The term *Latino* is even more confusing, since the indigenous groups of the Americas did not speak Latin but the Spanish priests that accompanied the Spanish conquerors did speak it in the Americas. Because the Latin language is no longer used, and much demographic information and research uses the term *Hispanic* in this chapter we will use the term *Hispanic* unless we are reporting specific research that used the term *Latino*.

The controversy around terminology is likely to continue for some time. Shorris (1992) makes an excellent point when he states that to lump cultures together under one rubric is to take away the name and to eradicate the individuality of the group. These authors wholeheartedly entreat helpers to avoid insensitivities and incorrect assumptions when counseling people with this background. Inquire about individual countries and cultures. It is better to ask clients which term they prefer, and use it accordingly.

CASE EXAMPLES

Jovita Gonzalez

Jovita Gonzalez and her family live in south Texas. They are illegal immigrants from Mexico who crossed the border to escape the severe poverty of their homeland and in search of a better education for the children. Jovita has been married to her husband, Juan, for almost twenty years, and they have three sons, ages sixteen, fifteen, and eleven. All her children attend public school. Neither parent speaks English very well, but their children can act as translators when it is needed. Because they are "illegals," no members of the family can obtain Texas driver's licenses, and Jovita cannot obtain a permit to be a hair stylist, her occupation when she lived in Mexico. Jovita cleans houses for a living but does not make a very high hourly wage because there are many "illegals" in this area and the competition has the tendency to drive wages down. Juan earns money by doing yard work and other manual labor. His income is more seasonal than Jovita's, so his two older sons often join him during warmer weather to make up for the lost income during the winter months.

The Gonzalezes are Jehovah's Witnesses. They attend church several times each week, and they consider the other church members to be family. Besides two used automobiles that they have purchased during their five years in the United States, they have bought few pieces of furniture or other household items. Instead they rely on the generosity of church members and customers of Jovita and Juan. Several times a year they return to Mexico, but they worry because in recent years the border has been much more heavily patrolled. They look forward to the day when they might return to their home but realize that until all the boys are through public school and college, they will need to live in Texas. Jovita often feels lonely, and as a member of a religion that does not celebrate holidays and birthdays she is periodically reminded that she and her family are different from others in her community.

Gustavo Ricardo-Garcia

Gustavo Ricardo-Garcia is a thirty-two-year-old man living in Miami. Most of his family is still in Puerto Rico, where he was born and raised. Gustavo moved to the mainland when he was twenty years old after attending several years of college in Puerto Rico. He had become unfocused and felt "burnt out" on education and island life. Several of his extended family had left Puerto Rico and had achieved some status as business owners in Florida and New York. Against his parents' warnings, he set out for New York City in search of adventure and financial success. His Americanized name is Gus.

After a period of "culture shock" that lasted about a year, he gradually became more accustomed to life in the States. He has been involved in several long-term relationships with women, his most recent being a four-year relationship with a Hispanic woman named Sophia. Sophia is a second-generation U.S. citizen whose family emigrated from Argentina. About three months ago Sophia discovered that she is pregnant. Her family is both excited about a new infant and also disappointed that her partner, Gus, is not a member of their ethnic group.

Gustavo's family says that it is time for him to come home to Puerto Rico. As the man of the family, it is his obligation to bring Sophia and to make sure that his child is raised with an extended family involved in his or her life. His father reminds Gus that he has never obtained the fame and fortune that he sought in New York and that if he returns to Puerto Rico, one of his relatives will certainly help him build a real career.

HISTORY

Mexican Americans

Most Mexican Americans are "mestizos," the combination of heritage between the Spanish and Mexico's indigenous people. The Mexican Indians believed that their most powerful religious icon—the feathered serpent Quetzalcoatl—would return to their world in the form of a White man. This optimistic hope eventually led them to be conquered by the Spanish virtually without resistance. The conquistadors landed at Vera Cruz in 1519, and Montezuma was sure that Cortez was Quetzalcoatl (Order of the Quetzalcoatl, 2002). The seeds of the current Mexican American social perspective were planted during the three hundred years that followed. Once conquered, Roman Catholic priests from Spain taught Catholicism to the Indians, who often combined it with their own religions. The Spanish, who were enslaving the Mexican Indians and keeping them in poverty, also insisted that they switch their beliefs to a new religion and desert their ancient religious way of life.

During the 1820s, Mexico allowed many Americans to settle in their territory, which is now Texas, and in 1835 the Americans led a revolt against the Mexicans that resulted in the establishment of the Republic of Texas. The disagreement over Texas led to the Mexican War (1846–48), in which the United States gained most of the land that is now Arizona, California, Colorado, Nevada, New Mexico, Utah, and Wyoming. More than 75,000 Mexicans living in these areas became United States citizens, and even today many consider the southwestern region of the United States to be culturally Mexican (Falicov, 1998). *Chicano(a)* is another term that is often used interchangeably with Mexican American.

Puerto Ricans

Puerto Ricans are a unique group because they are natural U.S. citizens. They are often not acknowledged or received as citizens, however, and are the poorest Latino group (Massey & Eggers, 1990). The island's indigenous population was virtually eradicated by the Spaniards, who replaced them with African slaves (Fitzpatrick, 1971). The relationship between Puerto Rico and the United States began in 1898 when the United States won the war with Spain and acquired the island. Puerto Rico was particularly attractive to the United States because of its military location and rich coffee plantations. The United States faced a dilemma that continues today about what to do with the 1 million Puerto Ricans who spoke only Spanish. Citizens of Puerto Rico are U.S. citizens who are subject to military duty but do not pay U.S. income taxes, are not full beneficiaries of federal social service programs, and are prohibited from voting (Falicov, 1998).

U.S. influence is pervasive on the island. Puerto Ricans have two languages, two cultures, two flags, two national anthems, and two basic philosophies of life—dichotomies that did not exist to the same extent when Spain was in possession of the island (Ramos-McKay, Comas-Díaz, & Rivera, 1988). When European migration to the United States ceased after World War I, the opportunities offered to Puerto Ricans were similar to the seasonal farm work offered to Mexicans. Puerto Ricans appeared mostly in the east and the midwest, but also in Arizona and Utah. During World War II, railroads and a variety of industrial employers attracted Puerto Ricans to the United States once more. The greatest immigration occurred at the end of the war when surplus airplanes and low airfares from Puerto Rico to New York boosted the movement. Dense colonies formed near workplaces on New York City's Lower East Side, Harlem, South Bronx, and Brooklyn (Falicov, 1998). Even though it became evident to Puerto Ricans by the 1950s that mainland cities did not offer the vast economic opportunities they sought, the back-and-forth flow of migrants has continued, sometimes reaching 2 million people a year. After accumulating small amounts of money on the mainland, Puerto Ricans often go back to the island to see their loved ones and nurture their cultural roots. These motivations are similar to those that propel Mexicans back and forth across the border. Although Puerto Ricans, unlike Mexicans, can legally and freely stay on the mainland, return to visit, conduct transactions with financial and governmental institutions, and retire back on the island they suffer high unemployment and poverty (Fal-icov, 1998).

Cuban Americans

The third largest Hispanic group is the Cubans, people who can trace their immediate ancestry to Cuba, the largest Caribbean island (Flores, 2000). The Cuban culture historically has been a blend of Spanish and African cultures (Bustamante & Santa Cruz, 1975). Most Cubans who immigrated to the United States from Cuba during the early phases of Castro's takeover, however, were of White European backgrounds (Bernal, 1982). Many of these political immigrants had professional training and quickly adapted their skills to the U.S. way of life. Political refugees from Cuba came in waves, many leaving behind economic hardships attributed to the new Cuban government. The Cubans in the second wave were poor and Black or of mixed ethnicity and race (Bernal, 1982).

Cubans have the greatest economic power of any of the Latino ethnic groups (Zapata, 1995). In Miami, Cubans represent 60% of the popula-tion and dominate the city both politically and economically. They be-lieve firmly in democracy and free enterprise and oppose communism and socialistic forms of government (Bernal, 1982). When wealthy Cubans arrived in the United States, they immediately created businesses and es-tablished a marketplace and commerce. Later, when poorer Cubans ar-rived in this country, the already established Cubans offered them jobs and sympathy concerning their oppressive experiences under Castro's regime. Their experience was different from those of Mexican Americans and Puerto Ricans, since Cuban Americans were welcomed into this country. There were several reasons for this. Cubans, particularly first-wave immigrants, brought with them upper-class financial and political resources and middle-class entrepreneurial skills. In addition, many were of a privileged lighter skin color and their flight from Castro's command was looked upon favorably by the United States. Due to their unique sta-tus, the federal government supported this group of immigrants finan-cially, educationally, and with job training (Bernal, 1982). Cubans were thought by some to be "model" immigrants because of their economic success in small businesses in such centers as Miami, parts of New Jersey, and New York. Economically, Cubans are now about as successful as Whites (Bernal & Gutierrez, 1988).

CURRENT ISSUES

The Hispanic population is more likely than non-Hispanic Whites to reside in the west and less likely to live in the northeast and the midwest (U.S. Bureau of the Census, 2000). The vast majority of this population is experiencing high growth rates, closely clustered around major urban hubs. This clustering, growth, and daily interaction with other Hispanics have helped to preserve and enhance the culture. Distinct knowledge, beliefs, values, customs, and religious traits have been maintained and passed from generation to generation. For this Hispanic author, for example, marrying outside the Roman Catholic faith was never considered an option.

As a result of a burgeoning growth rate and inner-city living many Hispanics experience poor schools, overcrowded classrooms, and campus violence. High unemployment and low-paying jobs mean an overall lower standard of living. Much of the current situation can be linked to the early immigration of this group. Many immigrants were unskilled, Spanish speaking, and objects of stereotyping, prejudice, and discrimination. They competed for scarce jobs that offered low pay and began a perpetual cycle of poverty and discrimination (Atkinson, Morten, & Sue, 1998). When the author's grandparents immigrated from Mexico in 1920 the only employment possibilities were various low-paying positions. Saving their earnings, they eventually were able to open a small grocery store in their Hispanic neighborhood, and it became profitable. Overall, the Hispanic group is a young population with relatively high rates of birth to teen and single mothers. Compared with non-Hispanic Whites, Hispanic parents are typically younger, less educated, employed at lower paying jobs, and financially poorer (Zayas, 1992).

Poverty and education status continue to be two issues that greatly affect many Hispanics. Predictably, poverty among Latinos is the main correlate of limited educational achievement (Chapa & Valencia, 1993).

Twenty-five percent of Hispanic eighth graders have repeated one grade, and over 15% have been retained two or more times during their school years (Gersten & Woodward, 1994). The highest illiteracy rate of any ethnic group belongs to Mexican Americans: 40% have not completed high school; only 1% have gone to college; one-third live in poverty (Lee, 1999). Puerto Ricans are the least educated Hispanic ethnic group and have the highest dropout rate. They are also most likely to be unemployed and poor, with 40% living below the poverty level (Sue & Sue, 1999).

Many of the educational problems relate to varied proficiencies with the English language. Spanish is the primary language spoken in over half the homes of Hispanics, and command of the English language can be limited (Sue & Sue, 1999). Despite continuing language barriers, bilingual education programs continue to be the subject of controversy. Sue and Sue (1999) state, "In general, schools have been poorly equipped to deal with large numbers of Spanish-speaking students. Teachers who do not have proficiency in Spanish have a difficult time preparing understandable lessons for students and have no means of effectively evaluating their performance" (p. 289). Additionally, there is a lack of role models, since Hispanics constitute only 1.5% of all college faculty and 1.1% of all tenured faculty (Kavanaugh & Retish, 1991).

While experts continue to believe that the future of the U.S. economy looks good, ethnic minorities face many problems as they prepare to be part of the labor force (Okocha, 1994). Okocha states, "One of these problems is the racist, oppressive, discriminating, sociopolitical, American mainstream society that often leads to inequality in the educational preparation of non-Whites versus Whites" (p. 107).

Traditional Latino values of community, cooperation, modesty, and hierarchical relationships can sometimes be misaligned with the modern values of many work environments, which include individualism, competition, achievement, and egalitarianism (Lee, 1999) Research suggests that even highly educated Latinos may place more restrictions on relocation than Anglos and African Americans. Family and community appear to be important considerations in relocating as well as high incentives and whether the new geographical area has a high Latino concentration (Edwards et al., 1993). Although one of the authors has relocated a number of times, the desire to return to locations close to family is ever present. In order to understand Hispanics' reasoning about careers, one must understand the dynamics of Hispanic families.

In many Hispanic families, grandparents, uncles, aunts, or cousins live with or near the nuclear family, temporarily or permanently. The family is very protective of the individual members, and in return it demands loyalty. In the case study, Gus was encouraged by his family to return to his home so they could care for him and his wife. His family realized that he was not able to fully provide and he was encouraged to return home, where the family felt he belonged. Autonomy and individual achievement are not particularly emphasized, especially among females.

Families are usually large, consisting of the parents and several children. Traditionally, limited economic resources and Roman Catholic beliefs have reinforced large families of four, five, or more children, with extended family involvement across the life span (Bean & Tienda, 1987). Birth rates among Mexican Hispanics are higher than Anglo American families, making family size a major structural influence on many aspects of life, as indicated by the expectation that children care for their parents in times of illness and in old age (Falicov, 1998). Although the presence of the extended family is common, the role of the parent is still the most significant. "In general, the status of the parent is high and that of the children is low, although there are spoiled Latino children too, particularly in the upper classes" (Falicov, 1998, p. 169).

One of the most important values instilled in children by their parents is *respeto* (respect). Although the word *respeto* has the same English translation; for Anglo Americans it reflects a fairly "detached, self-assured egalitarianism," whereas for Mexicans it means a relationship involving a "highly emotionalized dependence and dutifulness within a fairly authoritarian framework" (Diaz-Guerrero, 1975). The parents of one of the authors expects each of their children to eventually take over some part of the family business. This is something that is not asked of the children but expected. This author is compelled by a moral obligation to the family and feels that it is essential in the preservation of her family heritage. Besides blood relatives, familism also includes close relationships in which people are perceived as kin because they are closely associated with the family. Counselors unfamiliar with this cultural value can miss the opportunity to involve a nontraditional extended family in counseling.

Other ideals rooted in Spanish antecedents are the traditional roles of the husband and wife. There is some confusion about the concept of *machismo* and its current derivation *macho*. *Machismo* refers to a man's responsibility to provide for and protect his family. The term originally referred to honor, loyalty, and the following of a valiant ethical code (Lee, 1999). Loyalty and responsibility to friends, family, and community are all associated with the original concept. In the United States, misguided assumptions have led to negative stereotypes and the association of the word *macho* with sexist, male chauvinistic behavior. This is radically different from the Latino meaning of *machismo*, which conveys the notion of an honorable and responsible man.

The traditional Hispanic family is patriarchal. The father is authoritarian and the mother is submissive (Falicov, 1982). The husband often assumes the role of provider and protector of the family, and the wife assumes the expressive role of homemaker and caretaker. Kinship relationships extend beyond the boundaries associated with the nuclear family. This *familismo* (familism) emphasizes interdependence over independence, affiliation over confrontation, and cooperation over competition (Falicov, 1982). Traditionally, males and females are taught to behave by two very different codes of sexual behavior. Traditional Hispanic women are expected to be sentimental, gentle, intuitive, impulsive, docile, submissive, and dependent, whereas traditional men are expected to be rational, profound, strong, authoritarian, independent, and brave (Senour, 1977).

Catholicism is the prevalent religion among the Hispanic population. This can be linked to the Roman Catholic priests from Spain who taught Catholicism to the Indians. The Indians often combined it with their own religions, something that remains in practice even today. Mexican Americans, Puerto Ricans, and Cubans view religion in very distinct ways. Falicov (1998) states that "Mexicans are a devout group to which churchgoing and observance of religious holidays and rituals is considered vital. Therapists should ask if the client finds spiritual solace or any form of support through church attendance. For many Puerto Ricans, the church is a place for communions, weddings, or funerals. Church is not considered necessary, however, to reach God or the supernatural. Cubans partake of Catholic values and rituals but perhaps with less vigor. Exposure to other Protestant and Afro-Caribbean religions has led to the incorporation of other beliefs and rituals for a considerable number of Cuban-Americans" (p. 147).

The strong influence of Catholicism may have several implications for people who wish to work effectively with the Hispanic population. Some Hispanics interpret the teaching of Roman Catholicism to suggest that health and illness are influenced by God, and therefore some people may be less likely to seek preventative medical exams or procedures (Lee, 1999). Perhaps as a result, Hispanics have disproportionately high rates of AIDS, tuberculosis, and obesity (Sue & Sue, 1999). Religious beliefs may also deter them from artificial contraception. Catholic teachings also denounce divorce.

Some Hispanic cultures also include some elements of nonreligious spirituality, such as witchcraft, sorcery, belief in anthropomorphic or animistic supernatural beings, sacred objects, rites, and ceremonies (Fabrega & Nutini, 1994). They may also embrace the use of folk healers, called *curanderos*, to use herbs and spirituality to treat the supernatural roots of psychological disturbances (Lee, 1999). *Curanderos* might use a combination of candles, a rosary, an altar, incense, praying in Spanish, massage, or ointments made from natural sources (Davidson, 1993).

Partly because of exposure to new faiths in the United States, religions other than Catholicism are increasingly present in Latino communities. These include various branches of Protestantism, Judaism, Pentecostalism, Jehovah's Witnesses, and numerous evangelical and fundamentalist faiths (Falicov, 1998).

SUGGESTIONS FOR ENHANCING COUNSELOR EFFECTIVENESS

It is important to remember that the term *Hispanic* is an abstract construction and does not correspond to the ways in which individuals experience and designate themselves (Draguns, 2000). Counselors should assess a client's self-identification and his or her phase of acculturation. The degree of acculturation will depend on many factors, including the length of time since the client's family immigrated to the United States, and different phases of the acculturation process can be associated with related behaviors and beliefs. While some clients, as in the case of Jovita and Juan, may be recent immigrants, there are also many Hispanics who have lived in the United States for generations.

In order for counselors to truly understand the Hispanic client's current experiences, the counselors must have an understanding of the unique cultural milieu of the client being served. Enculturation, acculturation, and racial/ethnic identity development are processes that account for many of these differences (Aponte & Johnson, 2000). Enculturation is the process by which the individual is socialized to their indigenous culture; it usually takes place in an individual's family (Atkinson et al., 1998). The culturally sensitive counselor must determine the level of enculturation for each individual. Acculturation is a process that encompasses the psychosocial changes that occur when an individual interacts with a second culture (Casas & Pytluk, 1995). In the case study involving Gus, Sophia's family found it difficult to accept Gus because of cultural differences. Although they were happy about the pregnancy, they were disappointed that Gus was not of their ethnic group. When the Hispanic client interacts within the Anglo dominant culture, either willingly or unwillingly, the client's values, attitudes, and behaviors change. There are a number of models that have been articulated to explain the changes that occur during the acculturation process. Berry (1998) suggests that there are four modes of acculturation: assimilation, separation, marginalization, and integration. Each mode can be associated with stress, social competence, and support, and overall psychological adjustment. For instance, the marginalization phase leaves a person bereft of adaptive skills acquired in their original country, yet without the resources necessary for effective functioning in the person's new setting. The client facing marginalization faces the greatest risk for maladaptive behaviors and symptom formation (Berry, 1998).

There are many useful models for explaining an individual's awareness about his or her ethnic, racial, or cultural identity (Atkinson et al., 1998). These models describe psychological processes in which individuals from ethnic populations become aware of and assign meaning to racial or cultural experiences and then integrate this information into their overall self-concept (Aponte & Johnson, 2000). Counselors working with Hispanics and other cultural groups should investigate these identity models and adopt one that fits their personal and theoretical philosophy.

Helms (1995) describes five stages that all "people of color" may go through as they attempt to understand themselves as ethnic persons in relation to their own ethnic group, other ethnic groups, and the majority culture. She posits that the first phase is conformity, a time when an individual devalues his or her own ethnic/racial group and emulates White standards, values, and norms. Next, the individual moves to a time of dissonance, when the individual becomes aware of his or her ethnic/racial identity and what it means to be a part of this group. This time is often associated with ambiguous feelings and conflict. Next comes immersion/emersion, which entails a person idealizing and immersing in his or her ethnic/racial group beliefs and values and a total rejection of other standards and values. The internalization phase is characterized by an individual's new capacity for using internal standards to define himself or herself and respond objectively to majority individuals. Finally, in the integrative phase, individuals are able to use flexible and complex thinking to value the many aspects of their identities thus feeling more secure and less anxious.

We strongly urge counselors who wish to play an effective therapeutic role working with Hispanics to become competent with the research literature on working with ethnic minorities. Many of the theoretical models are applicable to this group and can be adapted accordingly. Those detailed in this chapter are recommended by these authors, but are in no way inclusive or exhaustive of what is available. Once a counselor has adopted a holistic model, he or she should then try to understand the individual Hispanic client through this lens. Some additional strategies for conceptualizing and assisting Hispanic clients are included here.

In times of extreme stress or crisis, Hispanics will frequently turn to a relative or the clergy for support. For marital or parent-child conflicts, a wide range of helpers, including relatives, friends, "compadres" (godparents), or priests, are consulted. For some emotional problems, such as anxiety and depression and situations that an individual does not relate to a family situation, a physician may be consulted (Falicov, 1998). Remember that the Hispanic family is a large and complex organism including extended family and other closely associated people who are viewed as relatives. Family unity, welfare, and honor are significant values (Garcia-Preto, 1996). When the extended family is in crisis, children are commonly transferred from one nuclear family to another.

It is easy to forget that Hispanics want to adapt to an American culture and long for a sense of acceptance while attempting to preserve what is familiar and comfortable within their traditions. A person's generation plays a major role on how they adapt to both cultures: In general, first-generation immigrants are primarily affiliated with the social groups from their country of origin and have yet to transfer their identification to a new group. Hispanics from second and later generations show more current contact and social identities with groups in the United States (Hurtado & Gurin, 1995). Although Hispanics may have commonalities, background information needs to be considered when formulating a counseling plan, such as how long the person and the family have been in the United States, what brought them to the United States, how well they understand either English or Spanish. One must remember that there is tremendous diversity among these groups, emphasizing the need to provide therapy that is individualized, without generalizations or assumptions.

Respect for authority often keeps Hispanic clients from speaking up and asserting their rights. Most Hispanics will go outside their family for help only as a last resort, and complicated situations, such as being in the States illegally, cause people to perceive therapy, social services, and health care as threatening (Garcia-Preto, 1996). Due to lack of education and poverty, many Hispanics live in communities that are riddled with social problems such as crime, drugs, rape, and AIDS. They feel distanced from their countries of origin and isolated and pressured to change in ways that are not always understood and that can also be disruptive and cause conflict in their lives. Eliciting and validating stories about a client's life in this country is helpful to the counseling process (Garcia-Preto, 1996).

It is paramount to realize that not all Hispanics are alike. Many variables are involved in creating a person's culture; birthplace is only a small component in the formation of personal beliefs and values. Factors such as the family member that may have raised the individual, his or her educational background, the financial situation in the home, the expectations placed on the individual by family, and traditions that may have been passed on through the generations are important considerations when formulating counseling strategies.

Bean, Perry, and Bedell (2001) make the following suggestions concerning the formulation of a framework for developing the initial counseling agenda:

1. Utilize family therapy as the preferred treatment modality.
2. Assess beliefs in folk medicine; be prepared to collaborate with folk healers.
3. Act as an advocate for the family with other helping agencies.
4. Gather information on the immigration experience.
5. Assess level of acculturation.
6. Try to speak in the preferred language of the clients.
7. Respect the father or father figure.
8. Conduct separate interviews with family subsystems.
9. Do not force changes in family relationships.
10. Provide the family with concrete suggestions that they can quickly implement.

Finally, make sure that the counselor and family members have a similar expectation for the provision of mental health services. Create a trusting and personal relationship by entering the client's frame of reference and seek to understand the world from within their familial context.

We urge counselors to undertake their own journey in exploring other cultures with which they wish to be helpful. If one wants to be of true assistance with the Hispanic culture, one must come to understand their experience at a deeper level. Counselors accomplish this by developing cultural awareness. The Framework for Cultural Awareness (Rafuls & Marquez, 1997) proposes four tenets. Counselors should adopt a broader perspective about culture. Rather than studying only demographic information about their Hispanic clients, counselors should broaden their perspectives by adopting a multidimensional definition of culture that is dynamic and ever changing. They should also strive to become continuously aware of their own assumptions, biases, values, and cultural context. Counselors should strive to interact with others in experiences of immersion or other opportunities to experience other cultures as they are lived by others. Finally, culturally aware counselors should examine their individual personal experiences, values, and beliefs about the Hispanic culture. Individuals must organize and process their own experiences with culture, prejudice, and oppression.

CONCLUSION

This chapter has presented a brief overview of the people who make up about one-eighth of the population of this country. While there are many differences among groups, there are also some commonalities. The most obvious similarity among these people is probably the common language that is spoken in most of the countries of their origin. Like many other ethnic groups, Hispanics have experienced prejudice, bias, and oppression. They experience many social problems, including teen pregnancy, underpreparation for high-paying jobs, poverty, and poor education. There are many issues that are prevalent in this population that can be addressed by effective teachers, counselors, and other helping professionals.

In order for helpers to connect and make a difference, they must understand the diverse people who are represented by the Hispanic label. Helpers need to appreciate and utilize the strong family systems in developing effective treatment approaches and to intervene in all phases of the educational experience to ensure that barriers are minimized and eliminated. We should embrace bilingualism and the spiritual beliefs of these people.

Helpers need to meet people where they are and adapt their skills and techniques accordingly. We should assess clients for their levels of enculturation, acculturation, and racial/ethnic identity development. Rather than making assumptions and operating from misinformation, we must actively seek to understand our clients' experiences, embrace their individual cultural differences, and provide assistance in ways that are most meaningful. Rather than ascribing to the Golden Rule, in which we "Do unto others as we would have them do unto us," we must elevate our approach to the Platinum Rule, "Do unto others as they want to be done unto."

ACTIVITIES FOR ENHANCED AWARENESS, KNOWLEDGE, AND SKILL

1. As the school counselor at public middle school in Texas, you are asked by a teacher to look into Jon Gonzalez's family situation. It seems he is exhibiting some signs of depression. The teacher suspects that his feelings are related to worrying about his mother, most particularly her loneliness and sadness. Jon is the son of the Jovita and Juan Gonzalez, the family detailed earlier in this chapter. Go back and read the case again. How would you intervene with this family?

2. Gustavo Ricardo-Garcia's employer has referred him to the Employee Assistance Program. The employer has noticed that Gus is distracted, irritable, and somewhat lethargic. You are the counselor assigned to this case. Go back and read this case. What will be your plan of action? What special cultural considerations will be applicable to this case?

3. Go to your local or campus library and review a popular Hispanic magazine over a one-year time span (some examples include: *Hispanic Magazine, Latina, Urban Latino, Vanidades, H6K, Hispanic Engineer*, and *Information Technology*). What are some themes that emerge across issues? How do they compare and contrast with the counseling issues identified in this chapter?

4. Meet with at least two community leaders (ministers, politicians, teachers) from the Hispanic community. Interview them about the needs and concerns of this group of people.

5. Interview several Hispanic students on your campus. What has their experience been like as members of this group? What are the values, beliefs, and customs they appreciate the most? What do they feel are the most misunderstood aspects of their culture?

REFERENCES

Atkinson, D.R., Morten, G., & Sue, D.W. (1998). *Counseling American minorities: A cross-cultural perspective* (5th ed.). Boston: McGraw-Hill.

Aponte, J.F., & Johnson, L.R. (2000). The impact of culture on the intervention and treatment of ethnic populations. In J.F. Aponte and J. Wohl (Eds.), *Psychological intervention and cultural diversity* (2nd ed; pp. 18–39). Boston: Allyn and Bacon.

Bean, F.D., & Tienda, M. (1987). *The Hispanic population of the United States.* New York: Russell Sage.

Bean, R.A., Perry, B.J., & Bedell, T.M. (2001). Developing culturally competent marriage and family therapists: Guidelines for working with Hispanic families. *Journal of Marital and Family Therapy, 27* (1), 43–54.

Bernal, G. (1982). Cuban families. In M. McGoldrick, J.K. Pearce, & J. Giordano (Eds.), *Ethnicity in family therapy.* New York: Guilford.

Bernal, G., & Gutierrez, M. (1988). Cubans. In L. Comas-Diaz & E.H. Griffith (Eds.), *Clinical guidelines in cross-cultural mental health.* New York: Wiley.

Berry, J.W. (1998). Acculturation and health: Theory and research. In S.S. Kazarian & D.R. Evans (Eds.), *Cultural clinical psychology: Theory, research, and practice* (pp. 39–57). New York: Oxford University Press.

Bustamante, J.A., & Santa Cruz, A. (1975). *Psiquiatria transcultural.* Havana: Editorial Cientifico-Tecnica.

Casas, J.M., & Pytluk, S.D. (1995) Hispanic identity development: Implications for research and practice. In J.G. Ponterotto, J.M. Casas, L.A. Suzuki, & C.M. Alexander (Eds.), *Handbook of multicultural counseling* (pp. 155–180). Thousand Oaks, CA: Sage.

Chapa, J., & Valencia, R.R. (1993). Latino population growth, demographic characteristics, and educational stagnation: An examination of recent trends. *Hispanic Journal of Behavioral Sciences, 15* (2), 165–187.

Cohn, D. (2001, May 10). Shifting portrait of U.S. Hispanics. *Washington Post.* Retrieved February 1, 2002, at www.washingtonpost.com/wp-d>yn/nation/specials/socialpolicy/census2000/.

Davidson, K. (1993, May 2). Doctors becoming versed in curses. *San Francisco Examiner,* pp. A1, A8.

Diaz-Guerrero, R. (1975). *Psychology of the Mexican: Culture and personality.* Austin: University of Texas Press.

Draguns, J.G. (2000). Psychopathology and ethnicity. In J.F. Aponte and J. Wohl (Eds.), *Psychological intervention and cultural diversity.* Boston: Allyn and Bacon.

Edwards, J.E., Rosenfeld, P., Thomas, P.J., & Thomas, M.D. (1993). Willingness to relocate for employment: A survey of Hispanics, non-Hispanic Whites, and Blacks. *Hispanic Journal of Behavioral Sciences, 15,* 121–133.

Fabrega, H., & Nutini, H. (1994). Sudden infant and child death as a cultural phenomenon: A Tlaxcalan case study. *Psychiatry, 57* (3), 225–243.

Falicov, C.J. (1982). Mexican families. In M. McGoldrick, J.K. Pearce, & J. Giordano (Eds.), *Ethnicity and family therapy* (pp. 134–163). New York: Guilford.

Falicov, C.J. (1998). *Latino families in therapy.* New York: Guilford.

Fitzpatrick, J.P. (1971). *Puerto Rican Americans: The meaning of migration to the mainland*. Englewood Cliffs, NJ: Prentice Hall.

Flores, M.T. (2000). Demographics: Hispanic populations in the United States. In M.T. Flores and G. Carey (Eds.), *Family therapy with Hispanics: Toward appreciating diversity* (pp. 297–311). Boston: Allyn and Bacon.

Garcia-Preto, N. (1996). Latino families: An overview. In M. McGoldrick, J. Giordano, & J.K. Pearce (Eds.). *Ethnicity and family therapy* (2nd ed.; pp. 141–154). New York: Guilford.

Gersten, R., & Woodward, J. (1994). The language-minority student and special education: Issues, trends, and paradoxes. *Exceptional Children, 60,* 310–318.

Helms, J.E. (1995). An update of Helms' White and people of color racial identity models. In J.G. Ponterotto, J.M. Casas, L.A. Suzuki, & C.M. Alexander (Eds.), *Handbook of multicultural counseling* (pp. 181–198). Thousand Oaks, CA: Sage.

Hurtado, A., & Gurin, P. (1995). Ethnic identity and bilingualism attitudes. In A.M. Padilla (Ed.), *Hispanic psychology: Critical issues in theory and research*. Thousand Oaks, CA: Sage.

Kavanaugh, P.C., & Retish, P.M. (1991). The Mexican American ready for college. *Journal of Multicultural Counseling and Development, 19,* 136–144.

Lee, W.M.L. (1999). *An introduction to multicultural counseling*. Philadelphia, PA: Accelerated Development.

Massey, D.S., & Eggers, M.L. (1990). The ecology of inequality: Minorities and concentration of poverty. *American Journal of Sociology, 95,* 1153–1189.

Okocha, A.A.G. (1994). Preparing racial ethnic minorities for the work force 2000. *Journal of Multicultural Counseling and Development, 22,* 106–114.

Order of the Quetzalcoatl. (2002). History of the Quetzalcoatl. Retrieved February 20, 2002, at www.quetzalcoatl.org/history.htm.

Rafuls, S.E., & Marquez, M.G. (1997). La familia Fernandez: Directions for counseling Cuban Americans. In C.C. Lee (Ed.), *Multicultural issues in counseling: New approaches to diversity* (2nd ed.; pp. 269–294). Alexandria, VA: American Counseling Association.

Ramos-McKay, J., Comas-Díaz, L., & Rivera, L. (1988). Puerto Ricans. In L. Comas-Díaz & E.H. Griffith (Eds.), *Clinical guidelines in cross cultural mental health* (pp. 204–232). New York: Wiley.

Schick, F.L., & Schick, R. (1991). *Statistical handbook on U.S. Hispanics*. Phoenix, AZ: Oryx Press.

Shorris, E. (1992). *Latinos: A biography of the people*. New York: Norton.

Senour, M.N. (1977). Psychology of the Chicana. In J.L. Martinez (Ed.), *Chicano psychology* (pp. 329–342). New York: Academic Press.

Sue, D.W., & Sue, S. (1999). *Counseling the culturally different: Theory and practice* (3rd ed.). New York: Wiley.

U.S. Bureau of the Census. (2000). *Statistical abstract*. Washington, DC: U.S. Government Printing Office.

Zambrana, R.E., Silva-Palacios, V., & Powell, D. (1992). Parenting concerns, family support systems, and life problems in Mexican-origin women: A comparison by nativity. *Journal of Community Psychology, 20,* 276–288.

Zapata, J.T. (1995). Counseling Hispanic children and youth. In C.C. Lee (Ed.), *Counseling for diversity: A guide for school counselors and related professionals* (pp. 85–108). Boston: Allyn and Bacon.

Zayas, L.H. (1992). Childrearing, social stress, and child abuse: Clinical considerations with Hispanic families. *Journal of Social Distress and the Homeless, 1,* 291–309.

CHAPTER 7

Counseling Arab Americans

Sylvia C. Nassar-McMillan

Sylvia Nassar-McMillan, Ph.D., is an associate professor of counselor education at the University of North Carolina, Charlotte. Her scholarship and service revolve around cross-cultural understanding, and her research includes work with Arab American populations, particularly refugees and other immigrants. She has been involved with the professionalization of counseling, both domestically and internationally, for over ten years. She currently serves on the Arab American Institute Foundation's Census Information Center Professional Advisory Board as well as the Board of Directors of the National Board for Certified Counselors. Both her parents migrated to the United States within the last half-decade, and her paternal heritage is Palestinian.

AWARENESS INDEX

Please test your knowledge by marking the following statements true or false before proceeding to the text in this chapter. Compute your score from the scoring guide at the end of the Awareness Index.

1. T F The Arab world represents most of the world's Islamic population.

2. T F Most Arabs in the Middle East are Muslim.

3. T F Most Arab Americans are Muslim.

4. T F Muslim Arab Americans and Christian Arab Americans represent vastly different cultures.

5. T F Islam condones violent means if they can be justified by a positive outcome.

6. T F Most of the world's terrorists are of Arabic descent.

7. T F The Arabic language is a singular one that can be understood by all Arabic speakers.

8. T F Arab nationals on expired temporary visas are treated like all other nationals if apprehended.

9. T F Afghanistan, Iran, Pakistan, and other countries involved in the "war on terrorism" at the time of this writing are members of the Arab League of States.

10. T F Arab women must wear veils in public.

Scoring guide: **1.** F; **2.** T; **3.** F; **4.** F; **5.** F; **6.** F; **7.** F; **8.** F; **9.** F; **10.** F.

INTRODUCTION

Arab Americans have long represented an "invisible" minority. Because many Arab Americans' physical features are not as distinctive as those characterizing other minority populations, they can more easily blend into the mainstream "melting pot." Although the Middle East spans both Asia and Africa, Arab Americans are not governmentally designated as a minority population, unlike their African and Asian counterparts. I, for example, while encountering many family assimilation issues, including socioeconomic adaptation to United States culture, first-generation college exposure, and the like, was never eligible for government-sponsored support programs.

In the media, however, Arabs have been portrayed negatively, in commercial films (Shaheen, 1988, 2001), comic series and strips (Shaheen, 1991), and even computer games (Wingfield & Karaman, 1995). Due to strained U.S.–Middle East political relationships, there has been little backlash toward the media. This lack of national awareness and the undertone of negative perception are reinforced by the reluctance of Arab Americans to express pride in their ethnic heritage for fear of negative reactions from others. I can recount many childhood experiences in which my father denied his Arabic heritage, much to my confusion. Later in life, for example, during the Persian Gulf War, perceiving "American patriotism" as synonymous with anti-Arab sentiment, I myself downplayed my heritage. Only in recent decades have Arab Americans organized themselves to demand the civil liberties afforded to other ethnic minority groups, and to celebrate their unique ethnic identity (Zogby, 2001).

CASE EXAMPLES

Alexandra

Alexandra is the granddaughter of Lebanese Christian immigrants from the early 1900s. Her parents were both born in America. She is in her mid-fifties and practices law in Birmingham, Alabama. She is one of three daughters. She, like her sisters, married a non–Arab American man. She remains close to her parents and her extended family, primarily comprised of Arab Americans. While the family gathers often, they are not connected with the Arab American community nearby. Most of her relatives still uphold their native Arabic and Maronite Catholic customs but do not speak Arabic. Alexandra has never been to Lebanon, but in recent years has grown interested in making that journey. Her husband, while supportive of relationships with her family, is not particularly interested in learning about the culture or visiting Lebanon.

David

David is a high school student in Houston, Texas. His paternal grandparents are Palestinian. They emigrated from their native land in 1948, due to the political strife related to the establishment of Israel. His father was born in the United States. His mother emigrated from Palestine to marry his father in the 1970s. David's family speaks Arabic at home. They all are involved with Arabic cultural groups in their community. David's parents are actively involved in a political group promoting the Palestinian right-of-return to their homelands. David understands that a goal of his parents, and many other Palestinians, is to someday be able to reside in Palestine.

In David's world history and politics class last year, there was a discussion about the Arab-Israeli conflict. The teacher and classmates wanted to know David's opinion about why the Arabs were so violent toward the Israelis and why they were so unwilling to accept any of the "peaceful" solutions offered to them. David explained, from his own perspective, that many Palestinian Arabs feel oppressed by the Israelis, occupiers of their own rightful homeland, and believe that their human rights are being violated. Since that time, students have been scornful of David and have labeled him a Jew-hater and terrorist.

Ahmad

Ahmad emigrated from Iraq to the United States during the early 1990s as a refugee of the Persian Gulf War. He had fought on the same side as the United States in that conflict. He had some distant family contacts in Detroit, Michigan, so he decided to move there first. He tried to help his brothers and parents to leave Iraq, but was unsuccessful. Only he, his wife, and their four children were able to emigrate.

In Iraq, Ahmad was a physician. In the United States, he cannot obtain any medical credentials without completely retraining. Due to limited English skills and lack of knowledge of nonmedical professions and skills, he initially had trouble finding employment. With no means of financial support, he finally resorted to a position as a gas station attendant. He worries that there are people "watching him," is distrustful of others, is depressed, has struck his wife in several domestic episodes, and has begun to gamble compulsively at the local coffeehouses. Even within the Arab community he has felt ostracized because of his limited English and his lack of "Americanization." Once a devout Muslim, he has stopped worshipping at the mosque with his family.

Samira

Samira came from Sudan twenty years ago when she was still a teenager. Her family had arranged a marriage with a Sudanese man in his early thirties who had established himself in the United States as a grocer. Happy with the arrangement, Samira quickly settled into her new role as a wife and, in the coming years, bore five children. She did not often leave the home, and when she did she was accompanied by her husband or her brother, who had also moved from Sudan to live with them. Being a devout Muslim, she never left the home without her head and face covered.

As her children have grown, conflicts have arisen. She is wary of her children's honesty in translating permission slips for her to sign. Her eldest daughter does not want to continue wearing her veil and has not been coming home from school on time. Samira has made a few contacts in the small local Arab community, but because she has limited English skills she has remained isolated.

A HISTORICAL OVERVIEW

The region geographically considered the Middle East includes, in addition to the Arab world, Iran, Turkey, and Israel, representing non-Arab cultures and languages. The League of Arab States, in fact, includes twenty-two countries: Algeria, Bahrain, Comoros, Djibouti, Egypt, Iraq, Jordan, Kuwait, Lebanon, Libya, Mauritania, Morocco, Oman, Palestine, Qatar, Saudi Arabia, Somalia, Sudan, Syria, Tunisia, United Arab Emirates, and Yemen (Microsoft Corporation, 1997–2000).

The term *Arab* has historically defined a people adopting Islam in the seventh century A.D. and with ancestral ties to the Saudi Arabian peninsula (Abudabbeh & Aseel, 1999). It is commonly assumed that all Arabs practice Islam and are Muslim, although only roughly 80% of the Arab Middle East is Muslim. The terms *Muslim* and *Arab* are not synonymous, since the Arab Middle East represents only approximately 15 to 20% of the world's Islamic population (Council on Islamic Education, 1995). Instead, *Arab Nation* (see, e.g., Abudabbeh, 1996; Gray & Ahmed, 1988) or *Arab World* (H.H. Samhan, personal communication, January 10, 2002) represent more appropriate terms for those embracing Arab culture or Arab language.

Immigration to the United States from the Arab regions of the Middle East has occurred in four waves. The first, between 1875 and 1925 (Orafalea, 1988), included laborers and merchants from Syria, Lebanon, Palestine, and Jordan, primarily poor, uneducated, and Christian. Their reason for immigration was to escape the Ottoman Empire (Naff, 1984). As they immigrated, they established closely knit ethnic enclaves in various cities around the United States.

The second wave, sometimes referred to as the Brain Drain (see, e.g., Orafalea, 1988), occurred after World War II. Emigrating due to regional tensions and strife were Palestinians, Egyptians, Syrians, Jordanians, and Iraqis, with smaller immigrant groups of Lebanese and Yemeni, mainly educated Muslims. This wave included Palestinians who fled their country in 1948 to neighboring countries as well as to other continents. My own paternal family first sought refuge in Lebanon for several years, and, subsequently utilizing preestablished contacts in Detroit's automotive industry, resettled in that city in the early 1950s.

A third group, also largely educated and Muslim, came to the United States in the mid-1960s in response to easing immigration restrictions in search of better economic opportunities. Palestinians, representing the largest group, also came with a primary goal of escaping Israeli occupation of Palestinian lands.

The most recent group of immigrants from the Middle East has resulted from the Persian Gulf War. Since the early 1990s, Iraqi refugees have fled their country of origin to seek asylum from their repressive government after having fought on the side of the United States in the war. As yet, there is little demographic data available about this group, but experts estimate the influx of Iraqi refugees to the southeast Michigan area alone at 25,000 (Arab-American and Chaldean Council, 1997).

Demographic Characteristics

Arab Americans' ambivalence toward completing demographic information forms reflects their collectively confused cultural identity. Individuals often waver between self-identifying as "other," "person of color," and "White." Arab Americans have played an active role in the 2000 Census in an effort to address some of these important issues (Samhan, 1999). Although ethnicity data is not yet available from that census, the American Arab Institute contends that the general demographic concentrations have not changed since the last census (H.H. Samhan, personal communication, November 18, 2001), conservatively estimating the population of Arab Americans in the United States at 3 million (Zogby, 1990).

The goal of ethnic preservation has promoted patterns of intra-ethnic marriages, larger than average families, continued use of the Arabic language, and valuing cultural traditions. Unlike most other ethnic minority populations in the United States, the Arab American community is comprised of large numbers of foreign-born, youthful immigrants (Zogby, 1990).

Although the more recent groups of Arab American immigrants are Muslim, the majority of Arab Americans in the United States today are not. Major religious affiliations of Arab Americans include: Catholic (42%), Orthodox (23%), Muslim (23%), and Protestant (12%) (Zogby, 2001). This data often comes as a surprise to non-Arab Americans as they mistakenly equate "Arab American" with "Muslim." During a recent public-speaking program presented to a Jewish women's group, I was told by several attendees that they had never met a non-Muslim or nonveiled Arab woman. Given that not all Muslim or Arab Muslim women choose to veil themselves (Read & Bartkowski, 2000), and that Arab Americans' physical features do not necessarily distinguish themselves as such, it is quite plausible that these participants, and mainstream Americans, indeed, often encounter Arab American women without realizing it.

Approximately 75% of employed Arab Americans work in managerial, professional, technical, sales, or administrative fields (Zogby, 1990). Labor force demographics for Arab Americans parallel national percentages. Arab Americans, however, are more likely to be self-employed, or to specialize in managerial and professional occupations and less likely to work for local government.

Particularly large urban populations of Arab Americans are centered in Washington, DC; Boston, Massachusetts; Bergen Passaic, New Jersey; Los Angeles–Long Beach, California; Cleveland, Ohio; Chicago, Illinois; Houston, Texas; Anaheim-Santa Ana, California; New York, New York; and Detroit, Michigan (Zogby, 1990). Other large groups of Arab Americans reside in smaller, more rural communities such as Allentown, Pennsylvania; Jacksonville, Florida; Portland, Oregon; and Utica, New York (Zogby, 1984).

Arab Culture

Because so much of the Arab world practices Islam, many Arabic and Muslim traditions are similar. Hence, in order to better understand Arab culture, it is beneficial to understand some of the key teachings of Islam.

The beginnings of Islam have been traced back to the period between the seventh and tenth centuries A.D., during which time the Prophet Mohammad appeared to the peoples of the Arabian Peninsula. He was their messenger of God, proclaiming God's will as communicated to him through the Archangel Gabriel. These teachings resulted in the Qur'an (Abudabbeh & Aseel, 1999). The tribes of Arabia united, and the growth of an Arab nation began. Other (Christian) denominations found in the Arabic Middle East are the Coptic Orthodox Church, Assyrian Church of the East, Syrian Orthodox Church, Eastern Greek Orthodox Church, and Eastern Rite Catholic Churches (Abudabbeh, 1996).

The keys to Islam are found in the Articles of Faith, directing followers to have faith in God, Holy Angels, books, and messengers, and the Judgment Day (Council on Islamic Education, 1995). The five Pillars of Islam include affirmation of the faith, praying five times daily, fasting during Ramadan, making pilgrimage to Mecca, and paying community taxes (Abudabbeh & Aseel, 1999). General Arabic values influenced by Islam include dignity, honor, and reputation; family loyalty above personal gain; a pious belief in God; and God-determined fate (Nydell, 1987). A recent study indicated that, in fact, many Arab Americans attribute their satisfaction with life in the United States to religion (Faragallah, Schumm, & Webb, 1997). Islam promotes a collectivist view of family and community as opposed to the independent thinking, needs, feelings, and thoughts of Western culture.

Arab cultures are patriarchal; hence, the head of the household is either the father or, in his absence, the eldest brother or other designated male representative. Although women often publicly demonstrate subservience to their husbands in public matters, they shoulder much of the responsibility for domestic decision making and childrearing. Expectations for men include religiosity, hospitality, and courage; for women, chastity; and for children, honoring of parents (Abudabbeh & Aseel, 1999).

CURRENT ISSUES

Models describing diverse populations typically include such variables as length of residence in the United States, age at immigration, traditionalism, time since the last visit to their homeland (Marsella et al., 1994), language preference, place of birth, generation level, socioeconomic status, preferred ethnic identity, ethnic-group social contacts (Ponterotto, 1987). In addition, Arab Americans face issues related to racial and religious hostility and discrimination (Stockton, 1994) and racial-religious-ethnic identification (Jackson, 1997).

Several small, exploratory studies within Arab American communities illuminate some of the major issues faced by Arab Americans today. These studies represent interviews of community service officials (Paine, 1986), individual therapists (Hakim-Larson, Kamoo, & Voelker, 1998), and a group of therapists (Nassar-McMillan & Hakim-Larson, in press). Based on these exploratory works, a number of variables emerge as particularly salient to working with individuals of Arab descent, including ethnic discrimination, country of origin, length of United States residency, religion, reason for immigration, gender, and language usage, among others. The case examples presented earlier in this chapter will be referred to again here for the purpose of illustrating the variables discussed.

Ethnic Discrimination

Negative images of Arab Americans abound throughout media and educational materials in the United States, perpetuating the notion that individuals of Arab descent are either violent terrorists, wealthy, womanizing sheikhs, or nomadic, desert-dwelling camel riders. Not surprisingly, 40% of Arab Americans recently polled reported having experienced ethnic discrimination. Some scholars believe that the connection between United States foreign policy and racism against Arab Americans is intertwined (Shain, 1996). Much of the negative stereotyping toward Arab Americans seems related to mainstream Americans' perceptions of the Arab-Israeli conflict. The media has doggedly continued to attempt to link the World Trade Center attacks with the Israeli conflict, when in fact no evidence has surfaced supporting such a connection (Arab American Institute, n.d.). Relatedly, the United States government has expanded its "antiterrorism" legislation to deport suspected terrorists by utilizing "secret evidence." This legislative action is not unlike the compulsory targeting and profiling conducted at other times in United States history against other groups, such as Japanese Americans during the 1940s and suspected communists during the 1950s (Arab American Institute, n.d.). Some of the attitudes that David experienced in his school and classroom may be related to recent global events.

Country of Origin

Arab countries each represent a slightly different culture and language dialect, many with differing histories and cultural influences. Individuals may originate, by birth or ancestry, from countries with a relatively small (e.g., Yemen, Sudan) or large (e.g., Lebanon) Western influence, potentially impacting their adjustment to United States culture. For example, Samira, coming from Sudan, had had relatively little exposure to Western culture prior to her immigration.

The political relationship between the United States and clients' country of origin also is likely to impact one's acculturation process. For Ahmad, American stereotypes of Iraqis in general had hindered his ability to assimilate without a level of discrimination, even despite his relative insulation in an urban Arab American enclave.

Length of Residence in the United States

The longer one's United States residency, the more opportunities exist to learn the new language, laws, and systems of the dominant culture, which may differ drastically from those of one's country of origin. Homeland visits also are important considerations, as such visits may indicate the desire to maintain a bond to the country of origin. Among my paternal family, within a fifty-year period of fleeing Palestine, only one sibling and one offspring had gone back for a visit. The bitterness and trauma of the initial emigration out of Palestine, and the family's "survival mode," which took the form of looking only to the future and toward economic resettlement, impacted my the cultural identity tremendously. Although my family used the Arabic language in the immediate family units, it was rarely spoken in public and not taught to offspring.

Immersion in the dominant culture versus living in a relatively insulated Arab American enclave also is a factor in cultural adjustment. In Samira's case, despite the small size of her local Arab American community, she remained relatively encapsulated in it. Regardless of length of residence, it is likely that intergenerational conflicts will be a part of the acculturation process of Arab Americans. Newer generations will struggle to meld their Old World values with the enticing, individualistic freedoms afforded by the new host culture. The conflicts between Samira and her children, particularly her daughter, provide examples of this phenomenon.

Religion

Level of acculturation may differ based on both religion and level of religiosity. Although Christian Arab Americans are influenced by Islam and non-Western ideals, they may find relatively easier acceptance into mainstream United States culture than their counterparts of Muslim background do. One highly visible issue for women is that many Muslim females follow the traditional custom of wearing a veil, although this custom is now debated among Arab and other Muslim females for a variety of reasons (Read & Bartkowski, 2000). Being either White or Black also may influence acceptance into the dominant culture; Whites tend to find easier acceptance (Jackson, 1997). Being Christian and "White" (although "not quite" by some standards), while helping my Arab American family in our acculturation process, still posed an obstacle in some situations, such as in dating relationships with Euro-Americans, and even in acceptance by the author's maternal relatives, in terms of their European American heritage and standards.

Reason for Immigration

Voluntary versus involuntary immigration influence persons' acculturation processes differentially (Al-Issa, 1997a). The first wave of Arab immigration to the United States included those who came of their own free will, seeking better economic conditions. In contrast, many of the immigrants from Iraq in the last decade were exiled because of their opposition to the political regime. Although the United States may serve as the host country for many voluntary and involuntary immigrants from the Arab Middle East, there may be, understandably, some residual resentment and anger toward the United States based on its policies toward the immigrant's country and region of origin, both in times of peace and war. These issues may affect adjustment to life in the United States and may inherently be passed on to younger generations. David and Ahmad might well hold such sentiments toward the United States, despite its host status.

Gender

Gender plays an important role in an individual's worldview (Ibrahim, 1999). For young American-born Arab American females, in particular, the Old World values regarding gender-appropriate behavior may feel restrictive. In addition, career and other life choices may be directly and indirectly influenced by culture of origin. For me, living away from an Arab American enclave, the educational status often sought and achieved by Arab American males became the goal, and even further removal from those Old Word values through such educational pursuits made them a distant reality.

Language Usage

The vast majority of young Arab Americans speak English fluently (Zogby, 1990). Among those who do, use of the Arabic language may reflect an Arabic cultural identity. For those who do not, as might be the case in more recent immigrants or those who are less educated, the lack of English-speaking ability might pose a barrier in career and other pursuits. Both Samira and Ahmad were surely impacted negatively in their career development by their limitations in speaking English.

Socioeconomic Status and Education

Descendants of the early Arab American immigrants have made great gains in economic and educational arenas. Among the second and third waves of immigrants, education was highly valued, a value reflected in offspring of those immigrants pursuing professional careers (Zogby, 1990). Such a scenario played out in the case of Alexandra, as well as in my own case. Socioeconomic status may be a critical issue for the most recent immigrants, especially those emigrating involuntarily or as refugees. They may not have had the means or the familial connections to successfully re-adapt economically. Even those who are well educated may be relegated to lower-level careers due to limited language abilities and economic resources. Ahmad represented such an unfortunate case.

Other Factors

Variables such as age, birth order, and ability or disability status also have been noted as important in assessing clients' worldviews (Ibrahim, 1999). Clients' perspectives of these factors may be influenced by both country-of-origin and new host country values. Developmental or mental disorders may be overdiagnosed if not considered in a cultural context. Some clients may, therefore, have been previously misdiagnosed.

In addition to the challenges already faced by those leaving their countries of origin as refugees, these individuals also are at high risk for Post-traumatic Stress Disorder (PTSD). In fact, refugees from war-torn backgrounds (e.g., Lebanese, Iraqis) present PTSD symptoms at alarming rates (see, e.g., Jamil et al., 2001; Takeda, 2000). In addition to symptoms typical of PTSD (e.g., nightmares, flashbacks), PTSD can exacerbate other disorders such as addiction, depression, and developmental delays (Nassar-McMillan & Hakim-Larson, in press) and can be accompanied by shame, fear, paranoia, and broken family ties, potentially leading to breakdowns in moral reasoning (Kira, 1999). It is quite possible that Ahmad's symptomology may have been the result of PTSD from his military experiences.

Cultural identification of Arab Americans truly represents a complex and sometimes difficult process. Models addressing psychosocial development of minority-group members may need to be expanded to include the amount of discrimination and bias based on domestic and foreign policies of the United States. Such issues may arrest or hinder the cultural identity development of Arab Americans today (McGoldrick, 1996).

SUGGESTIONS FOR ENHANCING COUNSELOR EFFECTIVENESS

Parameters of traditional counseling modalities must be reexamined and modified in working with clients of Arab descent. Multisystemic approaches, including engaging community leaders in service delivery, must be sought. In addition to immigration and acculturation issues, Arab

American refugees are also faced with a host of unique issues. Finally, an advocacy role may be necessary in working with individuals or groups of Arab descent.

Cultural Identity and Counseling

Self-perceptions of clients as Arab versus American poses an important consideration. Country of origin, length of United States residency, occurrence and frequency of homeland visits, and language usage may provide some insight into clients' cultural identity. Because a mistrust of outsiders is common in Arabic societies, non–Arab American counselors must be attuned to culturally appropriate ways of establishing relationships and rapport. For example, same-gender counseling may be indicated under some circumstances. For example, Samira might be more comfortable with a female counselor, while Alexandra might be comfortable with female or male. Further, depending upon the clients' level of identification with traditional Arabic values, it may be effective to employ couples or family counseling strategies, focusing on collective goals rather than individual goals. Counselors must also become aware of how ethnic discrimination has impacted clients' cultural identity development. For example, if such discrimination has caused them to hide their ethnicity out of shame, then empowerment through reclaiming their heritage in a different light might be indicated. In addition, reason for immigration, whether voluntary or involuntary, may prescribe grief counseling to come to terms with the culture that was lost. David and Ahmad might both benefit from addressing such issues.

It is important for counselors to understand Arab culture from their clients' individual or group perspective. In order to understand a client's unique cultural identity, it may be effective for the counselor to question the client on issues of worldview and cultural identity. For example, asking the client about spiritual beliefs or strength of the family unit could provide insight into additional supports to the counseling function. Bingham and Ward (1996) support the inclusion of client-counselor discussion of racial variables and issues throughout the counseling relationship, particularly in building rapport, administering culturally appropriate tests, and deciding on personal versus career counseling foci. For Samira and Ahmad, particularly, given their direct immigration status, it is imperative that these issues be addressed. In order to provide culturally sensitive counseling services, even David and Alexandra, representing later generations, might well benefit from exploring these issues.

Counseling Issues

In many Arab cultures, particularly the less Westernized ones, the concept of counseling may be nonexistent. Instead, mental health services and functions have been provided historically by physicians, priests, and imams (Loza, 2001), and magicians, fortune tellers, and Koranic healers (Al-Krenawi & Graham, 2000). It may be important to discuss clients' understanding of counseling services, and to clarify the roles and functions of both counselor and client. Ahmad and Samira, particularly, may hold non-Western ideas about helping relationships, and even David's and Alexandra's ideas may be influenced, albeit less directly, by Old World beliefs about "counseling" roles. Relationship building with Arab American clients may be particularly meaningful to the counseling relationship. Also, because Arab cultures believe so strongly in fate, Arab Americans tend to be more survival-oriented them insight-oriented (Sayed, Collins, & Takahashi, 1998). Focusing on the development of intra- or interpersonal insight may be counterproductive, causing anxiety on the clients' part. Thus, problem solving and cognitive behavioral strategies may be good tools for working with Arab American clients, and relationship-oriented (as opposed to interpretation- or exploration-focused) strategies may provide the most effective counseling interventions (Al-Abdul-Jabbar & Al-Issa, 2000).

Parameters of traditional Western counseling sessions may need expansion, particularly with individuals who identify greatly with Arab culture. They may take longer than the typical fifty-minute client hour and may include other family members, perhaps children, due to lack of child care, or husbands or elder sons who may wish to be present while their wife or mother is obtaining services from an "outsider." It may be necessary to visit an Arab client at home from time to time, perhaps because of difficulty with transportation or other barriers inhibiting the clients' attendance. Openness to such visits may serve as proactive investments in the clients' progress in counseling. In terminating counseling, it might be effective to schedule several follow-up sessions to prevent the perception of an abrupt end to the relationship.

Because rituals are important in Arab culture, developing a culturally appropriate ritual in the counseling setting might help facilitate rapport building (Jackson & Nassar-McMillan, in press). Beginning and ending with a handshake (Nobles & Sciarra, 2000), standing at the conclusion of the session (Karmo, 2001), or utilizing proverbs common to Arab American clients (Abou El-Azayem, 2001) all can serve to enhance rapport with clients.

In developing personal relationships with Arab clients (e.g., learning about their communities, churches, etc.) it would not be surprising for a counselor to receive an invitation to join an Arab family for a meal or other social function (Timimi, 1995). While typically seen as an insult to refuse such hospitality, a polite refusal might be acceptable if explained in the context of the counseling. Potential dual roles with Arab American clients also can confuse confidentiality issues. On the one hand, Arab clients may welcome the inclusion of a helping professional into their personal milieu, and on the other they may become wary of how confidential their personal information will be kept.

Another caveat involves delivering counseling directives from a "benevolent authority" perspective. While this approach might be most effective, it may occasionally be perceived as a threat to paternal authority, and also may elicit transference in the counseling relationship (Abudabbeh, 1996).

It is important not to interpret Arab American clients' behaviors from a traditional Western model. For example, if a client reacted to an insight-oriented directive by becoming anxious, he or she might be labeled as "resistant." In fact, Arab Americans are not socialized to be expressive about their emotions. Communication styles also are open to misinterpretation. For example, Arabs may repeat a concept several times, perhaps in different ways, use louder volumes than considered normal by Western standards, and use hand gestures when speaking. Any or all of these behaviors may be considered aggressive by Western standards, and counselors may become intimidated in working with clients who exhibit such behaviors (Via et al., 1997). Interpreting them in a cultural context creates a much more inviting and empathic environment for clients and counselors alike.

Because counseling has historically been provided, as such, by community leaders, it is important to include such individuals whenever possible. If there is a large local Arab American community, instituting a community approach to providing counseling services may be most effective. Arab American enclaves serve as an extension of the family unit, especially in the absence of extended family.

Refugees: Special Cases

Because refugees face immediate acculturation barriers such as new systems (e.g., legal) and languages, as well as heightened discrimination due to new immigrant status, they pose specialized challenges to counselors. From a social service perspective, these clients must be empowered to meet basic needs, such as food and shelter. Concurrently, facilitating economic adaptation must be paramount if these individuals are ever to become self-sufficient (Sayed, Collins, & Takahashi, 1998).

Refugees from war-ravaged countries also may suffer a host of emotional maladies (see, e.g., Jamil et al., 2001). Broken family ties can lead to shame and guilt as well as worry and financial pressure (Nassar-McMillan & Hakim-Larson, in press). Some refugees suffer from extreme paranoia, which, while unsurprising if interpreted in the cultural context of their recent military history, could lead to a psychopathological misdiagnosis nonetheless (Al-Issa, 1997b; Kamoo et al., 2001). Moreover, PTSD can be psychologically debilitating, and can exacerbate other symptoms such as developmental delays, ADHD, depression, or addictions.

Advocacy and Social Justice

Helping professionals have recently rediscovered the roots of their calling—client advocacy. In working with Arab Americans, counselors must be willing to advocate on their behalf, and to examine their own preconceived notions toward and about Arabs and Arab Americans based on the strained sociopolitical relationship between the United States and the Arab world. Multicultural counseling models have begun to include consideration of politics in relationship to providing effective services to clients (see, e.g., McGoldrick, 1996) and to overcome the polarization that naturally occurs through the oppression process.

In this context, it behooves counselors to become aware of immigration laws and their potential effect on Arab American clients (see, e.g., Arab American Institute, n.d., www.aaiusa.org/immigration/immigration1.html). In light of current global sociopolitical events, helping professionals also should become knowledgeable about racial profiling practices, as well as laws and rights protecting their clients (Arab American Institute, n.d.). In addition to empowering clients both by empathizing and providing information, it is appropriate for counselors to become involved in lobbying efforts at community, state, and national levels.

CONCLUDING REMARKS

Arab Americans, not unlike most other ethnic groups, have a long and rich history of citizenship in the United States. Perhaps due to the influence of differing religions and worldviews, perhaps due to the coveted natural resources of the Middle East (e.g., oil), this region itself has had periods of strife with the United States. Given the recent historical events of September 11, 2001, coupled with the heightened tensions and war in Israel, cultural misunderstandings have become intensified, affecting Arab Americans and their cultural identity as a group. Ironically, this tragic series of events has brought Arab culture into the forefront of public attention. While much of the current media focuses on negative images (e.g., Palestinian suicide bombers), perhaps the heightened attention will inherently raise awareness of Arab culture in general. Because stereotypes and misunderstandings often are perpetuated by a lack of information, this increase in awareness may help non–Arab and Arab Americans alike to discover similarities and appreciate differences among themselves.

EXPERIENTIAL ACTIVITIES

Individual

Consider the cases of Alexandra, David, Ahmad, and Samira. Describe how the following factors may have influenced (or currently influence) their cultural identity development.

1. Ethnic discrimination.
2. Country of origin.
3. Length of United States residency.
4. Religion.
5. Reasons for immigration.
6. Gender.
7. Language usage.
8. Other factors.

Group

1. Review the case studies presented in this chapter. What implications for counseling can you generate from each?
2. Generate additional information to add to each case study, based on the current political situation in the United States (e.g., heightened ethnic discrimination and racial profiling). What additional implications are indicated?
3. Review world history and geography textbooks for accuracy and bias, including negative and positive images of individuals of Arab descent.
4. Divide into two groups of four to six people (extras can observe). Prepare a debate on the Arab-Israeli conflict, researching accordingly.
5. Prepare media campaigns supporting each of two (or more) sides of the political conflict identified in the debate above.
6. Develop curricula to teach classes (any level) about some aspect of Arab or Muslim culture (e.g., religion, artistic or scientific contributions to the world). (See, e.g., Arab World and Islamic Resources and School Services, n.d.; Council on Islamic Education, n.d.)

Out of Class

1. Interview several individuals of Arab descent. Identify how their generation level, religion, country of origin, and other factors influence their cultural identity. What issues might they present in counseling as a result of their ethnic background? (Speculate hypothetically.)

2. Research some aspect of Arab culture (see, e.g., Arab World and Islamic Resources and School Services, n.d.; Council on Islamic Education, n.d.).

Questions for Reflection

1. Think about your perceptions of Arabs and Arab Americans. How did they begin? How have they evolved?
2. Assess your own self-knowledge about United States foreign policy toward various countries in the Middle East.
3. Assess your self-knowledge about domestic policies potentially impacting Arab Americans or other specific ethnic minority groups.

REFERENCES

Abou El-Azayem, A. (2001, May). *Programs for prevention of domestic violence in Arab cultures*. Paper presented at the Second Biennial National Conference on Arab American Health Issues, Dearborn, MI.

Abudabbeh, N. (1996). Arab families. In M. McGoldrick, J. Giordano, & J.K. Pearce (Eds.), *Ethnicity and family therapy* (2nd ed) (pp. 333–346). New York: Guilford.

Abudabbeh, N., & Aseel, H.A. (1999). Transcultural counseling and Arab Americans. In J. McFadden (Ed.), *Transcultural counseling* (pp. 283–296). Alexandria, VA: American Counseling Association.

Al-Abdul-Jabbar, J., & Al-Issa, I. (2000). Psychotherapy in Islamic society. In I. Al-Issa (Ed.), *Al-Junun: Mental illness in the Islamic world* (pp. 277–293). Madison, CT: International Universities Press.

Al-Issa, I. (1997a). Ethnicity, immigration, and psychopathology. In I. Al-Issa & M. Tousignant (Eds.), *Ethnicity, immigration, and psychopathology* (pp. 3–15). New York: Plenum.

Al-Issa, I. (1997b). General issues and research problems. In I. Al-Issa & M. Tousignant (Eds.), *Ethnicity, immigration, and psychopathology* (pp. 277–289). New York: Plenum.

Al-Krenawi, A., & Graham, J.R. (2000). Culturally sensitive social work practice with Arab clients in mental health settings. *Health and Social Work, 25,* 9–22.

Arab American Institute. (N.d.). Retrieved February 24, 2002, at: www.aaiusa.org/policypriorities.

Arab-American and Chaldean Council. (1997). *Arab-American and Chaldean Council mental health services project proposal for Iraqi refugees*. Lathrup Village, MI: Arab-American and Chaldean Council.

Arab World and Islamic Resources and School Services. (N.d.). Retrieved February 24, 2002, at: www.skatesaway.com/gui/awairproductinfo.html.

Bingham, R.P., & Ward, C.M. (1996). Practical application of career counseling with ethnic minority women. In M.C. Savickas & W.D. Walser (Eds.), *Handbook of career counseling theory and practice* (pp. 291–313). Palo Alto, CA: Davies-Black.

Council on Islamic Education. (1995). *Teaching about Islam and Muslims in the public school classroom* (3rd ed.). Fountain Valley, CA: Council on Islamic Education.

Faragallah, M.H., Schumm, H.R., & Webb, F.J. (1997). Acculturation of Arab-American immigrants: An exploratory study. *Journal of Comparative Family Studies, 28* (3), 182–203.

Gray, N.A., & Ahmed, I. (1988). The Arab-American family: A resource manual for human service providers. Dearborn, MI: Arab Community Center for Economic and Social Services.

Hakim-Larson, J., Kamoo, R., & Voelker, S. (1998, July). *Mental health services and families of Arab ethnic origin.* Poster session presented at the annual meeting of the Family Research Consortium II, Blaine, WA.

Ibrahim, F.A. (1999). Transcultural counseling: Existential worldview theory and cultural identity. In J. McFadden (Ed.), *Transcultural counseling* (pp. 23–59). Alexandria, VA: American Counseling Association.

Jackson, M.L. (1997). Counseling Arab Americans. In C.C. Lee (Ed.), *Multicultural issues in counseling: New approaches to diversity* (2nd ed.; pp. 333–349). Alexandria, VA: American Counseling Association.

Jackson, M.L., & Nassar-McMillan, S.C. (In press). Counseling Arab Ameicans. In C.C. Lee (Ed.), *Multicultural issues in counseling: New approaches to diversity* (3rd ed.). Alexandria, VA: American Counseling Association.

Jamil, H., Hakim-Larson, J., Farrag, M., Kafaji, T., Duqum, I., & Jamil, L. (2001, May). *A retrospective study of Arab American mental health clients: Trauma and the Iraqi refugees.* Paper presented at the Second Biennial National Conference on Arab American Health Issues, Dearborn, MI.

Kamoo, R., Hakim-Larson, J., Nassar-McMillan, S.C., & Porcerelli, J. (2001, May). *An integrative approach to acculturation and mental health in immigrans of Arab and Chaldean descent.* Paper presented at the Second Biennial National Conference on Arab American Health Issues, Dearborn, MI.

Karmo, T. (2001, May). *Mental health management in Arab-Chaldean Americans.* Paper presented at the Second Biennial National Conference on Arab American Health Issues, Dearborn, MI.

Kira, I.A. (1999, July). *Value processing and mental health.* Paper presented at the Sixth European Congress of Psychology, Rome, Italy.

Loza, N. (2001, May). *Insanity on the Nile: The history of psychiatry in Pharaonic Egypt.* Paper presented at the Second Biennial National Conference on Arab American Health Issues, Dearborn, MI.

Marsella, A.J., Bornemann, T., Ekblad, S., & Orley, J. (Eds.). (1994). *Amidst peril and pain: The mental health and well-being of the world's refugees.* Washington, DC: American Psychological Association.

McGoldrick, M. (1996). Ethnicity and family therapy: An overview. In M. McGoldrick, J. Giordano, & J.K. Pearce (Eds.), *Ethnicity and family therapy* (2nd ed.; pp. 1–30). New York: Guilford.

Microsoft Corporation. (1997–2000). Microsoft Encarta Online Encyclopedia 2001. *In Arab League.* Retrieved December 22, 2001, at http://encarta.msn.com.

Naff, A. (1984). The early Arab immigrant experience. In E. McCarus (Ed.), *The development of Arab American identity.* Ann Arbor: University of Michigan Press.

Nassar-McMillan, S. C., & Hakim-Larson, J. (In press). Counseling considerations among Arab Americans. *Journal of Counseling and Development.*

Nobles, A.Y., & Sciarra, D.T. (2000). Cultural determinants in the treatment of Arab Americans: A primer for mainstream therapists. *American Journal of Orthopsychiatry, 70* (2), 182–191.

Nydell, M. (1987). *Understanding Arabs: A guide for Westerners.* Yarmouth, ME: Intercultural Press.

Orfalea, G. (1988). *Before the flames: A quest for the history of Arab Americans.* Austin: University of Texas Press.

Paine, P. (1986). *A study of the Middle East community in the Detroit metropolitan area.* Detroit, MI: United Community Services of Metropolitan Detroit.

Ponterotto, J.G. (1987). Counseling Mexican Americans: A multimodal approach. *Journal of Counseling and Development, 65,* 308–311.

Read, J.G., & Bartkowski, J.P. (2000). To veil or not to veil? A case study of identity negotiation among Muslim women in Austin, Texas. *Gender and Society, 14* (3), 395–417.

Samhan, H.H. (1999). Not quite white: Race classification and the Arab American experience. In M. Suleiman (Ed.), *Arabs in America: Building a new future* (pp. 209–226). Philadelphia: Temple University Press.

Sayed, M.A., Collins, D.T., & Takahashi, T. (1998). West meets East: Cross-cultural issues in inpatient treatment. *Bulletin of the Menninger Clinic, 62* (4), 439–454.

Shaheen, J. (1988, February 29). The media image of Arabs. *Newsweek,* p. 10.

Shaheen, J. (2001). *Reel bad Arabs: How Hollywood vilifies a people.* New York: Interlink.

Shain, Y. (1996). Arab-Americans at a crossroads. *Journal of Palestine Studies, 25* (3), 46–59.

Stockton, R. (1994). Ethnic archetypes and the Arab image. In E. McCarus (Ed.), *The development of Arab American identity.* Ann Arbor: University of Michigan Press.

Takeda, J. (2000). Psychological and economic adaptation of Iraqi male refugees: Implications for social work practice. *Journal of Social Work Practice, 26,* 1–21.

Timimi, S.B. (1995). Adolescence in immigrant Arab families. *Psychotherapy, 32* (1), 141–149.

Via, T., Callahan, S., Barry, K., Jackson, C., & Gerber, D.E. (1997). Middle East meets midwest: The new health care challenge. *The Journal of Multicultural Nursing and Health, 3,* 35–39.

Wingfield, M., & Karaman, B. (1995, March–April). Diverse learners in the social studies classroom: Arab stereotypes and American educators. *Social Studies and the Young Learner*. Washington, DC: American Arab Anti-Discrimination Committee.

Zogby, J. (Ed.). (1984). Taking root: Bearing fruit—the Arab American experience. Washington, DC: American Arab Anti-Discrimination Committee.

Zogby, J. (1990). *Arab America today: A demographic profile of Arab Americans*. Washington, DC: Arab American Institute.

Zogby, J. (2001). *What ethnic Americans really think: The Zogby culture polls*. Washington, DC: Zogby International.

CHAPTER 8

Counseling Multiracial Americans

Carmen Braun Williams

Carmen Braun Williams received her Ph.D. in clinical psychology from Pennsylvania State University. She had a private practice in Boulder and Denver, Colorado, and was a psychologist in the counseling center at the University of Colorado at Boulder before joining the faculty at the University of Colorado at Denver (UCD). Dr. Williams currently is an associate professor in counseling psychology and counselor education at UCD. She has written and presented extensively in the areas of racial identity development and cultural competency.

Dr. Williams, born in Germany, is the first of five children of an African American career Army sergeant and a German mother. She first came to the United States at age three and traveled with her family between the United States and Germany throughout her childhood.

AWARENESS INDEX

Please test your knowledge by marking the following statements true or false before proceeding to the text in this chapter. Compute your score from the scoring guide at the end of the Awareness Index.

1. T F *Mulatto* is an acceptable term for biracial individuals.

2. T F Interracial marriages were illegal in some states until 1967.

3. T F According to census data, most multiracial individuals are part White.

4. T F Multiracial individuals should be encouraged to choose one racial group with which to identify to resolve their identity conflicts.

5. T F Racial identity development models for monoracial individuals are equally applicable to multiracial individuals.

6. T F Interracial couples often are warned by others about the negative consequences for their offspring of being multiracial.

7. T F The majority of multiracial individuals identify themselves as belonging to only two racial groups.

8. T F As a counseling strategy, it is generally appropriate to explore a multiracial client's choice about racial identification.

9. T F Social constructions of race strongly affect the psychological tasks confronting multiracial individuals.

10. T F Physical appearance (i.e., skin tone, facial features, hair texture, etc.) generally is a key factor in multiracial individuals' racial identification.

11. T F In the 2000 census (which for the first time gave respondents the option of reporting more than one race), approximately 10% of the U.S. population reported more than one race.

Scoring guide: **1.** F; **2.** T; **3.** T; **4.** F; **5.** F; **6.** T; **7.** F; **8.** T; **9.** T; **10.** T; **11.** F.

INTRODUCTION

The population of multiracial Americans is growing and consequently "transforming the 'face' of the United States" (Root, 1992). A potential effect of the increasing presence of racially mixed people is a reexamination of the way we think about race and racial identity. In this chapter, the term *race* is used to refer to a construct that is socially and politically (rather than biologically) rooted. According to this construction of race, people are assigned different levels of power, status, and access to economic and social resources based on their ascribed location within mutually exclusive demographic categories (Helms & Cook, 1999; Root, 1992; Spickard, 1992). People's placement within these categories is predicated on certain physical markers such as skin color, hair texture, and facial features. The definition of race as socially constructed has major implications for individuals whose heritage crosses racial boundaries and whose physical features often defy single categorization.

The term *multiracial* will be used throughout the chapter to describe individuals with more than one racial heritage. Interchangeable terms are mixed-race and racially mixed. Biracial will be used specifically to describe individuals whose heritage consists of two races only. The term *mulatto*, although still used occasionally to refer to individuals of mixed African American and White heritage, is considered offensive to many because of its etymology in the Spanish word for mule (Fernandez, 1992). The term *mestizo*, which originally referred to people of mixed American Indian and Spanish heritage (Fernandez, 1992), also is used less often in the contemporary literature on multiracial individuals.

Issues of language and terminology become significant as multiracial populations grow. The dismantling in 1967 of the remaining legal barriers to interracial marriages, along with the civil rights and women's rights movements of the same era, encouraged a marked shift in social resistance to marrying outside of one's ascribed race (Gibbs, 1987; Root, 1992; Solsberry, 1994). Beginning in the 1970s, interracial marriage has increased so dramatically that some have described the United States as being in the midst of a "biracial baby boom" (Root, 1992).

Until the 2000 census, there was no systematic collection of data about the numbers of multiracial people in the United States. Estimates placed the population of multiracial people at anywhere from 2 to 10 million (Morrissey, 1996; Poston, 1990). The 2000 census gave us the first set of tangible data about multiracial people. For the first time on the census questionnaire, respondents were permitted to choose more than one racial category to describe themselves. Results revealed that previous estimates had been fairly accurate. According to the 2000 census (U.S. Bureau of the Census, 2001), nearly 7 million people, or 2.4% of the total U.S. population, reported membership in more than one racial group. Among those reporting more than one race, the overwhelming majority (93%) reported exactly two races.

These data suggest that most multiracial individuals identify themselves as belonging to only two racial groups, or biracial. Census data further revealed that the most common racial combination for those reporting more than one race was White and another race. More than half of multiracial respondents fit this category. This information raises interesting questions about racial identification for individuals whose heritage reflects both the racial group in power (White) and a so-called minority group. Historical laws of hypodescent—i.e., laws assigning mixed-race people to the racial category of lowest status—sought to prevent biracial individuals from exercising the choice to identify as White (Root, 1992). Certainly even today, social norms that rest on such outdated racial practices continue to limit mixed-race people's choices. The implications of these data for counselors working with multiracial populations will be addressed in later sections of this chapter.

CASE EXAMPLES

Mario

Mario is a twenty-year-old biracial man whose parents urged him to seek counseling to address his loss of interest in academic and social activities. Mario is in his senior year in college and has applied for admission to several law schools. His parents are concerned about his chances for getting into a good law school if his grades start to fall. They have tried to talk to him, but Mario keeps saying, "Nothing's wrong. Just give me some space." In the meantime, Mario continues to be distracted and unmotivated.

Mario's racial background is White and Mexican American. He looks Mediterranean with his olive skin and wavy hair and often is asked, "What are you?" Mario's three-year relationship with a young White woman, Kayla, recently suffered a blow when her parents found out that Mario was part Mexican American. Mario and Kayla had become quite serious and had begun to consider marriage. When Kayla told her parents about Mario's racial background in preparation for their initial meeting, they told her she was not to bring him home and pressured her to end the relationship. Mario is upset with Kayla for allowing her parents to distance her from him.

Mario's parents initially also had difficulty supporting his relationship with Kayla but eventually accepted his choice of a non–Mexican American partner. Mario feels grateful that his parents were able to get past their racial bias but knows they remain disappointed. Mario followed his parents' suggestion to seek counseling. He too is concerned about his academic future but more important, wants guidance about how to handle the problematic racial issues confronting him.

Gayle

Gayle is a sixteen-year-old biracial adolescent adopted at birth by a White couple, Fred and Sandra Hermann. The Hermanns had two biological children (a daughter now seventeen and a twenty-one-year-old son) when they adopted Gayle. The Hermanns are concerned about the marked change in behavior they have noticed in Gayle over the past several weeks. They received a call from Gayle's high school reporting that she has skipped school frequently. When the Hermanns confronted Gayle about missing school, she told them angrily that what she did with her own life was nobody's business but her own.

The Hermanns are a couple in their early fifties who pride themselves on their choice to adopt Gayle despite their parents' objections about their decision to raise a part–African American child in a small White community. The Hermanns are unaware that race has ever been an issue in Gayle's life. They believe strongly that raising Gayle just as they did their other children (with no need to address racial issues) was a successful parenting strategy. They believe that if their families and other people would just treat everyone as human beings America wouldn't have so many racial problems.

Meanwhile, Gayle confided to her older sister that she sometimes skips school, takes the bus to a nearby city, and "kicks back" with Black kids. Gayle says she is angry with her parents for raising her to be White and not helping her to discover the other side of her heritage. The problem is, she doesn't always feel welcomed by the Black kids. They accuse her of "talking and acting White." Gayle says she would like to figure out "who I really am." She agrees to see a counselor when her parents tell her they have located a biracial female counselor who is White and African American like Gayle.

HISTORICAL OVERVIEW

Despite the increasing presence of multiracial persons in the United States, this population has been and largely remains enshrouded in myth (Root, 1992). One of the pervasive myths about multiracial individuals is that, because of their racial ambiguity, they are doomed to a life of psychological stress and conflict. Growing up as a biracial child, I often heard people caution interracial couples against marrying because of "all the problems the children will face." This comment implied that these couples were selfish and not thinking about how "difficult life will be for the kids." Statements like this often made me wonder what terrible things might be in store for me! Later on in life I understood these reactions for what they really were—prejudice masquerading as empathy.

Assumptions about the deficiencies of multiracial people have permeated social consciousness. Myths about multiracial people have been perpetuated through popular literature, movies, and other media. Popular literature dating back to the early 1900s contains pejorative descriptions of multiracial people doomed to lives of ostracism, alienation, and confusion (Zack, 1993). Until recently, clinical studies also have characterized the multiracial population in pathological terms. Early clinical studies described multiracial people as confused, suicidal, drug-addicted, delinquent, psychosomatic, depressed, and marginal (Benson, 1981; Sebring, 1985; Stonequist, 1937). The widespread assumptions that multiracial people have difficulty adjusting to their mixed racial status and are often rejected by one or more racial groups are reinforced by accounts of "hybrid degeneracy" resulting from the "unnatural" mixing of the races (Nakashima, 1992). As one young biracial man put it, "American society makes being biracial feel less like a blessing than a curse" (Courtney, 1995, p. 16).

It has been only since the 1980s that this deficit focus has given way to more realistic accounts of the resilience of multiracial people (Funderburg, 1994; Gay, 1987; Gibbs, 1987; Herring, 1995; Poston, 1990). This gradual shift to a more positive view of multiracial Americans has coincided with greater awareness by many of the racism embedded in mainstream U.S. culture. This person-in-culture perspective (Ivey, 1995) helps to elucidate factors that affect multiracial persons' construction of identity by shifting the locus of pathology from within multiracial people to cultural constructs about race that place people in mutually exclusive racial boxes. This determination to "box in" everyone racially is, in my experience, not limited to the "privileged" racial group (i.e., Whites). As a biracial woman who is part White and part African American, I have felt pressure from both races to claim one race and only one, and to deny my dual racial heritage.

CURRENT ISSUES

Resisting Myths and Stereotypes

Multiracial people live in a cultural context laced with racism. In racist cultures, stereotypes and distortions abound about people racially different from the group in power. Myths about multiracial people are consequences of prejudice against interracial marriage, which itself is a consequence of racism. With the possible exception of states like Hawaii, where acceptance of interracial marriage has a long history, prejudices surrounding marrying a person of another race are deeply ingrained in our culture (Solsberry, 1994). The case example of Mario is a striking illustration of these prejudices and their negative impact on family relationships.

Not all stereotypes about multiracial people appear negative. I remember at different times in my life being described as looking "exotic," which I did not mind. In college, friends told me I had "the best of both worlds" as a biracial woman. Other multiracial people I have known have shared similar accounts of being seen as special because of their multiracial status. Whether the stereotypes are positive or negative, I would urge multiracial people to examine the impact of these images and assumptions on their sense of self.

Reconciling Mixed Racial Identity

Models of racial identity development for people of color have proposed several stages individuals go through as they attempt to develop a positive sense of self that resists racist constructions (Cross, 1995; Helms & Cook, 1999; Jackson, 2001; Parham, 1989). These models typically describe a process whereby individuals move from naivete about racial issues to an internalization of societal racism, or racial self-hatred, as they are exposed repeatedly to negative images and messages about their racial group. According to these models, internalized racism eventually gives way to exploration of and eventually pride in one's racial heritage (Cross, 1995; Helms & Cook, 1999; Parham, 1989).

Models of White racial identity development similarly present a multistage process of examining and rejecting racial stereotypes, including beliefs about the superiority of White people. The journey for Whites, however, also involves recognition of their privileged racial status and exploration of the personal impact of racial privilege and its consequences for relations with devalued individuals (Hardiman, 2001; Helms & Cook, 1999).

Racial identity models have contributed a great deal to our understanding of the psychological processes involved in developing a healthy sense of self in a racially stratified cultural climate. When I first saw the research on racial identity development in graduate school, facets of my struggle for self-definition finally began to make sense to me. I read these models (Cross, 1991; Helms & Cook, 1999; Parham, 1989) excitedly because they reflected my own journey, first from nonconsciousness about racial divisions then, later, shame about my racial heritage, and eventually my immersion in and embracing of my Black identity.

Although monoracial models work to an extent for all people of color who grapple with racism, they do not address the multiracial experience. Since these identity models assume mutually exclusive racial identification (e.g., one is either Black or White; one is not permitted to be both Black and White), they fail to examine the process of coming to terms with a dual racial identity. Thus, the research could not help me reconcile being part White with my emerging Black identity. The task of integrating my experience as a person who is racially and culturally both African American and European American was something I had to figure out for myself.

Another problematic aspect of applying monoracial identity models to multiracial people is that social withdrawal from White people, posited as a potentially healthy aspect of identity development, may actually impede attainment of a positive sense of oneself as a biracial person with White heritage. The healthy integration of dual White and minority status is likely to follow a different course than that proposed by monoracial models.

Parham (1989) identified three possibilities for movement through stages of racial identity: stagnation, linear progression, and recycling. For multiracial people, I believe that another possibility exists: simultaneity. That is to say, I experience my biracial consciousness as placing me in several "stages" at the same time. For example, within every context in every interaction, I am in the same moment both White-identified and Black-identified. I usually do not experience this dual consciousness as split, but as fluid, seamless parts of who I am. It is only when I feel forced to conform to people's expectations based on social constructions of race that my racial identity feels constricted (Williams, 1999).

There are few racial identity development models that capture this simultaneous reality (see Kerwin & Ponterotto, 1995; Poston, 1990; and Wijeyesinghe, 2001). Indeed, as I write about my experience, I struggle to find words that do not compartmentalize, words that do not divide. Yet, our cultural beliefs about race are mired in dualistic constructs: good and bad, right and wrong, us and them, black and white. Finding words that convey both/and rather than either/or is challenging. Describing an experience that does not fit dualistic constructions is even more difficult. By placing people into either/or categories, we force people's experiences into simplistic paradigms that fail to capture their multiracial complexity (Williams, 1999).

Several researchers have proposed alternative models that delineate as a key psychological task of biracial identity development integrating dual racial heritage into a coherent sense of self (Herring, 1995; Jacobs, 1992; Kich, 1992; Poston, 1990). These models describe a linear movement from nonawareness about race and social status, to identification with one part of one's racial heritage, to pride in mixed racial identity. According to these models, integration of a dual racial heritage is the hallmark of healthy identity development.

Other alternatives to monoracial identity models propose a circular process of multiracial identity development in which individuals internalize social, cultural, familial, and political factors in different ways at different times in their lives (Kich, 1992; Root, 1990; Wijeyesinghe, 2001). In this cyclical process, racial identification may shift throughout the course of one's life. Central to these models is the idea that "the biracial person has the right to declare how they wish to identify themselves racially—even if this is discrepant with how they look or how society tends to perceive them" (Root, 1990, pp. 201–202). Thus, it is the multiracial person who chooses her or his identity—and the choice may be innovative. Golf professional Tiger Woods's self-labeling as "Cablanasian" comes to mind as a creative alternative to forced choice that allows him to fully embrace his multiracial heritage.

Juggling Racial Allegiance and Betrayal

Social definitions of race assign membership to categories based on what some theorists call "blood quantum" (Root, 1992; Spencer, 1997; Spickard, 1992: Wilson, 1992). Thus, "one drop" of Black blood (i.e., having a Black relative, no matter how distant) has historically barred one from membership in the White category and relegated one to the socially undesirable Black category (Russell, Wilson, & Hall, 1992; Spickard, 1989, 1992). Similar efforts to advance the idea of "racial purity" are evident among some Native Americans (Wilson, 1992) and some Asian Americans, for whom a biracial person "half Asian and half anything else, particularly [B]lack, is identified by the blood of the non-Asian parent" (Root, 1990, p. 188). Similarly, the racial assignation of biracial individuals whose heritage consists of two non-White groups often is that of the group with less social status (Root, 1990).

Claiming multiracial identity in a society invested in maintaining exclusive racial boundaries often is not tolerated well by others. Accounts by multiracial individuals are saturated with reports of criticism from others vested in claiming the multiracial person as a member of their group (Courtney, 1995; Funderburg, 1994; Nakashima, 1992). Multiracial people who are part White often are viewed as attempting to disassociate themselves from their minority heritage by claiming their biracial status instead of their minority-group status (Funderburg, 1994; Russell et al., 1992). Rarely is biracial identification understood as an affirmation of the whole of one's identity and supported as such by other people.

Appearance is a key factor in these dynamics. Funderburg (1994) tells of a biracial woman who looked White but identified as Black, and constantly encountered arguments from others, particularly Whites, who challenged her choice of identity. Conversely, multiracial people who choose to "pass" as White may be viewed by their peers of color as racially disloyal (Bradshaw, 1992; Daniel, 1992). These conflicts are not limited to those who are part Black. Many multiracial people who are part Asian also experience considerable conflict with other racial groups due to their mixed heritage and appearance (Bemak & Chung, 1997; Kich, 1992; Valverde, 1992). In this often hostile social climate, it is not surprising that many multiracial individuals choose to identify with the racial group with which their appearance most closely fits (Root, 1990). This may be particularly true during adolescence, when the need for belonging and acceptance among peers is high (Gibbs, 1987). The multiracial person often faces a choice between racial allegiance and self-allegiance, between racial betrayal and self-betrayal.

Breaking New Racial Ground

Multiracial people, since they lie outside the boundaries of racial-group categories, must find ways to construct their own positive meanings about racial identity. This is a daunting task, for, unlike members of other racial populations, multiracial people have no historical heritage that can serve as a source of emotional grounding and strength (Rosenblatt, Karis, & Powell, 1995; Zack, 1993). Neither can they look to their parents and extended family for role models, as they are usually the only members of their family who fall between racial boundaries. As Funderburg (1994) states, "They are a one-time-only generation, and so necessarily have to break new ground in their own relationships. And just as they cannot replicate their parents, they cannot look to public images—media, literature, films—for models, since there they remain virtually invisible" (p. 197).

The multiracial person then faces the challenge of sifting through societal myths, negative images, and rigid racial definitions to construct a coherent sense of self. This task consists in part of sifting through early family messages about race and identity (Jacobs, 1992). Families' attitudes about racially different family members may take many forms, including acceptance, rejection, silence, denial, avoidance, and special treatment of multiracial family members (Funderburg, 1994; Rosenblatt et al., 1995).

Likewise, multiracial children and adolescents internalize family dynamics around racial issues in various ways. Gibbs's (1987) clinical study of biracial youth indicated much conflict and ambivalence toward self, parents, and peers. The youth in this study struggled with self-acceptance, alternately rejecting one or the other parent's race, sometimes feeling ashamed of their own physical features, and fighting fears of peer rejection born of their racially mixed status. These appeared to be fairly common problems for multiracial adolescents whose families were themselves ambivalent, conflicted, avoidant, or silent around issues of race (Funderburg, 1994).

On the other hand, parents who directly addressed their children's multiracial identity and provided clear, positive messages about multiple racial heritage appeared to instill a strong sense of self in their children (Rosenblatt et al., 1995). These parents tended to talk with other family members about their children's racial status, worked at maintaining extended family connections with other multiracial children, and helped their children learn how to respond to inquiries about their racial status (Rosenblatt et al., 1995). Families that dealt directly and affirmatively with being multiracial appeared to lay a strong foundation for multiracial individuals' self-affirmation.

SUGGESTIONS FOR ENHANCING COUNSELOR EFFECTIVENESS

Training and supervision in multicultural counseling, a component of most counselors' professional preparation (Das, 1995), offer few specific guidelines or resources for working with multiracial people. Training for multicultural competency has focused on three major areas: counselor self-awareness, knowledge about various racial groups, and skill in delivering effective services to culturally different clients (Arredondo et al., 1996; Sue, Arredondo, & McDavis, 1992). These areas serve as a useful framework for identifying strategies for enhancing counselor effectiveness in working with multiracial individuals.

Awareness

A legacy of viewing multiracial individuals as cursed, tainted, impure, and maladjusted pervades our social consciousness; however, there are also positive images of multiracial people. Counselors must examine their own biases, negative and positive, about multiracial individuals that they may have inherited from this cultural framework. Counselors are encouraged to ask themselves questions such as: How do I feel about interracial marriage? What do I believe about the children of interracial marriages? What assumptions do I make about problems they experience? What stereotypes am I aware of about mixed-race people? Do I have any? Do I know any multiracial people? Have I ever questioned or challenged a multiracial person's choice of identity, even silently? Do I make assumptions about people's identity based on their physical appearance? How might I react if someone's stated racial identification did not "match" their appearance or my assumptions about them?

I urge counseling students to challenge themselves by engaging in awareness-building exercises around these questions. Case scenarios describing biracial clients could serve as a springboard for students' exploration of their reactions to clients who choose to identify racially in unconventional ways. To illustrate, let us take another look at the case of Gayle. Let us say that Gayle has fair skin, green eyes, and blond hair. You meet her and assume she is White. She tells you she self-identifies as African American. What is your reaction to Gayle's claim of a racial identity not reflected in her physical appearance? What are your assumptions of how African Americans look?

Gayle goes on to tell you that although she is biracial, she never volunteers this information to her Black friends. Perhaps, she reasons, if they believe both her parents are Black, however light-skinned, they will be more accepting of her. For the same reason, Gayle does not disclose that her family is White. Gayle makes a point of telling Whites she meets that she is part Black. She tells you she enjoys shocking them and finding out how accepting they are of racial differences. How do you feel about the choices Gayle is making? How would you help a young biracial client sort through her own and other people's assumptions about her? Your reactions to cases such as this can be a springboard for honest discussions of how we have internalized society's beliefs and expectations about race.

Knowledge

Counselors should inform themselves about the prevalence of interracial marriages, the hostility such marriages often draw from others within and outside the family, and the range of cultural attitudes toward the offspring of these marriages. Counselors also should understand the "one-drop rule" and how it continues to limit multiracial people's identity choices.

This knowledge affords the counselor a picture of important aspects of the social environment of multiracial individuals. In addition, counselors should be aware that in this context forced choice of a single racial identification is standard operating procedure, often reinforced by family members and peers (Rosenblatt et al., 1995).

Knowledge about models of racial identity development is also important. Counselors should familiarize themselves with both monoracial and multiracial models of identity development. Many multiracial individuals who are part White and choose to identify primarily or even exclusively with the non-White part of their background may relate well to monoracial identity development models. Counselors knowledgeable about these models can anticipate some of the issues and questions their client may raise. Similarly, counselors informed about multiracial identity models and processes can anchor their work with clients in an understanding that racial identity often is fluid rather than fixed, circular rather than linear.

Counselors can increase their knowledge about multiracial people's life experiences and identity choices by getting to know people who self-identify as biracial or multiracial. Multiracial people often are quite receptive to genuine inquiries about their racial identity and may be especially so if they know they ultimately may be helping others in their journey. Seeking consultation and supervision from multiracial persons also can be very helpful. Educational films such as *Just Black?* (Twine, Warren, & Martin, 1991) introduce viewers to some of the dilemmas and pressures multiracial people face, adding to counselors' knowledge base.

Skill

One of the key skills in multicultural counseling is the ability to bridge the silence within counseling sessions surrounding issues of race (Comas-Diaz & Greene, 1994; Helms & Cook, 1999; Sanchez-Hucles, 2000). Racial status has profound implications for quality of life and psychological well-being, yet many counselors report reluctance to raise racial issues in therapy (Helms & Cook, 1999; Sanchez-Hucles, 2000). How can a counselor be culturally competent if she or he is hesitant to discuss racial issues with clients? How forthcoming will clients be if they sense their therapists' discomfort? Counselors should take every opportunity to examine racial and cultural issues as they arise in their lives and find opportunities to discuss these issues with others. Desensitizing oneself to fears about discussing racial issues is an important step toward greater effectiveness with multiracial clients.

Skill in working with multiracial clients begins with the counselor's credibility with regard to issues of race and identity development. Sue (1991) identifies two kinds of therapist credibility: ascribed and achieved. The rare multiracial counselor will likely enjoy a measure of ascribed credibility with a multiracial client if she or he identifies as multiracial and is able to connect with the client on the basis of shared racial status. Achieved credibility, on the other hand, "refers more directly to the skills and actions of the therapist in treatment" (p. 71). These skills, bolstered by self-awareness and knowledge, are augmented by experience dealing with racial issues.

Counselors should seek opportunities for focused skill building in working with multiracial people. Role playing is an excellent medium for acquiring greater ease in exploring multiracial issues and can easily be integrated in counselor education classrooms and supervision sessions. Postmodern counseling approaches such as narrative therapy may be particularly applicable to the examination of racial identity and internalized racism (Semmler & Williams, 2000). Creative therapeutic techniques such as music therapy and art therapy also have been effective with persons struggling with racial identity issues (Alexander & Sussman, 1995).

CONCLUDING REMARKS

Multiracial individuals comprise a large and growing population that faces unique challenges regarding racial identity. Social constructions of race that limit identity to a single racial category fail to consider individuals whose identities cross over racial boundaries. Outworn conceptions of race, along with negative myths and stereotypes about people with mixed-race heritage, hinder our understanding of multiracial people's development. The case examples of Mario and Gayle illustrate some of the questions, concerns, and dilemmas multiracial individuals encounter in this confusing social environment.

Counselors working with multiracial clients should be aware of the contradictions inherent in a cultural climate that has sought to assign racial membership on the basis of physical characteristics. Counselors should examine their own beliefs about race and the extent to which they have subscribed to racial myths and stereotypes about mixed-race people. It is critical that counselors understand how they feel about a multiracial person's right to choose her or his racial identity. Finally, through ongoing involvement in professional development opportunities addressing multiracial issues, counselors' skill and expertise with this emerging population will grow.

EXPERIENTIAL ACTIVITIES

Shattering Stereotypes

Race is a complicated and emotionally charged topic. Often White counseling students I work with are anxious when talking about race, especially if there are students of color in the classroom. White counselors also share a fear that they will offend their clients by talking about race, something society teaches us to pretend to ignore. One of the most important things I believe I do as a counselor educator is help people begin to break the silence and tension around issues of race and culture.

A classroom exercise designed to open up dialogue about race and multiracial people begins with a brainstorming session. Ask students to share aloud cultural stereotypes about multiracial people as you write them on the board. Students should share "societal or cultural stereotypes" rather than their own, thereby allowing them to feel freer to participate in the brainstorming. Next, students label each stereotype as positive, negative, or both. Ask students to look at the list for a few moments, commenting on any patterns or inconsistencies they notice. Discuss how these stereotypes, whether held by the client or counselor, might affect the counseling relationship.

Visualizing the Multiracial Experience

Ask students to imagine themselves in the shoes of a multiracial person and to share their thoughts about what this life might be like. A good question to start the discussion is: How many of you would, if you could, choose to live as a mixed-race person? Give students a few minutes to take note of their reactions. Ask students what thoughts, images, and feelings came to mind as they imagined this scenario.

Follow up with an imagery exercise. Begin by asking students to close their eyes and imagine themselves as multiracial: Look at yourself in the mirror. What color is your skin? Your eyes? Your hair? As you look closely at yourself, how do you feel about how you look? Imagine you're with your family. What does your mother look like? Your father? Do you have brothers and sisters? What do they look like? Now imagine that as you go out into the world each day, you notice people staring at you. Some people even approach you and ask, "What are you?" In everyday conversations with peers, people always ask about your racial background. How does it feel to be constantly asked this question? What do you tell people? Sometimes people challenge you by saying, "But you don't look like you're _____. You look more like you're _____. Or maybe even like you're _____." Once in a while, people even become angry with you, demanding to know your reasons for your racial identification. How do you feel about their anger? Now imagine you're filling out an application and come to the optional question about race. You are given six choices and asked to mark only one: Caucasian, African American, Hispanic American, Asian American, American Indian, or Other. Which one do you mark?

Give students a few moments to tune in silently to their feelings, then ask them to tell the class (1) the heritage they chose for themselves, (2) their physical features in the visualization, and (3) how they marked the application form. Ask students to share their thoughts, feelings, and reactions during the visualization. Helpful questions include: At any point during the visualization, were you surprised you reacted as you did? What was most difficult about visualizing yourself as multiracial? What was easiest? How might the visualization help you to understand the experiences of multiracial people?

Creating Alternative Identities

Earlier in the chapter, I offered the idea that multiracial individuals are free to claim whatever racial identity they believe suits them best, whether or not their physical appearance matches their choice. In this exercise, the instructor presents students with a dozen or so pictures of multiracial individuals cut from magazines, or pictures of people whose features could be considered racially ambiguous. The exercise is most effective when the photos represent a range of skin colors, hair textures, and facial features.

Ask the students to write down racial group or groups they believe to be in the person's background, and their best guess about how the person identifies racially. An interesting aspect of this exercise is the range of responses students in the class may have to the same photo. When this is the case, ask students to discuss what triggers our assumptions about a person's racial identity. Their discussion becomes the springboard for examining a variety of issues particular to multiracial people's experiences.

Questions for Reflection

Questions such as the following can be catalysts for deeper understanding of multiracial people's realities: What do you think it is like to go through life having others project onto you their assumptions about your racial background? How would it feel to you to know that your choice of racial identification is confusing to others? What strategies would you use to reconcile others' definitions of you with your own self-definition? How could these strategies be helpful when working with multiracial clients?

REFERENCES

Alexander, C.M., & Sussman, L. (1995). Creative approaches to multicultural counseling. In J.G. Ponterotto, J.M. Casas, L.A. Suzuki, & C.M. Alexander (Eds.), *Handbook of multicultural counseling* (pp. 375–384). Thousand Oaks, CA: Sage.

Arredondo, P., Toporek, R., Brown, S., Jones, J., Locke, D.C., Sanchez, J., & Stadler, H. (1996). *Operationalization of the multicultural counseling competencies.* Alexandria, VA: American Counseling Association.

Bemak, F., & Chung, R.C. (1997). Vietnamese Amerasians: Psychological adjustment and psychotherapy. *Journal of Multicultural Counseling and Development, 25,* 79–88.

Benson, S. (1981). *Ambiguous ethnicity.* London: Cambridge University Press.

Bradshaw, C. (1992). Beauty and the beast: On racial ambiguity. In M.P.P. Root (Ed.), *Racially mixed people in America* (pp. 77–88). Newbury Park, CA: Sage.

Comas-Diaz, L., & Greene, B. (Eds.). (1994). *Women of color: Integrating ethnic and gender identities in psychotherapy.* New York: Guilford.

Courtney, B.A. (1995, February 13). Freedom from choice. *Newsweek,* p. 16.

Cross, W. E. (1991). *Shades of Black.* Philadelphia: Temple University Press.

Cross, W.E. (1995). The psychology of Nigrescence: Revising the Cross model. In J.G. Ponterotto, J.M. Casas, L.A. Suzuki, & C.M. Alexander (Eds.), *Handbook of multicultural counseling* (pp. 93–122). Thousand Oaks, CA: Sage.

Daniel, G.R. (1992). Beyond black and white: The new multiracial consciousness. In M.P.P. Root (Ed.), *Racially mixed people in America* (pp. 333–341). Newbury Park, CA: Sage.

Das, A.K. (1995). Rethinking multicultural counseling: Implications for counselor education. *Journal of Counseling and Development, 74,* 45–52.

Fernandez, C.A. (1992). La Raza and the melting pot: A comparative look at multiethnicity. In M.P.P. Root (Ed.), *Racially mixed people in America* (pp. 126–143). Newbury Park, CA: Sage.

Funderburg, L. (1994). *Black, white, other: Biracial Americans talk about race and identity.* New York: William Morrow.

Gay, K. (1987). *The rainbow effect: Interracial families.* New York: Franking Watts.

Gibbs, J.T. (1987). Identity and marginality: Issues in the treatment of biracial adolescents. *American Journal of Orthopsychiatry, 57,* 265–278.

Hardiman, R. (2001). Reflections on white identity development theory. In C.L. Wijeyesinghe & B.W. Jackson (Eds.), *New perspectives on racial identity development: A theoretical and practical anthology* (pp. 108–128). New York: New York University Press.

Helms, J.E., & Cook, D.A. (1999). *Using race and culture in counseling and psychotherapy: Theory and process.* Needham Heights, MA: Allyn and Bacon.

Herring, R.D. (1995). Developing biracial ethnic identity: A review of the increasing dilemma. *Journal of Multicultural Counseling and Development, 23,* 29–38.

Ivey, A.E. (1995). Psychology as liberation: Toward specific skills and strategies in multicultural counseling and therapy. In J.G. Ponterotto, J.M. Casas, L.A. Suzuki, & C.M. Alexander (Eds.), *Handbook of multicultural counseling* (pp. 53–72). Thousand Oaks, CA: Sage.

Jackson, B.W. (2001). Black identity development: Further analysis and elaboration. In C.L. Wijeyesinghe & B.W. Jackson (Eds.), *New perspectives on racial identity development: A theoretical and practical anthology* (pp. 8–31). New York: New York University Press.

Jacobs, J.H. (1992). Identity development in biracial children. In M.P.P. Root (Ed.), *Racially mixed people in America* (pp. 190–206). Newbury Park, CA: Sage.

Kich, G.K. (1992). The developmental process of asserting a biracial, bicultural identity. In M.P.P. Root (Ed.), *Racially mixed people in America* (pp. 304–317). Newbury Park, CA: Sage.

Kerwin, C., & Ponterotto, J.G. (1995). Biracial identity development: Theory and research. In J.G. Ponterotto, J.M. Casas, L.A. Suzuki, & C.M. Alexander (Eds.), *Handbook of multicultural counseling* (pp. 199–217). Thousand Oaks, CA: Sage.

Morrissey, M. (1996, November). Rising number of interracial children presenting new challenges for counselors. *Counseling Today,* pp. 1, 8, 24.

Nakashima, C.L. (1992). An invisible monster: The creation and denial of mixed race people in America. In M.P.P. Root (Ed.), *Racially mixed people in America* (pp. 162–178). Newbury Park, CA: Sage.

Parham, T.A. (1989). Cycles of psychological Nigrescence. *The Counseling Psychologist, 17,* 187–226.

Poston, W.S.C. (1990). The biracial identity development model: A needed addition. *Journal of Counseling and Development, 69,* 152–155.

Root, M.P.P. (1992). Within, between, and beyond. In M.P.P. Root (Ed.), *Racially mixed people in America* (pp. 3–11). Newbury Park, CA: Sage.

Root, M.P.P. (1990). Resolving "other" status: Identity development of biracial individuals. In L.S. Brown & M.P.P. Root (Eds.), *Diversity and complexity in feminist therapy* (pp. 185–205). New York: Harrington Park Press.

Rosenblatt, P.C., Karis, T.A., & Powell, R.D. (1995). *Multiracial couples: Black and White voices.* Thousand Oaks, CA: Sage.

Russell, K., Wilson, M., & Hall, R. (1992). *The color complex: The politics of skin color among African Americans.* New York: Harcourt Brace Jovanovich.

Sanchez-Hucles, J. (2000). *The first session with African Americans: A step-by-step guide.* San Francisco, CA: Jossey-Bass.

Sebring, D. (1985). Considerations in counseling interracial children. *Journal of Nonwhite Concerns in Personnel and Guidance, 13,* 3–9.

Semmler, P.L., & Williams, C.B. (2000). Narrative therapy: A storied context for multicultural counseling. *Journal of Multicultural Counseling and Development, 28,* 51–62.

Solsberry, P.W. (1994). Interracial couples in the United States of America: Implications for mental health counseling. *Journal of Mental Health Counseling, 16,* 304–317.

Spencer, R. (1997). Race and mixed-race: A personal tour. In W.S. Penn (Ed.), *As we are now: Mixblood essays on race and identity* (pp. 126–139). Berkeley: University of California Press.

Spickard, P.R. (1989). *Mixed blood: Intermarriage and ethnic identity in twentieth-century America.* Madison: University of Wisconsin Press.

Spickard, P.R. (1992). The illogic of American racial categories. In M.P.P. Root (Ed.), *Racially mixed people in America* (pp. 12–23). Newbury Park, CA: Sage.

Stonequist, E.V. (1937). *The marginal man: A study in personality and culture conflict.* New York: Russell and Russell.

Sue, S. (1991). Ethnicity and culture in psychological research and practice. In J.D. Goodchilds (Ed.), *Psychological perspectives on human diversity in America* (pp. 51–85). Washington, DC: American Psychological Association.

Sue, D.W., Arredondo, P., & McDavis, R.J. (1992). Multicultural counseling competencies and standards: A call to the profession. *Journal of Multicultural Counseling and Development, 20,* 64–88.

Twine, F.W., Warren, J.F., & Martin, F.F. (1991). *Just Black?* [Film]. New York: New York Filmmakers Library.

U.S. Bureau of the Census. (2001). *Overview of race and Hispanic origin: Census 2000 brief.* Washington, DC: Government Printing Office.

Valverde, K.C. (1992). From dust to gold: The Vietnamese Amerasian experience. In M.P.P. Root (Ed.), *Racially mixed people in America* (pp. 144–161). Newbury Park, CA: Sage.

Wijeyesinghe, C.L. (2001). Racial identity in multiracial people: An alternative paradigm. In C.L. Wijeyesinghe & B.W. Jackson (Eds.), *New perspectives on racial identity devel-*

opment: A theoretical and practical anthology (pp. 129–152). New York: New York University Press.

Williams, C.B. (1999). Claiming a biracial identity: Resisting social constructions of race and culture. *Journal of Counseling and Development, 77,* 32–35.

Wilson, T. (1992). Blood quantum: Native American mixed bloods. In M.P.P. Root (Ed.), *Racially mixed people in America* (pp. 108–125). Newbury Park, CA: Sage.

Zack, N. (1993). *Race and mixed race.* Philadelphia: Temple University Press.

CHAPTER 9

Counseling Women from Feminist Perspectives

Victoria A. Foster
Kathleen M. May

Victoria A. Foster is an associate professor in counselor education, coordinator of the doctoral program in counselor education, and the director of the New Horizons Family Counseling Center at the College of William and Mary. She has clinical experience in family, couples, and sex counseling, crisis counseling, and in treating emotionally disturbed youth in residential settings. She is a licensed professional counselor, a licensed marriage and family therapist, and a National Board of Certified Counselors–approved supervisor. Her areas of interest include gender/diversity issues in family counseling, family-school collaboration, counseling supervision, and cognitive developmental theory.

Kathleen May is an associate professor in the counselor education program at the University of Virginia. She teaches courses in couples and family counseling as well as mental health counseling. She is a licensed mental health counselor in Florida, a National Certified Counselor, and a National Board of Certified Counselors–approved supervisor. At present, she enjoys considering the place of feminist theory in counseling, training, and supervision.

AWARENESS INDEX

Please test your knowledge by marking the following statements true or false before proceeding to the text in this chapter. Compute your score from the scoring guide at the end of the Awareness Index.

1. T F Dissatisfaction with the applicability of traditional counseling approaches to women's lives motivated a call for change in how women are counseled.

2. T F Characteristics attributed to gender are not "true" attributes of females and males but are socially constructed categories that serve to maintain the status quo.

3. T F Feminist therapists should support competence in women in both traditional and nontraditional roles.

4. T F Most couples today share equally in household and parenting responsibilities when both members have careers outside the home.

5. T F Racism contributes to the experience of power imbalance in couples of color, resulting in complicated gender roles.

6. T F A stance of neutrality is recommended when counseling women.

7. T F Managing both career and family responsibilities creates gender-specific physical and psychological difficulties for women.

8. T F A feminist model for counseling women is derived primarily from Rogerian counseling theory and technique.

9. T F Feminist models advocate demystifying the process of counseling.

10. T F A new Feminist Code of Ethics should replace traditional guidelines for those who wish to utilize a truly feminist orientation in counseling.

Scoring guide: **1.** T; **2.** T; **3.** T; **4.** F; **5.** T; **6.** F; **7.** T; **8.** F; **9.** T; **10.** F.

INTRODUCTION

A chapter on counseling women written by two White women in their forties, living heterosexual lifestyles, well educated and financially stable, can be both presumptuous and dangerous. We do not want to become the "new experts" (replacing White males), speaking for all women. We do believe, however, that feminist therapies operate from principles with relevance for transforming women's definitions of themselves and challenging the dominant discourses within counseling and society. These principles include a strong emphasis on advocacy, client-therapist collaboration, therapist self-disclosure, and an analysis of social context.

Feminism

When we speak of feminism, we speak of a philosophy that recognizes that men and women have different experiences of self, of others, and of life, and that men's experience has been widely articulated whereas women's has been ignored or misrepresented. When we speak of feminism, we speak of a philosophy that recognizes that this society does not permit equality to women; on the contrary, it is structured so as to oppress women and uplift men. This structure is called patriarchy. When we speak of feminism, we speak of a philosophy that recognizes that every aspect of public and private life carries the mark of patriarchal thinking and practice and therefore is a necessary focus for re-vision (Goodrich et al., 1988, pp. 1–2).

The above definition of feminism clarifies the need for feminist perspectives in counseling women. Feminist perspectives on counseling emerged from the women's movement of the 1960s, a time when women began challenging the restrictive and devalued nature of traditional sex roles for women. This movement called for equal rights and an end to the discrimination against women that was commonplace in American society. Feminist approaches to counseling developed in response to the growing awareness that the oppression of women was as present and damaging in counseling as it was in the society at large (Laidlaw & Malmo, 1990).

While we both were exposed to feminism in undergraduate school, we each had different experiences as we continued our education. Graduate studies in counseling then provided limited opportunities for a focused study of feminist theory and applications to counseling. Our personal paths to the stance presented in this chapter developed primarily from our relationships with others who also searched for alternatives to patriarchy, and from readings by those groundbreaking feminists who challenged the dominant culture. Personal and professional friendships, conversations at conferences and in classrooms, over dinners and on the phone, provided the stimulus for developing new frameworks to expand our thinking about women's issues and for respectful counseling approaches. We learned from ourselves, our students, and most especially our clients, who taught us to listen without imposing biases that we didn't even know we had.

Feminist philosophies that guide the practice of feminist counseling are diverse and are best understood as ranging along a continuum of perspectives rather than as separate stances. However, they all challenge traditional theories and practices to be more inclusive of diversity and to focus on societal transformation. Feminist approaches are not exclusively for counseling women, nor are only women able to be feminist counselors. Feminist approaches to counseling can be effective in working with men and boys, who are also oppressed by the patriarchal system. Further, men who embrace feminist principles and adhere to feminist practices can be effective feminist counselors.

SITUATIONAL EXAMPLES

Evelyn

Evelyn is a thirty-eight-year-old African American single mother. She holds a Ph.D. and is an industrial engineer employed in a governmental organization. Evelyn describes herself as quiet and reserved. She has always had high expectations for herself and is committed to success in her endeavors. She is proud of her achievements. Evelyn feels that she has little flexibility in her work schedule. She believes she must work long hours to demonstrate that she is as dedicated to her profession as are her colleagues, who are mostly men. She would like to date, but so far she has not met anyone who seemed interested in her. Evelyn worries that if she did meet someone, her daughter would resent it. Evelyn isn't eating or sleeping well. She has no family or close friends nearby. She reports feeling depressed and unhappy with her personal life, although she finds her career rewarding.

Evelyn is most troubled by her relationship with her daughter, Alyssa, who is seven years old. Although Alyssa has qualified as a gifted student, she is performing poorly both academically and behaviorally. Evelyn has a hard time coping with Alyssa's indifference to schoolwork and "silly," distracting behaviors. Evelyn has "always felt that playing with children doesn't come easily," but problems with her daughter have escalated to the point that she now wonders whether she has the "aptitude to be a good mother." While Evelyn knows that Alyssa would like to have more time with her, she feels overwhelmed by her daughter's behavior and is very critical of her. Her physician suggested counseling.

Cate

Cate is a twenty-eight-year-old Irish American woman who is beginning her last year in the military. Cate asserts that she is comfortable with her sexual orientation, although she has never openly acknowledged that she is lesbian for fear of family and job repercussions. She and her eight-year-old daughter, Deborah, currently live with twenty-year-old Sue, who is biracial. Sue's father is Puerto Rican and her mother identifies as White. Sue, who is unemployed, is enrolled in some computer courses at the community college. Cate and Sue share parenting and household responsibilities. Career concerns brought Cate to counseling initially. She said, "I have no idea what I want to do for a living. I don't know what I might be good at or able to do, but I do not want to stay in the navy." In the military she worked primarily in food services, which she did not find enjoyable or satisfying.

In her second session, Cate shared her uncertainties about what it means to be both a mother and a lesbian. She has never known another lesbian who was also a parent, and she has not sought out gay and lesbian groups or resources for fear of losing her military position and its attendant benefits. Indeed, Cate knows only a few gay women and men. Cate loves Sue, but she is not sure if their relationship has much future because of the age difference. Cate also reports that Sue would like to be more open about their lives.

GENDER IN CONTEXT

We live in a highly gendered society with powerful norms that shape our lives as men and women. A gendered society is one in which males and females learn and internalize society's expectations concerning what it means to be male or female and what is and is not appropriate behavior for one's sex. This socialization begins at birth. "From that first moment of life, people feel compelled to 'genderize' babies—the pink and blue blankets" (Rampage, 2001, p. 173). Gender "influences core information regarding what we and others come to believe about ourselves" (Robinson & Howard-Hamilton, 2000, p. 100). Based on one's biological sex, gender roles both define and constrain the behaviors deemed socially suitable. According to Cook (1992), we perceive and treat men and women differently on a systemic basis, such that in many respects, the "two sexes essentially live in different worlds" (p. 5).

A premise of male superiority constructs the social world; that is, gender and the power asymmetries predicated upon gender are the foundations upon which human relationships are organized (Fine, 1992). A feminist construction of gender redefines the nature of men's and women's lives and relationships in terms of the expression and maintenance of power. In our culture, men are socialized to develop an instrumental identity, which consists of a sense of personal agency expressed in behavior that is rational, analytical, competitive, and self-directed (Bakan, 1966). For example, men may believe that the expression of pain or grief is "unmanly." They may fear that expression of such feelings is an admission of vulnerability or a loss of control. By contrast, women are socialized to develop an expressive identity. Communal traits such as mutuality, nurturance, and cooperation characterize an expressive identity (Bakan, 1966). Women may deny their own needs and desires in order to meet the needs and wishes of others. They may feel responsible for relationships and work to maintain even those that are harmful. Gender-role socialization results in oppression. Individuals who are oppressed lack the power and privilege of the dominant group. Oppression is the unwarranted reduction in options, or freedom to choose among options, available to members of a group defined by one or more morally irrelevant characteristics (Baylis & Downie, 1997). Examples of irrelevant characteristics are gender, race/ethnicity, class, and sexual orientation. Both men and women are harmed by gender-role socialization, but the harm to women is greater because society devalues the stereotypical characteristics and traditional roles assigned to them.

Although progress has been made in reducing oppression based on gender, it has not been eliminated. For example, Lieutenant Colonel Martha McSally was a top performer in her class at the Air Force Academy and the first woman to fly combat. Nonetheless, she found herself in the position of challenging military regulations that she believed to be oppressive and discriminatory toward women. In 1999, McSally was assigned to Saudi Arabia. It was then that she encountered the "abaya rule" concerning travel requirements for women serving in the U.S. military in the region. When traveling off base, female staff are required to be accompanied by a man; to sit in the back of a vehicle; and to wear the abaya, the traditional Islamic head-to-toe robe. Although the wording in the abaya rule recently changed from "requiring" to "urging" women to wear the abaya, many enlisted women will interpret this as a direct order. At the time of this writing, McSally is the plaintiff in a lawsuit that names Defense Secretary Donald Rumsfeld as the defendant and challenges these military orders as unlawful because they discriminate against women (Mulligan, 2002).

A recent congressional study, prepared by the General Accounting Office (as cited in Henry, 2002), dispels the general sense that women have edged closer to equality with men in many areas, including career advancement and compensation. The study found that the male-female salary gap actually worsened during the economic boom years of 1995 to 2000. For example, in 1995 one full-time female communications manager earned 86 cents for every dollar a male made in her industry, but in 2000 she earned only 73 cents on the male's dollar. In addition, data from this same study may indicate that women often find it more difficult than men to balance family and career. A comparison of married women and men in management positions found that only about 40% of female managers have children at home, while more than 60% of the men have children. Given the fewer numbers of married women with children in the upper-level workplace, expectations for job performance and commitment combined with parenting may seem insurmountable for many women.

Gender is not the only characteristic that results in oppression. Although all women in our society are oppressed, "gender oppression must be viewed in the context of other oppressions in which it is embedded: racism, colonization, classism, heterosexism, and homophobia" (Almeida et al., 1998, pp. 416–417). Greater attention to the experiences of women in the context of their race, class, and sexual orientation can underscore the limitations of applying a solely gender analysis to women's issues. Women who are not White and heterosexual experience multiple oppressions. For example, an African American lesbian may experience triple oppression—sexism, racism, and heterosexism. She also may experience internalized homophobia. Because of racism, sexism, and heterosexism in the dominant culture and sexism and heterosexism in African American cultures, African American women may find heterosexuality the only privileged status they hold and thus be reluctant to relinquish it (Greene & Boyd-Franklin, 1996).

Women of color are financially undercompensated for their work and generally have minimal access to benefits (Almeida & Hernandez, 2001). African American women are overrepresented in low-paying service jobs and underrepresented in professional positions (Goldenberg & Goldenberg, 2002). According to Lamison-White (1997), nearly 34% of families headed by females live in poverty. Of these, 27% are headed by White women, 40.7% by African American women, and 51% by Hispanic women. No improvements are reported in the numbers of women and children living in poverty over the last decade (Goldenberg & Goldenberg, 2002; Ziemba, 2001). Women have higher rates of poverty than men, and single mothers, widows, and divorced women are most affected (Hendley & Bilimoria, 1999; Ziemba, 2001).

Identifying multiple oppressions can facilitate clients' ability to see the world from the dominant point of view, as well as from their own unique perspective. The various "isms" to which women are subjected result in an elaborate layering of experiences. Gender "braids with social class, race/ethnicity, age, disability (or not) and sexual orientation as well as social context to produce socially and historically constituted subjectivities" (Fine, 1992, p. 3). Traditional beliefs regarding gender differences persist, although research findings clearly indicate that differences within genders are as great as those between them. In other words, women can be as different from each other, as a result of the interactions among age, social class, race, and other characteristics, as they are different from men (Hare-Mustin, 1991, 1998). Counselors must not operate under the false premise that differences are less important than the patriarchy and gender oppression that unite us.

While acknowledging diversity and the complexity of women's lives, it is equally important not to lose sight of women's common struggles. Women experience oppression *as women,* mediated by other structural factors in both the public and private realms of their lives (Coppock, Haydon, & Ritcher, 1995). "A major challenge or balancing act for feminist therapists . . . is to attend simultaneously to that which unifies women's experiences as well as that which makes each woman's concerns unique" (Enns, 1997, p. 64). Unless we address such influences in counseling women, our therapy will be oppressive for what it includes as well as excludes (Hare-Mustin, 1998).

FEMINIST CRITIQUES OF THE TRADITIONAL COUNSELING PARADIGM

Feminists recognized the inherent male bias within the traditional theories of psychological development, diagnosis and assessment of psychopathology, and models of counseling. A number of serious criticisms emerged from the feminist critique:

- the omission of women from the knowledge base of psychology;
- the depiction of male-typed traits as the norm and female-typed traits as deficient;
- the dominant assumption that intrapsychic factors are the source of women's psychological disturbances;
- the maintenance of female-male dichotomies (such as women as passive and men as aggressive) and male-dominated power structures through sexist models of counseling and therapy; and
- the practice of attributing blame and responsibility to women who are victims of sexual and physical violence (Hare-Mustin & Marecek, 1990; Kitzinger, 1991; Marecek, 2001).

Over the years, feminist perspectives have "recast theories of clinical disorders, focusing particularly on problems of high prevalence among women" (Marecek, 2001, p. 306). A social and contextual construction of gender relocates women's problems from the individual and internal to the social and external. This relocation shows how women's problems or symptoms can be understood as methods of coping and surviving rather than as signs of dysfunction or mental illness. For example, a woman with low sexual desire may be resisting sexual relations with a partner who is insensitive to her need for mutuality and intimacy. Her symptom could represent a refusal to subjugate her own sexuality to that of her partner. Feminist counselors "view clients as individuals coping with life events to the best of their ability" (Enns, 1997, p. 10). "Not all symptoms are neurotic. Pain in response to a bad situation is adaptive, not pathological" (Klein, 1976, p. 90).

A personal example from the experience of one of the authors highlights the need for such contextual considerations:

> Some years ago, I entered counseling because I was struggling to manage the stress of a full-time job, graduate school, and the breakup of a long-term relationship that shortly was followed by my parents' very surprising late-in-life divorce. My symptoms included difficulty sleeping and anxiety about performance in school. While I had initiated the breakup, I was nonetheless struggling with the changes in my daily life as a newly single woman. And I was very sad about the dissolution of my parents' marriage. My counselor was an older woman who was highly recommended. I readily shared my concerns with her, and wanted some assistance in managing my anxiety initially, and then to explore some of the losses in my life. My counselor, however, kept asking me about my relationship with my father. She was very persistent in her psychodynamic approach, and seemed quite skilled. But she failed to take into account my immediate needs, my strengths and resources, and the possibility that my relationship with my father was not pathological or even neurotic. I believed, in fact, that both my parents were sources of support for me, and were fine parents, despite their struggles in their own marriage. I was not unwilling to explore family influences, but that wasn't helping me sleep at night. I felt pigeonholed into a stereotype.

Feminists maintain that conventional theories mask the limitations placed on subordinate groups by the dominant groups. Further, much of the language of traditional counseling theories, including couples and family counseling theories, reflects concepts that devalue women. Diagnostic terms focus on the individual and conceal the sociocultural conditions and values that reinforce particular behaviors and maintain stereotypical standards for women and men. Research identified three reactions to women in counseling: (1) the discouragement of and disapproval of behavior that contradicted the stereotypical roles, such as that of mother; (2) the disparagement and inhibition of expressions of anger, bitterness, criticism, and other affects considered negative; and (3) the omission of confrontation, interpretation, and exploration of passive-submissive and compliant behavior in the client (Bernardez, 1987). Both male and female counselors exhibited these reactions to their female clients, although female counselors displayed greater empathy and promoted more self-disclosure than their male counterparts. Such findings indicate the potential harm of counseling practices that maintain gender stereotypes. The failure of the traditional counseling paradigm to adequately address the mental health needs of women led to the creation of feminist approaches to counseling.

EMERGING COUNSELING THEMES FOR CONTEMPORARY WOMEN

A critical analysis of gender issues in a multilayered context results in identifying emerging client populations whose needs and goals are not addressed by conventional counseling theory and practice. In recent decades, political and technological changes have transformed the gender landscape so that the link between reproduction and sexuality is no longer absolute. Changes in family structure, behavioral norms, and demographics have altered social systems (Fine, 1992; Maddock, 1990; McGoldrick, Giordiano, & Pearce, 1996; Vance, 1984); however, while women's experiences are changing, the sociological structures surrounding them have remained comparatively unchanged. For example, controversy persists regarding access to safe and affordable contraception for women at all stages of their reproductive lives. Housework and carework remain socially constructed as women's work, despite women's acquisition of outside employment (Parker, 1997). Even with the greater involvement of fathers in the family and changes in family configurations, mothers still carry most of the burden of child care, elder care, maintaining family relationships, holiday preparations, and housekeeping. According to McGoldrick (1999), the family is seen as "supporting the male worker for his performance on the job, whereas women are seen as depriving their families by working" (p. 110).

Compared to our predecessors of twenty or more years ago, women today are likely to remain single more frequently and for longer periods of time, separate and divorce more often, repartner or remarry, function as single parents and heads of household with young children at home, experience interrupted careers, and live longer. These family role changes present particular coping issues for women who seek counseling. Counselors must be prepared for responding to concerns related to sexual relationships, divorce, single living, blended families, child adjustment and custody, financial stress, establishing support systems, and acquiring new social skills, among other more predictable life-span adjustments. As women outlive men, issues related to financial security and retirement, social security benefits, housing, and living alone emerge.

Today women struggle to manage both work and family responsibilities and their associated physical and psychological distress (Bromet, Dew, & Parkinson, 1990; Facione, 1994; Frone, Russell, & Cooper, 1991; Theorell, 1991). Current data indicate that the organization of employment and the national distribution of income, wealth, and poverty follow the same patterns as two decades ago. Women and children comprise the fastest growing homeless population in America (Boettcher, 1999). A large proportion of women still serve in sex-segregated, low-paying jobs (Lewin, 1997) and still earn only 70% of what men earn. At the same time, fully one-third of American women provide more than half of their family's entire income. As women combine paid labor, homemaking, and parenting, fatigue, depression, and stress increase (Derry & Gallant, 1993; Wheatley, 1991). Not only does the working woman need to make vocational choices that will enhance her self-esteem and autonomy, she needs to develop coping strategies that will enable her to function effectively in her multiple roles (Christian & Wilson, 1985). In addition, women may face challenges such as employment discrimination, the glass ceiling, and sexual harassment.

Other special issues related to gender and counseling include women and violence, women and body, and women in high-risk groups (Worell & Remer, 1992). Public attention to the crimes of rape and incest has resulted in a greater likelihood that women will seek treatment for these violations. Attempts to conform to stereotypical images have increased the frequency and severity of eating disorders among women. Other medical and physical concerns such as infertility, contraception, abortion, menopause, AIDS, and addictions necessitate counseling intervention for women throughout the life span.

FEMINIST COUNSELING PERSPECTIVES AND PRINCIPLES

The development of feminist theory has served as a guide for further research and its application to professional practice. Feminism represents a continuum of broad social and political philosophies that "stand outside any particular system of therapy" (Marecek, 2001, p. 307). Nonetheless, feminist counseling models have a common focus on safety, connectedness, and equity.

Based on the principles of empowerment, feminist counseling approaches expand the goals for change beyond that of the individual to the social and political spheres. Empowerment first involves identifying both internal and external contributions to women's distress. Discriminating between these two sources is crucial and assists women in freeing themselves from self-blame. Feminist counselors do not believe in "neutrality," because a neutral stance is effectively a sexist stance. Ignoring differences between men and women and among women means supporting stereotypes, and, consequently, doubly disadvantages women. Feminist counselors acknowledge that values enter into all human endeavors and that therapeutic practice cannot be value free.

Moreover, feminist counselors are pluralistic in their thinking and recognize the huge differences among women. Each of our lives contains multiple realities or narratives about who we are and how we interact with others. These stories are heard in their gender, class, racial/ethnic, and sociocultural contexts. It is important to avoid assuming that all women have a common experience with oppression.

Together the counselor and client should explore the client's experience of gender, ethnicity, and the salient issues of potential oppression such as sexual orientation. African American women frequently sense conflict or discomfort when the counselor emphasizes gender. For them, race is a defining and prominent issue, and they do not want that point misconstrued (Robinson & Howard-Hamilton, 2000). Myopic thinking may result in the devaluing or denying of the experiences of women who experience oppression in unique ways (Coppock et al., 1995). A growing body of literature has identified common features of feminist counseling that help to define practice. Feminist counselors use these core components in a manner that is fair and equal to both genders. The following descriptions represent a general introduction to feminist counseling practice.

Relabeling and Reframing

Feminist counselors recognize the power of language and language's creation of images and assumptions. Feminist counselors work to reexamine these concepts in order to discern the environmental conditions that may sustain or require behavior perceived as deviant or defective. The purpose is to avoid labels that imply that the attribute belongs to the individual rather than to the situation, and to move from weakness to sources of strengths (Hare-Mustin, 1998). For example, traditional counseling approaches often apply the term *enmeshment* to women in response to their concern for and involvement with their children or other family members. The double bind for women is that they are held responsible for the emotional and social well-being of their family while at the same time are pathologized for their involvement. While such a label imposes the male standard of independence and autonomy, a feminist perspective reframes the relationship as one of deep concern or connection.

In another example, a woman's assessment that she complains and badgers her partner about his inattention could be recast as her taking too much responsibility for the relationship. This shift in terminology alters the negative connotations of her behavior and casts them in a more positive light. Such reframing helps the client consider alternative ways to manage her level of responsibility in the relationship and to explore her partner's contributions to its maintenance.

Equality and Collaboration

Feminist counseling provides models that reject manipulation, demystify the process of counseling, and emphasize the equalization of power between the counselor and client. A collaborative therapeutic relationship builds on the strengths and capabilities of the client and addresses her special needs. Each woman's subjective experiences and constructed knowledge are valued alongside the counselor's expertise. The counselor helps each client to set her own personal goals and trust her own experience. Having conversations about counseling itself facilitates this collaborative relationship. Included in these conversations are both the meaning and the limits of the therapeutic relationship. Appropriate counselor self-disclosure can foster a sense of communal experience among women and also acknowledge relevant differences among them.

Feminist counselors also provide information that facilitates the client's understanding of the change process and equips the client with tools for monitoring and evaluating her own progress. Developing a contract can establish mutual responsibility between the client and the counselor. A contract delineates the goals, processes, and measurable outcomes of therapy. The process and pace of counseling vary according to the needs of each client. These strategies help to decrease the power differential between the client and the counselor, reducing the hierarchical nature of the therapeutic relationship found in many traditional approaches.

Counselors should help clients articulate their struggles and make meaning of them in such a way as to see and act for change both within themselves and within society. Alternatives to traditional individual counseling, such as group work, may be especially helpful to women who can benefit from mutual support systems, validation, and an expanded exploration of various experiences and possibilities in life choices. Career counseling services, community resources, women's centers, churches, and other avenues of growth are valuable options for women seeking change.

Empathy and Whole-Person Development

Empathy is the capacity to be fully present to the affect and experience of another without being overwhelmed by or defensively resisting it. Affect expresses itself in myriad ways, according to each woman's culture and personal history. Empathy and openness to all aspects of emotional expression are critical elements in creating safe processes in the counseling relationship. An exploratory rather than a directive stance enables each client to express herself with authenticity. Listening with respect and receptivity promotes self-discovery and commitment. The client is the expert on her life and collaborates with the counselor to create change or cope more effectively. The counseling process encourages women to explore and honor aspects of self that have been maligned, rejected, or labeled as dysfunctional. The feminist counselor can support the client in reclaiming and redefining her sense of self in ways that promote self-esteem and agency.

Gender-Role Analysis

As an alternative to or in addition to traditional models of assessment and diagnosis, feminist counselors employ gender-role analysis. This involves a collaborative examination by counselor and client of the impact of gender on the presenting problems (Herlihy & Corey, 2001; Santos De Barona & Dutton, 1997). Gender-role analysis helps clients to identify how societal messages, expectations, and structures related to traditional gender arrangements have influenced their lives. This type of analysis facilitates clients' awareness of how gendered roles are one-dimensional, the male role restricting connectedness to others and the female role limiting the experience of self. A focus on the environmental context shifts the therapeutic emphasis away from an intrapsychic source of distress. Individual patterns of behavior and responsibility are conceptualized through an understanding of the unequal patterns of power distribution in social structures. Facilitative questions, such as the following, invite clients to deconstruct their cultural premises about gender roles:

1. What is the traditional role for women in your culture?
2. What aspects of the traditional roles have the women in your family followed and which have they not followed?
3. How do you see yourself as similar and different from the women in your family?

Gender-role analysis aims to help clients bring an end to the allocation of roles and functions on the basis of gender. Instead, interests, abilities, and personal choice determine each individual's course in life. Through gender-role analysis, counselors can promote androgyny in the sense of encouraging women to combine "male" and "female" qualities within themselves. When constructively challenged, women develop or repossess those previously rejected or ignored "masculine" aspects of themselves, and may reconstruct concepts of "feminine" qualities. Clients discover how gender stereotyping both constrains and controls them. For example, preconceived ideas about mothering as a natural role for women contradicts the struggle that Evelyn (in the situational example) experiences as a single parent with a career that is important to her. She has never felt comfortable or adequate in her mothering role. Through gender-role analysis, Evelyn might reconsider what "mothering" means to her and learn to appreciate her strengths as a professional woman and a role model for her daughter. New ways of confirming her identity and reaching out to her daughter could emerge from this analysis.

Power Analysis

A power analysis is a strategy used to explore the power differential between women and men or oppressed and dominant groups (Herlihy & Corey, 2001; Marecek, 2001; Morrow & Hawxhurst, 1998). Power analysis helps clients to identify what kinds of power they possess or have access to, and for what reasons. Such an analysis assists clients in understanding both the destructive and effective use of power.

The concept of power is socially constructed; indeed, there are some cultures that have no word for "power." According to Robinson and Howard-Hamilton (2000), "gender is the blueprint for all power relationships because power is the infrastructure of the sex-gender system" (p. 253). Definitions of power include the capacity to compel obedience and to direct others to accomplish goals. Power includes control over resources. Power is also considered a delegated role or privilege, according to one's status. Certain groups of people are identified with power and privileges at the expense of other groups. The various contexts in which we live influence and define power differently (Kitzinger, 1991). For example, power within the family is a different kind of power than in the workplace. Power may have different meanings for a Latina than for an Asian woman.

Morrow and Hawxhurst (1998) advocate exploration of power within three dimensions—personal (power within), interpersonal (power with others), and sociopolitical (power in society)—as a strategy for feminist counseling. The counselor and client analyze power within each dimension and identify potential action plans. Each dimension embodies the conditions for empowerment—permission, enablement, and information.

The first condition, permission, considers the personal dimensions of recognizing, knowing, naming, and believing that one deserves to have individual rights and freedoms, which are the prerequisite conditions for a rich quality of life. The client identifies and explores her right to have personal control of her life.

At the interpersonal dimension, permission addresses questions of ownership, obligation, entitlement, and consequences in relationships. The counselor encourages the client to consider all these aspects of power in her family of origin, her current family and partner, her children, and others that are influential in her personal life. Permission within the sociopolitical dimension is related to analyzing the laws, rules, norms, and values that support or challenge a person's rights and freedom. For example, by educating herself regarding policies, written and unwritten, regarding roles and power in her workplace or educational setting, the client is better prepared to advocate for change.

Enablement within the personal dimension involves identifying skills, abilities, and resources or the means to enhance those resources through education, training, employment, and other endeavors. At the interpersonal level, the counselor encourages activities such as mentoring, networking, and group work as means to facilitate empowerment. By meeting others who share similar goals, the client will contradict her isolation, expand her avenues of support, and supply support to others.

In the broader sociopolitical dimension, actions that implement social justice and civil rights laws and policies promote access to the resources and opportunities of human rights. Attending community meetings to support access to quality child care and participating in organizations that advocate for equal pay for equal work are examples of empowerment in the sociopolitical dimension.

Information, the third condition for empowerment, takes the form of self-awareness across an array of personal characteristics, needs, capacities, and circumstances. Within the interpersonal dimension, counselors share information in the context of relationships in order to validate women's experiences, to counteract isolation, and to acknowledge both the commonality and the diversity of women's stories. In the sociopolitical dimension, counselors encourage women to critically examine sources of information that emanate from the dominant culture, and to identify the ways of using information to maintain or restrain power relationships.

Exploring each of these areas and identifying the influence of power dimensions on a woman's personal and career decisions can reframe attendant problems as social and cultural conflicts. Counseling from an empowerment and developmental perspective supports the client within her present framework and subsequently challenges the client to open herself to a more complex evaluation of herself and her relationship to her environment. Addressing sexuality, gender, and race is necessary to create a context for understanding power and linking it to the larger culture, thus enhancing multiple perspective taking. This model can assist women in clarifying the meaning of their experiences through a focus on power arrangements in their lives and in enhancing their capacity to solve their own problems through analysis and action planning.

Feminist Ethics

All counselors ascribe to the ethical code of their profession; however, feminist counselors' critiques of these ethical codes have raised issues about their compatibility with feminist counseling principles. "Traditional ethical codes tend to do the following: (1) define ethics in reactive rather than proactive terms, (2) describe issues in either-or terms rather than representing the complexity of ethical decisions, (3) pay limited attention to prevention and growth issues, (4) devote minimum attention to diversity as they influence ethics, and (5) often frame issues in overly concrete, lengthy and cumbersome language" (Enns, 1997, p. 205).

Because of deficiencies such as these, a "Feminist Code of Ethics" (Feminist Therapy Institute, 1990) promotes the consideration of feminist counseling principles in all aspects of therapy, from assessment to evaluation. This code of ethics is not meant to replace traditional codes but rather represents a guideline to professional practice that explicitly addresses gender, race, class, and oppression in the therapeutic relationship. Although recent revisions of codes of ethics in counseling and related fields do give greater attention to diversity, from a feminist perspective they remain incomplete.

A feminist code of ethics stresses the counselor's obligation to reflect consistently on her own biases and possible oppressive practices. "How does my and my client's gender, race, and class shape my beliefs, affect the process of counseling, and influence the decisions I make?" is the question that feminist counselors ask themselves. Feminist counselors believe that all counselors bring a value commitment to counseling, but feminist counselors make their values overt. The code also encourages the feminist counselor to consider the emotional-intuitive responses of the counselor; the sociocultural context of the counselor and client, particularly as it relates to issues of power; and the client's participation in the decision-making process (Hill, Glaser, & Harden, 1998). Feminist counselors always consider the context of clients' lives and engage clients as active participants in the counseling process. They explore and respect clients' moral codes and ethical principles and make decisions collaboratively. Finally, a feminist code of ethics takes into account the connections between social changes and personal changes.

SUGGESTIONS FOR ENHANCING COUNSELOR EFFECTIVENESS

Research indicates that counselors operating from stereotyped perspectives of sex roles may actually restrict female clients to narrowly defined roles and to psychologically unhealthy life circumstances (Foster, 2001; May, 2001). Societal sex-role stereotypes and expectations shape therapists' perceptions and interventions (Ivey, 1995). Without gender-conscious practice, counseling fails to address fundamental aspects of the human self (Orbach, 1990). Counselors are responsible for educating themselves about women's issues and for continually looking at their own personal biases about sex roles (Ritchie, 1994; Stabb, Cox, & Harber, 1997).

In order to be fully effective, feminist counselors must become aware of how privileges based on race, class, and sexual orientation may shape their lives and influence their counseling practice. According to Robinson and Howard-Hamilton (2000), "it is not possible to empower clients without the counselor being culturally competent" (p. 289). Counselors must deepen their recognition and appreciation of culture as a source of identity and meaning that should be respected and honored. For example, the heterosexual female counselor of color may need to acknowledge and work through the issue of heterosexual privilege, even though sexism and racism are a part of her personal experience. Despite differences in race, sexual orientation, class, and gender, similarities can create a point of connection and understanding between counselor and client.

The importance of encouraging counselors to engage in critical examination of their own beliefs and values regarding counseling women cannot be overstated. Counselors must be willing to examine the role they play in the social construction of gendered therapy. Counselors must be willing to ask themselves how they are situated in relation to their clients and how they might address their own contradictory position as oppressor and oppressed. We must continue to look for liberation for all even when our own subjective realities reveal contradictory and conflicting experiences and struggles.

Finally, counselors should not assume that the experiences of White middle-class women are universal. Many researchers studied only dominant-culture populations in the development of psychological theory. Assuming that their findings in regard to normalcy and deviance hold true for all people is unsound practice. The counselor has an obligation to recognize how stereotypes about a client's group membership (whether it is class, sexual orientation, ethnicity, or some other dimension) may affect the therapeutic relationship. If counselors do not recognize and explore bias, they may unintentionally evaluate all women using their own self-reflecting lens.

CONCLUSION

Writing this chapter enlarged our perspectives on gender issues in counseling, and, through our collaboration, we recognized and challenged our own biases. We did not always agree, but by acknowledging and (sometimes) reconciling our differences, we better understood the complexities of the work we had undertaken. We each drew on our experiences in roles both common and disparate: as students, counselors, and clients; as sisters, mothers, and daughters; as partners in our respective committed relationships; as professionals and as friends. And all of these relationships grew and changed as a result of what we learned in this project. Working together gave each of us a new vision of feminism that expanded our counseling framework and our fundamental philosophies of human growth and development.

Feminist approaches to counseling women rest on a vision of personal and social transformation even in the midst of dramatic political and cultural change. Feminist therapists recognize and honor the importance of personal experience as a source of knowledge. Interventions should reflect the realities of women's socially defined subjectivities and the conditions of their lives. Counseling women effectively requires counselors to validate differences and challenge universal claims to truth. We must acknowledge the diversity of women's lives and move beyond mere tolerance of this diversity to affirmation and celebration.

EXPERIENTIAL ACTIVITIES

Individual Activities

1. Look back on your life. What messages have you received about what it means to be a woman or a man in this society? Critically examine these messages to decide which ones fit your life experiences.
2. Read a novel written by a woman from another culture or background. Imagine the characters as clients. Describe their worldviews. How would you provide relevant services?
3. Identify the interlocking issues of racism, sexism, and homophobia that Cate faces in her life. List the competencies that you have that would enable you to provide capable assistance to her as a counselor. Next, list your limitations. How could you address your limitations?

Group Activities

1. Form or join a consciousness-raising group for counselors that explores the impact of gender, race, culture, and power upon your decision to become a counselor and your counseling practice.
2. Make a group presentation at a professional conference on these issues.
3. Encourage your local professional organization to sponsor participatory workshops on gender and counseling.

REFERENCES

Almeida, R.V., & Hernandez, M. (2001). Reflections on current feminist training in family therapy. In T.S. Zimmerman, *Integrating gender and culture in family therapy* (pp. 234-249). New York: Haworth Press.

Almeida, R., Woods, R., Messineo, T., & Font, R. (1998). The cultural context model: An overview. In M. McGoldrick (Ed.), *Re-visioning family therapy: Race, culture, and gender in clinical practice* (pp. 414–431). New York: Guilford.

Bakan, D. (1966). *The duality of human existence*. Chicago: Rand-McNally.

Baylis, F., & Downie, J. (1997). Child abuse and neglect: Cross cultural considerations. In H.L. Nelson (Ed.), *Feminism and families* (pp. 173–187). New York: Routledge.

Bernardez, T. (1987). Gender-based countertransference of female therapists in the psychotherapy of women. In M. Braude (Ed.), *Women and therapy* (pp. 25–39). New York: Haworth Press.

Boettcher, K. (1999, August). Clinton's poverty tour an insult to millions. *The People, 109* (5), 3.

Bromet, E.J., Dew, M.A., & Parkinson, D.K. (1990). Spillover between work and family: A study of blue-collar working wives. In J. Eckenrode & S. Gore (Eds.), *Stress between work and family* (pp. 133–151). New York: Plenum Press.

Christian, C., & Wilson, J. (1985). Reentry women and feminist therapy: A career counseling model. *Journal of College Student Personnel, 26,* 496–500.

Cook, E.P. (Ed.). (1992). *Women, relationships, and power: Implications for counseling.* Alexandria, VA: American Counseling Association.

Coppock, V., Haydon, D., & Richter, I. (1995). *The illusions of "post-feminism": New women, old myths.* Bristol, PA: Taylor and Francis.

Derry, P., & Gallant, S. (1993). Motherhood issues in the psychotherapy of employed mothers. *Psychiatric Annals, 23,* 432–437.

Enns, C.Z. (1997). *Feminist theories and feminist psychotherapies: Origins, themes, and variations.* Binghamton, NY: Haworth Press.

Facione, N. (1994). Role overload and health: The married mother in the waged labor force. *Health Care for Women International, 15,* 157–167.

Feminist Therapy Institute. (1990). Feminist Therapy Institute code of ethics. In H. Lerman & N. Porter (Eds.), *Feminist ethics in psychotherapy* (pp. 37–40). New York: Springer Publishing.

Fine, M. (Ed.). (1992). *Disruptive voices: The possibilities of feminist research.* Ann Arbor: University of Michigan Press.

Foster, V.A. (2001). A feminist perspective on sexuality issues in family therapy. In K.M. May (Ed.), *Feminist family therapy* (pp. 141–161). Alexandria, VA: American Counseling Association.

Frone, M.R., Russell, M., & Cooper, M.L. (1991). Relationship of work and family stressors to psychological distress: The independent moderating influence of social support, mastery, active coping, and self-focused attention. In P.L. Perrewe (Ed.), Handbook on job stress (special issue). *Journal of Social Behavior and Personality, 6,* 227–250.

Goldenberg, H., & Goldenberg, I. (2002). *Counseling today's families* (4th ed.). Pacific Grove, CA: Brooks/Cole.

Goodrich, T.J., Rampage, C., Ellman, B., & Halstead, K. (1988), *Feminist family therapy: A casebook.* New York: Norton.

Greene, B., & Boyd-Franklin, N. (1996). African American lesbian couples: Ethnocultural considerations in psychotherapy. In M. Hill & E.D. Rothblum (Eds.), *Couples therapy: Feminist perspectives* (pp. 49–60). New York: Haworth Press.

Hare-Mustin, R.T. (1991). Sex, lies, and headaches: The problem is power. In T.J. Goodrich (Ed.), *Women and power: Perspectives for family therapy* (pp. 63–85). New York: Norton.

Hare-Mustin, R.T. (1998). Challenging traditional discourses in psychotherapy: Creating space for alternatives. *Journal of Feminist Family Therapy, 10* (3), 39–56.

Hare-Mustin, R.T., & Marecek, J. (1990). *Making a difference: Psychology and the construction of gender.* New Haven, CT: Yale University Press.

Hendley, A.A., & Bilimoria, N.F. (1999). Policy paper: Minorities and social security: An analysis of racial and ethnic differences in the current program. *Social Security Bulletin, 62* (2), 59–64.

Henry, S. (2002, January 24). Male-female salary gap growing study says. *Washington Post,* p. A9.

Herlihy, B., & Corey, G. (2001). Feminist therapy. In G. Corey (Ed.), *Theory and practice of counseling* (6th ed.; pp. 340–381). Belmont, CA: Brooks/Cole.

Hill, M., Glaser, K., & Harden, J. (1998). A feminist model for ethical decision-making. In M. Hall & E.D. Rothblum (Eds.), *Learning from our mistakes: Difficulties and failures in feminist therapy* (pp. 101–121). Binghamton, NY: Haworth Press.

Ivey, D.C. (1995). Family history, parenting attitudes, gender roles, and clinician perceptions of family and family member functioning: Factors related to gender inequitable practices. *American Journal of Family Therapy, 23* (3), 331–347.

Kitzinger, C. (1991). Feminism, psychology, and the paradox of power. *Feminism and Psychology, 1,* 111–129.

Klein, M.H. (1976). Feminist concepts of therapy outcome. *Psychotherapy: Theory, Research, and Practice, 13,* 89–95.

Laidlaw, T.A., & Malmo, C. (1990). Introduction: Feminist therapy and psychological healing. In T.A. Laidlaw, C. Malmo, & associates (Eds.), *Healing voices: Feminist approaches to therapy with women* (pp. 1–11). San Francisco, CA: Jossey-Bass.

Lamison-White, L. (1997). Poverty in the United States: 1996 Current population reports, (pp. 60–198). Washington, D.C.: U.S. Bureau of Census.

Lewin, T. (1997, September 5). Equal pay for equal work is no. 1 goal of women. *New York Times,* p. A4.

Maddock, J.W. (1990). Promoting healthy family sexuality. *Journal of Family Psychotherapy, 1,* 49–63.

Marecek, J. (2001). Bringing feminist issues to therapy. In B. Slife, R. Williams, & S. Barlow (Eds.), *Critical issues in psychotherapy* (pp. 305–319). Thousand Oaks, CA: Sage Publications.

May, K.M. (2001). Feminist family therapy defined. In K.M. May (Ed.), *Feminist family therapy* (pp. 3–14). Alexandria, VA: American Counseling Association.

McGoldrick, M. (1999). Women in the family life cycle. In M. McGoldrick & B. Carter (Eds.), *The expanded family life cycle: Individual, family, and social perspectives.* Needham Heights, MA: Allyn and Bacon.

McGoldrick, M., Giordiano, J., & Pearce, J.K. (1996). *Ethnicity and family therapy.* New York: Guilford.

Morrow, S.L., & Hawxhurst, D.M. (1998). Feminist therapy: Integrating political analysis in counseling and psychotherapy. In M. Hill (Ed.), *Feminist therapy as a political act* (pp. 37–50). New York: Haworth Press.

Mulligan, J.E. (2002, January 29). Bucking the system earns a pilot a prime seat at State of Union. *Washington Post,* pp. A4, A7.

Orbach, S. (1990). Gender and dependency in psychotherapy. *Journal of Social Work Practice,* 1–15.

Parker, L. (1997). Keeping power issues on the table in couples work. *Journal of Feminist Family Therapy, 9* (3), 1–24.

Rampage, C. (2001). An interview with a leading feminist family therapist. In K.M. May(Ed.), *Feminist family therapy* (pp. 165–189). Alexandria, VA: American Counseling Association.

Ritchie, M.H. (1994). Cultural and gender biases in definitions of mental and emotional health and illness. *Counselor Education and Supervision, 33,* 344–348.

Robinson, T.L., & Howard-Hamilton, M.F. (2000). *The convergence of race, ethnicity, and gender: Multiple dimensions in counseling.* Upper Saddle River, NJ: Prentice-Hall.

Santos De Barona, M., & Dutton, M.A. (1997). Feminist perspectives on assessment. In J. Worell & M.G. Johnson (Eds.), S*haping the future of feminist psychology: Education, research, and practice* (pp. 37–56). Washington, DC: American Psychological Association.

Stabb, S., Cox, D., & Harber, J. (1997). Gender-related therapist attributions in couples therapy: A preliminary multiple case study investigation. *Journal of Marital and Family Therapy, 23,* 335–346.

Theorell, T. (1991). Psychosocial cardiovascular risks—on the double loads in women. *Psychotherapy and Psychosomatics, 55,* 81–89.

Vance, C. (1984). Pleasure and danger: Towards a politics of sexuality. In C. Vance (Ed.), *Pleasure and danger: Exploring female sexuality* (pp. 1–30). Boston: Routledge and Kegan Paul.

Wheatley, D. (1991). Stress in women. *Stress Medicine, 7,* 73–74.

Worell, J., & Remer, P. (1992). *Feminist perspectives in therapy: An empowerment model for women.* West Sussex: John Wiley & Sons.

Ziemba, S.J. (2001). Therapy with families in poverty: Applications of feminist family therapy principles. *Journal of Feminist Family Therapy, 12* (4), 205–237.

CHAPTER 10

Counseling Men

Robin L. Daniel

Robin Daniel, LPL, holds a Ph.D. in counseling and counselor education from the University of North Carolina, Greensboro. He is director of Counseling and Disability Services at Greensboro College and has a part-time private practice counseling individuals, couples, and families. Since 1995 he has counseled male batterers in the Domestic Violence Intervention Program at Family Service of the Piedmont in Greensboro. He enjoys teaching and has regularly served as a visiting lecturer at the University of North Carolina, Greensboro.

AWARENESS INDEX

Please test your knowledge by marking the following statements true or false before proceeding to the text in this chapter. Compute your score from the scoring guide at the end of the Awareness Index.

1. T F One in three working women earns more income than her husband.

2. T F Men's level of education is a major factor in marital stability.

3. T F A stepfather should be the disciplinarian in his stepfamily.

4. T F Investment is a function of success for men in relationships.

5. T F Creativity is a key component of counseling men.

6. T F Men approach counseling as a task to be performed.

7. T F Reflection of feeling is a counseling skill that is better avoided when counseling men.

8. T F Men readily acknowledge and express fear and sadness.

9. T F Divorced men emotionally disengage from their noncustodial children because they feel unable to fulfill their parental role.

10. T F Men like to talk and resist experiential counseling interventions.

Scoring guide: **1.** T; **2.** T; **3.** F; **4.** T; **5.** T; **6.** T; **7.** F; **8.** F; **9.** T; **10.** F.

INTRODUCTION

Only when it is realized that each man's environment is unique to himself, can how he feels be understood.

—John Bowlby, 1969

Early in my counseling training, I worked in an in-patient hospital during the day and led domestic violence groups two nights per week. The Adult Open Unit (anxiety and depressive disorders) was populated predominantly by women, and the domestic violence group members were all men. Hearing members of each gender/population articulate their reasons for being in treatment and describe the situations they confronted led me to make some generalizations about gender differences. Women appeared to focus on the primary emotions of sadness and fear, and men appeared to focus on secondary emotional responses including frustration, anger, resentment, and hostility. Subsequently, most men appear to benefit from learning to identify, acknowledge, and manage their primary emotional responses to situations in the workplace and with intimate partners. Men fear they will not be able to provide well for their families. Some fear that they will be ignored or abandoned. Many men become frustrated when confronted with expressions of emotions they do not understand. And some men want to be "right" to the degree that they frequently respond to disagreements or conflict in an inappropriate or self-defeating manner.

In this chapter, the phenomenon of men in counseling is discussed primarily with regard to societal developments that have shaped the evolution of men's roles in couples' relationships, the family, and the workplace. Such a discussion is warranted because men may be participating in counseling not necessarily motivated by desire for personal growth, but rather in response to environmental factors that they perceive as threatening to their personal identity and societal role(s). A changing economy and accompanying workplace instability, increases in the rates of divorce and remarriage, and societal intolerance of violence against women are examples of dynamics that put men in positions heretofore unimaginable to them. More frequently than ever before, men appear to be sharing more of the burden of adjustment in the workplace, in relationships, and in the family.

In my work with male batterer groups, heterosexual couples, and individuals, men have repeatedly demonstrated the ability to accept help, provide help, and assume responsibility for personal change within counseling contexts. In the section on enhancing counselor effectiveness, descriptions of various clinical interventions and techniques, borrowed and developed by me, are explained using the case studies that follow.

CASE EXAMPLES

Akil

Akil is a thirty-four-year-old African American male who is divorced and remarried. His mother and father divorced when Akil was eight years old. He has two older sisters and a younger brother. He maintains infrequent contact with his mother and siblings and no contact with his father. Akil has two stepsons, ages eleven and fifteen. He has no contact with his biological daughter, age nine, from his first marriage. He is a high school graduate and served in the military for approximately four years. At the time he initiated contact with the counselor, Akil worked as a legal secretary. He quit that job and held a variety of others acquired through a temporary employment service until finding permanent employment as a researcher and archivist for an industrial newsletter. Akil is neat, well groomed, interpersonally engaging, and extremely adept at articulating his perceptions, emotions, and self-awareness. He is a self-taught cartoon artist and hopes to develop his talent further. Although his general demeanor could be described as gentle, he initiated counseling to satisfy conditions of his parole for felony child abuse of his biological daughter (who was five months old at the time the abuse occurred).

Lou

Lou is a thirty-seven-year-old married white male with two children, a daughter age three and son age six. He is the only son of an intact marriage. He is an attorney and real estate developer. His daughter suffers from a congenital digestive/nervous disorder that causes her to experience severe convulsive episodes. She requires continuous connection to a feeding pump that requires adjustment, frequently in the middle of the night. Family vacations and other events are frequently disrupted by the daughter's convulsions and medical needs. His wife of ten years is the primary caregiver to their daughter and son. Unlike his wife and six-year-old son, Lou is unfamiliar with the mechanisms and processes associated with the care of his daughter. Lou is well groomed, impeccably dressed, and possesses a generally abrasive, abrupt demeanor. He participated in counseling as a collateral client in the treatment of his son for frequent somatic complaints at school and oppositional behavior toward his mother.

Jerry

Jerry is a forty-four-year-old white male who attends couples counseling sessions with his wife of fifteen years, Tina. This is Jerry's second marriage and he has no children from either marriage. He graduated from high school and achieved the top rank as a machinist in his previous job, from which he was laid off. Tina also lost her job as a human resources director. They moved south to find work and gain closer proximity to Tina's family. Jerry took an entry-level job with a high-tech company. Tina completed certification as a trainer in the human resources field and took a job that takes her away from home for two weeks of each month. In just a few months, her rate of income exceeded Jerry's by over 50%. Jerry entered the counseling process at Tina's insistence. She complained of poor communication, feelings of isolation, and an unsatisfactory level of sexual activity.

Although Akil, Lou, and Jerry differ in race, socioeconomic status, family history, relationship history, family structure, and path into the counseling process, they share very similar values and personal issues. Each man desires to provide financial support for his family. Each expressed a desire to be "a good father and [or] husband." And each man acknowledged experiencing extreme frustration with fulfilling one or more of those roles in the manner he perceived to be "right." Frustration and anger are significant influences on the quality of each man's marital, family, and peer relationships.

A HISTORICAL OVERVIEW

Since World War II, men have experienced changes in career development, family structure, gender roles, and societal norms. Initially, conscientious, hard-working men provided money for the family and were readily perceived as "head of the household." Since that time, the lives of men have become inherently more complex. Dad is not the only one going out to work. Children do not necessarily live with their fathers, although many men have children and stepchildren. Society will no longer tolerate households controlled by violence and intimidation. For the better part of the last three decades, men have increasingly experienced interpersonal and intrapersonal challenges that seldom existed half a century ago.

Gradually in the 1960s and accelerating in the 1970s, the number and proportion of women entering the workforce began to increase steadily (White, 2000). Accompanying the increase of women in the workplace during the 1970s came a dramatic increase in the divorce rate (Norton & Miller, 1993) and, in turn, gradual shifts in family structure and perceptions of gender roles. As more women gained economic autonomy, traditional families with the father cast primarily as provider and the mother as homemaker and caregiver represented a decreasing proportion of total households. Through divorces and subsequent remarriages, many men began experiencing challenges associated with nonresidential parenting and stepparenting. The maintenance and development of relationships with children produced in previous relationships may be negatively affected by geographical distance and acrimony in relationships with former spouses (Hanson, McLanahan, & Thomson, 1996). Research strongly suggests that the quality of stepfamily relationships and functioning is significantly affected by stepparent role management and the quality of relationships with former spouses and nonresident biological children (Barber & Lyons, 1994; Hanson et al., 1996; Vuchinich et al., 1991).

Accompanying the challenges associated with changes in family structure, gender-related changes in workforce participation, income, and tenure test the coping ability of many men. Between 1990 and 1998, the proportion of working women aged twenty-five to fifty-four years increased from 74% to 77%, while the proportion of working men decreased from 94% to 92% (White, 2000). Examination of individual earnings (in constant dollars) between 1963 and 1997 reveals that the median income for men with bachelor's degrees increased 22%, while the incomes of men with a high school diploma decreased by 12%. Concomitantly, women's incomes during that period have increased for all levels of education, including a 53% increase in the median income of women with bachelor's degrees. Between 1983 and 1998, the median employee tenure declined for men (4.1 years to 3.8 years) and increased for women (3.1 years to 3.4 years) (White, 2000). Such trends in employment may challenge male assumptions about the necessity of maintaining the role of primary provider in the family unit. As a result, many men perceive decreases in self-efficacy and experience more emotional distress in response to environmental forces associated with daily routines and situations.

Men in general are encountering many new challenges. They face economic challenges in the form of employment stability and child support. As spouses produce more income, men may have more responsibility for child care. Increasingly complex relationships, including parenting children from previous relationships, contribute to the sense that men are no longer the undisputed kings of their castles. In many instances, they may be struggling to determine how they fit into the systems of work and family they once ruled without question.

CURRENT ISSUES

In this section, male counseling issues are discussed with regard to clinical observation and published research.

Career

Jerry was a union member machinist with a high degree of seniority before moving to the southeast when Tina lost her job and one of her parents became ill. As Jerry and Tina attempted to establish a new life in the southeast, they were confronted with some difficult challenges: loss of income, the illness of a parent, and adjustment to a new job market. Although the couple reported that the initial stage of the transition was fairly smooth, their marital problems emerged when Tina pursued new training and applied her skills in a new area that involved more travel and a much higher income. Meanwhile, Jerry found little demand for his skills and grew increasingly frustrated about the level of compensation offered in the jobs available to him. As the weeks became months, Jerry became increasingly withdrawn from Tina, even after beginning a promising new job.

Research on the relationship between income and marital stability has produced mixed results. Although generally higher levels of income tend to be positively correlated with higher levels of marital stability (Hoffman & Duncan, 1995), dual-income couples with a low male to female income ratio appear to be at greater risk of divorce (Heckert, Nowak, & Synder, 1998; Ono, 1998). Jerry and Tina fit the latter scenario very well: Tina earned as much as 50% more than Jerry.

Early in the counseling process, Jerry denied perceiving problems in the marriage and attempted to normalize Tina's concerns as a natural function of her frequent absences. He frequently mentioned how much he enjoyed cooking for Tina when she was not traveling. As counseling progressed, Jerry admitted feeling unsure about his ability to succeed in his new job. He later acknowledged that doubts about his viability as a partner in the relationship led to his emotional withdrawal from Tina.

Marriage and Family Relationships

Shifts in workplace demographics and career predictability of men have been accompanied by shifts in couples' and family relationships. Dual-income households or families with special needs typically require a higher degree of shared responsibility for household matters such as cleaning, laundry, meal provision, and auto maintenance. When children are a part of the family system, the potential for distress related to such responsibilities can be heightened considerably as children place added demands on time, finances, and physical and emotional energy. In some relationships, women may wield more economic power than their male companions. Indeed, census data indicates that nearly one in three married women makes more money than her husband (Goldstein, 2000).

When their wives do not work in an income-producing capacity, men may work long hours or unusual schedules to provide acceptable levels of income. Lou's family exemplifies a scenario involving special family needs and long hours of work for a man with primary provider status. From Lou's perspective, two problems existed in his household: (1) his wife was too lenient in dealing with the children, contributing to the behavior problems of his son, and (2) since his wife did not work outside the home and they were able to hire support persons, the home should be neat and orderly at the end of each day. By report of Lou and his wife, Lou's typical response to a disorderly home was an angry outburst directed toward all family members and ordering the children to "clean up" before any other activity took place.

By report of Lou's wife, Lou had little empathy or support for the challenges she faced in managing their daughter's medical needs and supporting the children's school and recreational activities. He felt justified in his expectations of a neat house based on his long hours of work and ability to provide household help. In the first session, Lou responded to his wife's assessment by stating, "In difficult situations, everyone just needs to work harder." Lou's wife repeatedly stated that although she understood Lou's work-related stress, the family did not feel supported by him because of his unwillingness to participate in his daughter's care and make time for a least one or two family meals each week. Lou's only response was, "I can't help that."

During an individual session with Lou, he absolutely stated, "I don't need to change." After meeting with the family members, it became apparent that Lou was attempting to define the role of each family member with no regard for the special challenges presented by his extremely long hours at his job and the special attention required by his daughter. Additionally, Lou was unaware that his son's demanding and oppositional behavior toward his mother was directly reflecting Lou's attitude toward his family.

Akil experienced a different type of marital issue regarding his reported sense of responsibility for the happiness of his wife and stepsons. He reported frequent frustration with communication failure between himself and his wife. Once they began to argue, his wife would withdraw from the conversation and ignore his overtures to reengage. Akil stated that he was much more prone to engage in angry tirades and hostile behavior (demanding that she tell him what is wrong, yelling, slamming doors, etc.) when his wife withdrew from him emotionally. During their three years of marriage, demand-withdraw interactions had occurred with increasing frequency, significantly diminishing the relationship.

Akil's response to his wife's withdrawal can be conceptualized within the framework of attachment theory (Bowlby, 1969) and labeled as proximity-seeking behavior, which is intended to ensure availability of the attachment figure. Paradoxically, Akil's pursuing behavior apparently served to intensify his partner's desire to remain physically and emotionally separated from him.

Researchers studying communication patterns in relation to battering behavior found that couples engaging in frequent demand-withdraw interactions reported lower levels of marital satisfaction and a higher incidence of interpersonal conflict than couples who avoided such interactions (Berns & Jacobson, 1999; Christensen & Heavey, 1990). A higher frequency of violent behavior was associated with the male partner assuming the demanding position and the female partner assuming the withdrawing position in the interaction.

According to Akil, he almost always assumed that he was the cause of his wife's anger, sadness, and anxiety, and therefore had a low tolerance for his wife's physical and emotional withdrawal. Akil reported having trouble managing his own emotions in the presence of intense emotions displayed by his wife. If she became angry, no matter the provocation, he would become angry as well. Akil reported that those situations often resulted in intense conflict with his wife, even when her emotions were connected with a situation that did not involve him. In his interview, Akil acknowledged that he was generally unable to feel calm and/or happy unless his wife appeared to feel calm and/or happy. Such behavior is consistent with research on male batterers suggesting that some men may be hypersensitive and reactive to the emotional state of their intimate partners (Daniel, 2000).

The conceptualizations of etiology of the behaviors of Lou and Akil may differ, but their responses to the situations they faced were very similar. Each man intensified efforts to control the situation he confronted, caused more harm than good, and continually felt frustrated, angry, and unappreciated.

Parenting and Stepparenting

Though Akil acknowledged seeking counseling services as a condition of his parole, much of his attention was focused on stepfamily-related issues. He reported that much of the conflict he experienced in his marriage was generated by disagreements with his wife regarding his parenting of his stepsons. Researchers have consistently found evidence suggesting that adolescent males and females are unaccepting of stepparent discipline and perceive stepparents as more strict than biological parents with similar parenting styles (Ganong & Coleman, 1995). Akil described using an authoritarian approach with his stepsons markedly similar to the parenting style employed by his own father and mother. Although he readily acknowledged his mistakes in attempting to discipline his stepsons, Akil expressed intense frustration with his role in the household. He frequently experienced his stepfamily role as a "double bind." He perceived that he was supposed to provide necessary structure and discipline for the boys and felt such actions to be at the expense of his wife's approval and their marital intimacy.

Akil's separation from his biological daughter is familiar to many men. According to a census report, 90% of children with divorced parents live with their mothers (Norton & Miller, 1993). Akil, while attempting to be a "good father" to his stepsons, was grieving the loss of his daughter and filled with regret regarding the circumstances of their separation.

Summary

Although Akil, Lou, and Jerry vary in age, family structure (Akil is a parent and stepparent, Lou is a parent of a disabled child, Jerry is childless), marital status (Lou is once married, Akil and Jerry are divorced and remarried), and career paths, their behaviors and presenting problems appear driven by a common theme: a sense of or fear of powerlessness. From this counselor's perspective, male behavior appears to be especially sensitive to shifts in perceived power. In the next section, issues related to the perception of power and influence will be explained within the context of describing counseling interventions applied to the problems faced by Akil, Lou, and Jerry.

SUGGESTIONS FOR ENHANCING COUNSELOR EFFECTIVENESS

Rapport building, though often taken for granted as a component of the counseling process, is a significant element of counseling men. I have observed that men are generally wary of counseling processes because they perceive counseling as a threat to their personal autonomy. Liddle (1986) discussed resistance in supervision as "a response to a perceived threat," and that conceptualization applies to men in counseling. Counselors working with men should respect those concerns and proactively address them.

Building counseling rapport with men, individually or in groups, can be enhanced by prudent use of a fundamental active listening skill—reflection of feeling. Many men may hesitate to articulate strong emotions, especially anger, even though these same emotions may drive their behavior. Counselors willing to reflect feelings will communicate empathy and understanding of the client's position.

Men generally appreciate respectful and direct feedback, and counselors can gain trust with men by stating certain facts about the process that imply respect for client autonomy. I often state that change does not happen during the counseling session, but only occurs when clients take the risk of behaving differently. That type of statement contains three implicit messages that are important to men: the counselor is not attempting to change anyone; the counselor acknowledges that change involves risk and respects the client's ability to take risks; and the client is in charge of changing. Men like to know who is in charge and they generally welcome responsibility. Counselors who respectfully assume charge of the counseling process and communicate respect for the male client's ability to control himself and his behavioral changes will have more success in counseling men. Men need to hear that their autonomy is respected.

Assumption of responsibility for current behavior or changes in behavior can be a delicate process in working with men. Though "homework" may be poorly received, suggestions or challenges may be more readily embraced. The delivery of prescriptive interventions may unintentionally disrespect a man's sense of autonomy and right to choose. Counselors who employ between-session intervention strategies may experience more success by putting men in a position to make choices or ask for suggestions. This can be accomplished with a technique I call setting the table, a subtle expression of doubt about client readiness for change.

Setting the table involves descriptions of alternative scenarios that address a specific problem described by a client. This intervention is based on the premise that people will eat foods that taste good and avoid foods that taste bad. Similarly, they will typically choose to behave in ways that reflect a positive self-image and avoid behavior that reflects a negative self-image. For male clients, the perception of having choices, even circumscribed as in the following example, is a key component in promoting change.

Jerry complained that Tina's seeking affection from him immediately following her return from a trip made him feel pressured and invaded. To avoid her advances on weekends, he would take long rides on his motorcycle—leaving her just as she had left him two weeks earlier. Processing of this behavior revealed that Jerry wanted to set some of the terms for reengaging with Tina. He wanted to be an affectionate husband, but he rebelled at Tina's insistent approach to him. Jerry was encouraged to entertain two very different scenarios: one scenario included continuing to avoid Tina, the other included planning a trip on his motorcycle and extending an invitation to Tina *before* she left on her business trip. He agreed that the latter scenario seemed plausible. When asked what he would do if it rained on the day of the excursion, he smiled and said, "It's not that far to the motel."

As simple and transparent as it may seem, men generally enjoy challenges. In cases where a prescriptive intervention appears appropriate, a counselor's subtle expression of doubt about a male client's readiness for change predisposes the client to accepting the risk associated with trying new behavior. A suggested modification of behavior may be preceded by some casual reference to readiness ("It may be too early for you, but I've seen [alternative behavior] work well for some people"). An alternative method of expressing doubt can be delivered the form of thinking out loud ("A possibility just occurred to me, but you probably . . . No, maybe later"). Typically, a man's response is to ask about the possibility, explore the potential benefits, and assume ownership of implementing the proposed change.

Imaging, Visual Aids, and Movement

Just as the combination of imagery and sound make motion pictures and television more powerful mediums than radio, visual aids, tokens, and movement appear to enhance counselor effectiveness when used in conjunction with the verbal counseling process. It has been my observation that men respond positively when interventions contain a visual component or activity. Many of the interventions serve as metaphors for the issue discussed and invite male clients to use visual and kinesthetic modes of processing information to embrace new ideas and learn new skills. The following interventions consistently engender unsolicited feedback from clients.

Imaging exercises and role playing are proven cognitive-behavioral interventions that men appear to generalize effectively. Researchers have studied the use of these interventions as components of behavior-modification (Meichenbaum, 1977) and stress inoculation training (Meichenbaum, 1985) and concluded them to be effective in treatment of various problems such as anger management (Novaco, 1979) and post-traumatic stress disorder (Foa et al., 1991).

Akil reported having a problem with becoming angry when his wife verbalized angry emotions. I asked him to act out an example of his wife's angry outburst. When finished with the role playing, I directed him to close his eyes and imagine himself taking a shower with the water running over his head and describe himself in the shower. He described having his face tilted forward to avoid having water run into his nose and mouth. Next, I directed him to imagine his wife verbally expressing her anger about something and imagine her words coming out of her mouth as letters and falling on him like the water from a shower. Akil immediately observed that the letters did not "soak-in," they fell away as harmlessly as the water rolling off his head. He soon reported using the shower image successfully and generalizing his imaging skills to other types of situations.

Lou reported feeling frustrated by what he considered to be the disorganized state of his home on some days and a perceived lack of discipline demanded of the children by his wife. When asked how he dealt with the disorder and inefficiency routinely exhibited in real estate development, he reported approaching each day positively because he anticipated that problems would occur. I directed Lou to close his eyes, imagine parking his car in the driveway, and to talk about the problems he might upon entering his house. Further processing of that image allowed Lou to explore his expectations of his home and family. He acknowledged that he placed unrealistic expectations on his family because he felt so frustrated and out of control in his business. Lou and his wife then constructed a "husband/father reentry plan" that accounted for both expected and unexpected household disorder.

During Akil's participation in a domestic violence prevention program, he and other participants acknowledged consistently feeling unappreciated and taken for granted in their family and intimate relationships. Further exploration of this issue suggested that to a large extent these men relied on the emotional state of intimate partners to indicate their personal worth and acceptability. Further group discussion yielded conceptualization of the issue as a form of emotional/psychological dependency.

To illustrate the point, two volunteers were recruited for an exercise directed by the counselor. With spotters behind them, each man grasped the wrists of the other and slowly moved their feet closer together while keeping arms straight and leaning against the other man. Processing of the exercise revealed that the position felt uncomfortable because if one man slipped, both would fall. That dynamic was then generalized to emotions in intimate relationships. As the volunteers slowly returned to individually stable stances, the counselor pointed out that ownership of self and allowing others the same responsibility affords many more options for effective coping. Many men participating in or observing this exercise have reported using that image of physical dependence as a reminder to analyze situations where emotional or psychological dependence may motivate maladaptive behavior.

A similar movement-based intervention involves having a man stand inside a circumscribed area (hula hoops tend to work well) and attempt to lift an object (a chair will do), placed approximately three feet away, straight up from the floor. When he is unable to perform this task, his failure can be observed to be analogous to attempting to take ownership and control of another person's emotions. Lifting them is all but impossible.

Akil, Lou, and Jerry each acknowledged responding to frustrated and angry feelings with the initiation or intensification of controlling behavior. To illustrate the potential for negative outcomes from controlling behavior, I placed a smooth ball of play dough in each man's open hand and instructed the men to close their fists. Each man observed that with the support of an open hand, the shape of the ball was retained and exerting pressure resulted in distortion of the ball. Likewise, relational and perceptual distortions may be produced by intensification of power and control in family and couples' relationships. I encouraged each man to keep the dough and carry the lid in a pocket as a cue to monitor his controlling behavior. Lou's wife reported a significant reduction in the degree and frequency of explosive behavior by her husband after the dough intervention.

Paper money is a readily available visual aid that can be used to illustrate several themes, including value, communication, and reciprocity. During a session with Jerry and Tina, a dollar bill was used to help Jerry understand the dynamics of defusing power struggles. With Jerry and Tina facing each other in opposite chairs, I held the bill between them and each described what they observed. Each acknowledged observing the same object from different points of view. When asked what he might do to better understand what Tina described, Jerry acknowledged that moving to a different point of view would help him see her side. He walked around the bill, sat next to Tina, became tearful, and said, "I'm always trying to convince her that I'm right, instead of trying to understand her side." Communication was a frequently discussed topic in the couples' sessions, and communication exercises given to the couple as homework had produced mixed results and some frustration. Jerry reported understanding conversations with his wife in a totally different way after the session with the dollar intervention.

Recently, the domestic violence program that employs me part-time shifted from a format that relied heavily on group process to more of a psychoeducational format. I initially resisted the change because I was concerned that the focus on individual issues, learning, and attention would be lost or greatly diminished. To my surprise, I found that the format change produced results totally contrary to my expectations.

The new format featured video vignettes depicting interpersonal issues and behaviors commonly associated with battering behavior. After viewing and processing the behaviors and interpersonal dynamics in the video, group members completed worksheets intended to provoke individual introspection and ownership of patriarchical and controlling behaviors and shared their work with the group in the next session. Groups that were often difficult and demanding of the counselors were transformed into forums of self-inspection, honest respectful observation and feedback, and exploration of alternative responses to conflict.

Initially focusing on the video apparently allowed counseling participants to analyze the dynamics of the situation, empathize with the characters, and begin to compare their own behaviors to the behaviors they observed. The process of tackling a task or engaging in problem solving produces an environment that most men experience as safe, productive, and rewarding. In this way male clients generally learn to understand themselves, learn more effective methods of coping, and have a sense of being in charge of the process.

CONCLUDING REMARKS

My experiences with counseling men in private practice, in-patient hospital, and community agency settings have allowed observation of themes in presenting problems that men from all walks of life appear to share. Feelings of isolation and expressions of frustration and anger predominate their emotional responses to challenging and stressful situations. A patriarchical sense of responsibility for intimate partners and children often produces disrespectful behavior toward others. Because many men highly value personal autonomy and respect, they often have a low tolerance for feeling a sense of powerlessness.

Men's investment in relationships—marital, parental, or counseling—is largely a function of their perceived potential for success. Indeed, some researchers studying fathers suggest that the parental involvement of men is much more a matter of conditions than commitment (Fox & Bruce, 2001). Unfortunately, male responses to situational stressors frequently imply that men are insensitive and/or uncaring. Men feel pain; they fear losing income and the ability to provide for their family; they grieve separation from their children; and they often manage these primary emotions poorly.

In counseling male clients, it can be easy for counselors (both male and female) to focus on inappropriate and hostile behaviors and difficult to empathize with the person who exhibits them. Revealing and exploring the primary emotions associated with anger and hostility facilitates empathy and trust. Counselors working with men must assume responsibility for clear definition of the process and communicate respect for each client's personal autonomy. In groups, couples, and individual counseling contexts, men appear to feel more confident in working with tangible and observable mechanisms of intervention. Using visual aids, props, and exercises allows male clients to focus on the lessons to be learned and applied to specific situations without a need to feel wary or guarded. When men feel respected and in charge of their part of a process, they can exhibit a high capacity for emotional sensitivity and support for their partners and each other. Men enjoy helping and solving problems, and counselors may work with male clients more effectively when modeling a problem-solving approach to presenting problems.

Many men struggle to cope with systemic changes in Western society. Women continue to claim more prominent positions in the workplace, politics, and other areas of society. Changes in job markets and career paths provoke self-doubt. Divorce, remarriage, and other changes in family structure continue to challenge the traditional male image as "head of the household," though many men still embrace the role of provider and protector. Counselors who can realize that "each man's environment is unique to himself" can understand how he feels—and help him.

EXPERIENTIAL ACTIVITIES

1. In groups or three or four, develop a visual or kinesthetic intervention that is applicable to an issue you consider important to men. Have the class participate in a practice delivery of the intervention.
2. Interview clinicians, including those in programs to prevent violence against women or child abuse, providing counseling services for men in your community. What are the formats for treatment? What is the duration of those programs? At what level are those services utilized? Observe a session or intake if confidentiality policy allows.
3. Divide your class according to gender. What is the percentage of men in the class? Discuss the possible impact of counselor gender in the provision of counseling services to men.
4. Visit a support group or class for divorced parents. Are men under- or overrepresented? What is said regarding parenting roles and challenges?
5. Visit a class/seminar for remarried couples or new stepfamilies. What does the curriculum emphasize as important for stepfathers to know? How do the men in attendance respond?

REFERENCES

Barber, B.L., & Lyons, J.M. (1994). Family processes and adolescent adjustment in intact and remarried families. *Journal of Youth and Adolescence, 23* (4), 421–436.

Berns, S.B., & Jacobson, N.S. (1999). Demand-withdraw interaction in couples with a violent husband. *Journal of Consulting and Clinical Psychology, 67* (5), 666–675.

Bowlby, J. (1969). *Attachment and loss, vol. 1.* New York: Basic Books.

Christensen, A., & Heavey, C.L. (1990). Gender and social structure in the demand/withdraw pattern of marital conflict. *Journal of Personality and Social Psychology, 59,* 73–82.

Daniel, R. (2000). Emotional caretaking in male batterers: Instrument development and testing. Ph.D. diss., University of North Carolina, Greensboro.

Foa, E.B., Rothbaum, B.O., Riggs, D.S., & Murdock, T.B. (1991). Treatment of posttraumatic stress disorder in rape victims: A comparison between cognitive-behavioral procedures and counseling. *Journal of Consulting and Clinical Psychology, 59* (5), 715–723.

Fox, G.L., & Bruce, C. (2001). Conditional fatherhood: Identity theory and parental investment theory as alternative sources of explanation of fathering. *Journal of Marriage and Family, 63* (2), 394–404.

Ganong, L.H., & Coleman, M. (1995). Adolescent stepchild-stepparent relationships: Change over time. In K. Pasley & M. Ihinger-Tallman (Eds.), *Stepparenting: Issues, theory, and practice.* Westport, CT: Greenwood Press.

Goldstein, A. (2000, February 28). 1 in 3 women earns more money than her husband: Rise in income has altered balance of power in marriage. *Washington Post*, p. A1.

Hanson, T.L., McLanahan, S.S., & Thomson, E. (1996). Double jeopardy: Parental conflict and stepfamily outcomes for children. *Journal of Marriage and Family, 58* (1), 141–154.

Heckert, D.A., Nowak, T.C., & Synder, K.A. (1998). The impact of husbands' and wives' relative earnings on marital disruption. *Journal of Marriage and Family, 60* (3), 690–703.

Hoffman, S.D., & Duncan, G.J. (1995). The effect of incomes, wages, and AFDC benefits on martial disruption. *Journal of Human Resources, 30,* 19–42.

Liddle, B.J. (1986). Resistance to supervision: A response to a perceived threat. *Counselor Education and Supervision, 26* (2), 117–127.

Meichenbaum, D. (1977). *Cognitive behavior modification: An integrative approach.* New York: Plenum Press.

Meichenbaum, D.H. (1985). *Stress inoculation training.* New York: Pergamon.

Norton, A.J., & Miller, L.F. (1993). Marriage, divorce, and remarriage in the 1990s. U.S. Bureau of the Census, Current Population Reports, Series P23, No. 180. Washington, DC: Government Printing Office.

Novaco, R. (1979). The cognitive regulation of anger and stress. In P.C. Kendall & S.D. Hollon (Eds.), *Cognitive behavioral interventions: Theory, reseach, and procedures* (pp. 84–101). San Diego, CA: Academic Press.

Ono, H. (1998). Husbands' and wives' resources and marital dissolution. *Journal of Marriage and the Family, 60* (3), 674–689.

Vuchinich, S., Vuchinich, R.A., Hetherington, E.M., & Clingempeel, W.G. (1991). Parent-child interaction and gender differences in early adolescents' adaptation to stepfamilies. *Developmental Psychology, 27* (4), 618–626.

White, L. (2000). Economic circumstances and family outcomes: A review of the 1990s. *Journal of Marriage and the Family, 62* (4), 1035–1063.

CHAPTER 11

Counseling People
with Physical Disabilities

Richard Holicky

Richard Holicky, M.A., is a counselor in Denver, Colorado, whose practice includes people with a variety of disabilities. He investigated many aspects of living and aging with spinal cord injury while a research associate at Craig Rehabilitation Hospital, and has written extensively on disability issues for several consumer publications. He has lived with a disability since 1989.

AWARENESS INDEX

Please test your knowledge by marking the following statements true or false before proceeding to the text in this chapter. Compute your score from the scoring guide at the end of the Awareness Index.

1. T F Income levels of people with disabilities are only slightly lower than those of able-bodied people.

2. T F People with disabilities are better educated than their nondisabled counterparts.

3. T F Since the passage of the Americans with Disabilities Act, employment of people with disabilities has rapidly increased.

4. T F Because of Medicare and Medicaid, people with disabilities receive, on average, better health care than most Americans.

5. T F People's quality of life is most adversely affected by the severity of their physical impairment.

6. T F Substance abuse is a greater problem for people with disabilities than for the general population.

7. T F Before the Nazis began executing Jews, they instituted a program of sterilization and euthanasia of the physically disabled.

8. T F Most people with disabilities don't experience changes in relationships with others because of their conditions.

9. T F People with disabilities socialize with close friends, relatives, or neighbors just as much as their able-bodied peers do.

10. T F Depression is a predictable and inevitable secondary condition of disability.

Scoring guide: **1.** F; **2.** F; **3.** F; **4.** F; **5.** F; **6.** T; **7.** T; **8.** F; **9.** F; **10.** F.

INTRODUCTION

According to most recent government estimates and the U.S. Bureau of the Census, over 50 million Americans possess some type of disability. These disabilities consist of various physical impairments in mobility, dexterity, sight, hearing, and sensation, or the presence of adverse conditions or functions, such as chronic pain, spasms, and contractures. The Americans with Disabilities Act (ADA) defines disability as a physical or mental impairment that substantially limits one or more major life activities, a record of such impairment, or being regarded as having such an impairment. Major life activities consist of caring for oneself, performing manual tasks, walking, seeing, hearing, speaking, breathing, and working. These activities manifest for children as attending school or engaging in play, and for nonelderly adults as working, managing a home, and taking care of oneself or others.

The majority of people with disabilities are of working age. Individuals experiencing work limitation account for 11.9% of the population between the ages of eighteen and sixty-nine. More than half of that group reports a total inability to work (Kaye, 1997). The U.S. census figures (U.S. Bureau of the Census, 2001) show that more than 33.2 million people older than fifteen report some limitation of physical function. These limitations take the form of difficulty seeing words or letters, hearing impairments, difficulty lifting or carrying a ten-pound object, trouble walking a quarter mile or climbing stairs without resting, or requirement of an ambulatory aid, such as a wheelchair, cane, crutches, or walker. Activities of daily living (ADL), such as bathing, dressing, cooking, and driving, provide narrower definitions of disability and address limitations of self-care and home-management activities. Approximately 9.5 million Americans over the age of fifteen require personal assistance in one or more self-care or home management activities. These figures do not include an estimated 2.1 million Americans with disabilities residing in long-term care facilities, prisons, college dormitories, or mental hospitals (Kaye, 1997).

More than 17% of individuals who are limited in at least one life activity live below the poverty line, compared to 11.2% of their able-bodied counterparts. Children with disabilities are nearly twice as likely to live in poverty as are elderly people with disabilities. Among working-age Americans, the income for those unable to work because of chronic disease or impairment is less than half the national average (Kaye, 1997).

Points to Remember

- People with disabilities are the largest minority group in the country.
- Nearly one-third of all families (29.2%) include a member with a disability. Disability eventually affects most families.
- Over two-thirds of people with disabilities are under age sixty-five.
- The majority of people with disabilities under the age of sixty-five report their health to be good to excellent. Many disabilities *do not* require constant medical monitoring.

CASE EXAMPLES

Dennis

Dennis is a twenty-five-year-old White man with quadriplegia, the result of an automobile accident that occurred two weeks after graduating from high school and three weeks before he was scheduled to join the navy. Following four months of rehabilitation at a nearby facility, Dennis returned to his semirural hometown to live with his parents and be cared for and supported by them. He rarely goes out to socialize in this town, as little is accessible to him. He's never heard from the others who were involved in the accident with him, none of whom was injured. He often wonders what he did to deserve his condition.

Dennis has only moderate use of his hands and arms. He has insufficient strength to independently transfer in and out of his wheelchair or the dexterity to button his shirts or tie his shoes. He requires assistance getting in and out of bed, showering, and managing his bowel and bladder care, of which he lacks voluntary control. Once he is in his chair, he is quite independent and self-sufficient. He continues to perform some physical therapy and has been involved in several clinical drug trials for possible cures. His van is equipped with a wheelchair lift and hand controls, making him fully mobile on the road.

Dennis is about to graduate from a local four-year college with a degree in information technology. After commuting fifty miles a day to college, he now would like to live in the city but has experienced difficulty making and maintaining friends there. Though he wants to work, he is concerned about how he will pay for the necessary attendant care and medical supplies in addition to all the usual expenses of living independently, especially if he takes a job with little or no health care coverage.

Nancy

Nancy is a fifty-eight-year-old single woman. A moderate stroke left her with mild hemiplegia (paralysis affecting one side of the body), some memory loss, and some difficulty speaking. Due to the length of her acute care and extensive outpatient physical therapy, she lost her job as an educational consultant and writer.

Presently, Nancy is involved in a wrongful termination lawsuit with her former employer. Because of growing medical bills she contemplates applying for Social Security Disability Insurance, though she describes herself as "not really disabled" because she's not in a wheelchair. She hates asking for help, feeling that any physical problems are hers alone; as a result, she continues to seek further rehabilitation. She believes she should pay her own way through employment; however, although highly qualified and experienced in her field, she has not found work.

Nancy has lived alone for over ten years and rarely sees either of her adult sons, both of whom live out of town. She has lost considerable weight since the stroke, rarely sleeps more than five hours a night, and complains of trouble concentrating. She does not get out very much, in part because she is concerned about her driving, but also due to her self-consciousness about her appearance and speech. She finds the stares from others embarrassing and feels that the help she needs is an imposition on others. Her unemployment and decreased social activity have caused her considerable isolation and loneliness.

A HISTORICAL OVERVIEW

People with disabilities have a long history of being shunned, segregated, discriminated against, publicly ridiculed, imprisoned, and involuntarily sterilized. Literature ranging from the Bible and Shakespeare to contemporary fiction characterizes people with disabilities as objects to be feared and shunned or as punished for some serious moral transgression. Disability itself has often been used as a metaphor for some shortcoming, deficit, or spiritual malaise ("The Invalids," 2001). Contemporary arts such as motion pictures perpetuate the images and stereotypes in films such as *Forest Gump, Scent of a Woman,* and *Born on the Fourth of July* (Norden, 1994). Furthermore, the practice of making people with disabilities the subject of medical experiment or extermination neither began nor ended in Nazi Germany (Wolfe, 1993).

Exclusion and pity for people with disabilities are recurring themes throughout history. Not until the post–World War II era and the return of a great many disabled veterans did this country begin to respond to need for equality, inclusion, and opportunity. Though the *Brown v. Board of*

Education decision of 1954 began to bring an end to "separate but equal" for most forms of segregation, another twenty-six years would pass before such segregation would be outlawed for people with disabilities.

Medical advances and legislative reform have served to extend and enhance the lives of people with disabilities in the second half of the twentieth century. Major legislative advances include the Vocational Rehabilitation Act Amendments of 1943, the Architectural Barriers Act of 1968, the Rehabilitation Act of 1973, and the Americans with Disabilities Act (ADA) of 1990. The Vocational Rehabilitation Act increased services and funding, expanded the basic definition of rehabilitation, and increased the number of people served. The Architectural Barriers Act began eliminating physical obstacles to accessibility, and the Rehabilitation Act of 1973 first addressed civil rights for people with disabilities. As the forerunner of the ADA, it outlawed employment discrimination against people with disabilities and provided for equal access to programs, services, and education. Despite its promise, it applied only to agencies receiving federal funds. In addition, enforcement was unenthusiastic and spotty (Olkin, 1999).

The ADA (1990) expanded the Rehabilitation Act of 1973 and placed nearly all public and private facilities, institutions, and employers under its jurisdiction. Its intent being full integration of people with disabilities into the mainstream, the five titles of the ADA address most facets of everyday life. Unfortunately, the ADA's promise remains unfulfilled due to numerous loopholes, lackadaisical enforcement, judicial review, the cry of "unfunded mandate," and resentment and backlash over what is perceived as special treatment (Shapiro, 1993; Russell, 1998).

CURRENT ISSUES

Thinking of disability as a social construct—that is, viewing it in terms of how society perceives it—provides valuable insight for clients and counselors alike. The three primary models of disability—the moral model, the medical model, and the minority model—furnish perspectives on just what problems disability presents and causes (Olkin, 1999).

The *moral model* views disability as the result of some moral lapse or defect, or as punishment for past sins. Phrases such as "There but for the grace of God . . ." and "God gives only as much as we can handle" suggest "divine retribution for sinful deeds, . . . preparation for the hereafter, as warning to one who strays from the path of the devout, or as a test of a person's faith" (Florian, 1982, p. 292). Such thinking suggests that the person with the disability is somehow responsible for his condition and should use it as an opportunity to learn a valuable lesson. Those who feel shame or embarrassment about their disability, who try to hide or minimize it, who rarely request help because they consider the disability as their problem, or who view their disability as a punishment adhere to the moral model. This was the case with Donald, who wondered what he had done to deserve the punishment of his quadriplegia.

The *medical model*, most common in this country, views disability as a biological breakdown, something to be fixed (Olkin, 1999). People become conditions to be treated and, as such, bear the responsibility of receiving treatment to the full capacity of medical science. The medical model views the individual as an empty vessel to be filled with procedures, medications, treatments, information, and services provided by skilled professionals, with the desired outcome being that the individual learns to adjust to both the condition and the environment. Those who think they should be able to figure out how to do things without assistance, who dress in ways to conceal their disability or emphasize positive features, or who believe that research should focus on prevention and cure fall into the medical model. While far less judgmental than the moral model, the medical model also implies that whatever problems exist lie solely within the individual and not within the culture. This was the case with Nancy, who fruitlessly pursued medical and physical therapy as antidotes for interpersonal and employment difficulties.

Rather than focusing on the individual, the *minority model* focuses on the culture and environment. This model views people with disabilities as a minority group with a long history of discrimination and exclusion. Functioning effectively with disability becomes a process of looking outward and formulating methods of dealing with a culture rife with negative attitudes and stereotypes and an environment that poses numerous physical barriers. Issues involve physical and attitudinal accessibility, and equal protection under laws that lack aggressive enforcement. The minority model essentially shifts the focus from personal pathology to social oppression (Olkin, 1999). Indications of minority-model thinking include identifying as part of a minority based upon disability; viewing disability-related legislation as civil rights legislation; affirming quality of life through changing policies, procedures, funding, and laws; and believing that people with disabilities thrive in an environment of full integration.

There is no right model, and most people hold beliefs in at least two of them. Presenting and working with the models help clients identify where they feel most comfortable and what works for them in managing their disabilities. Most clients can benefit from examining their attitudes and beliefs regarding their disabilities for internal negative messages, poor self-image, low self-esteem, and self-hatred. The notion of "acceptance" of disability, however, is a misnomer, as adjustment is an endless process (Olkin, 1999).

One additional view, provided by the World Health Organization (WHO), defines three aspects of disablement as impairment, disability, and handicap. Impairment identifies actual physical consequence at an organ level (paralysis, hearing loss, etc.); disability identifies an individual's ability to perform normal activities of daily living (bathing, dressing, eating, driving, etc.); and handicap defines how various social conditions (attitudes, physical environment, etc.) limit or prevent the fulfillment of normal and appropriate roles as a member of society. Impairment and disability both reside within the individual, while handicap is a social construct and phenomenon (World Health Organization, 1980). Studies concerning the negative effects of disablement on quality of life have shown that the greatest impediments to subjective well-being are commonly related to aspects of handicap; that is, facing various negative social factors—prejudice, inaccessibility, unemployment, attitudinal obstacles, and other disadvantages that affect social roles. In general, subjective well-being appears to have little, if any, relation to paralytic impairment and rather inconclusive relation to disability or one's ability to perform activities of daily living (Fuhrer, 1996). This was evident in the cases of both Donald and Nancy.

Because quality of life encompasses a constellation of domains, including emotional, social, intellectual, spiritual, economic, and physical, clients may need help incorporating these areas into their lives. Clients may also need assistance with managing disability, which does not mean denying or feeling positive about it, but rather separating one's total identity from it so it is not the defining issue of one's life. In addition, clients may need to learn various methods of *containing* their disability by becoming more comfortable with it, being able to compartmentalize it, and gaining the skills necessary to put others at ease with it so it does not dominate all interactions with others.

Much like any other multicultural group, people with disabilities have a multitude of predictable and associated problems. A common misconception is that the disability is the primary and defining issue and presenting problem. Many other issues often accompany the disability and present far greater obstacles to life satisfaction.

Poverty and Unemployment

The unemployment rate (72.2%) and poverty level (30%) for people with disabilities have remained remarkably stable over the past fifteen to twenty years. Neither decreased significantly following passage of the ADA (Kaye, 1997). People with disabilities earn an average of about one-third less than nondisabled individuals working a similar number of hours. People with disabilities continue to confront discrimination and misconceptions on the part of employers, who may fear that disabled employees will miss more work, perform poorly, or require excessive and costly job accommodations (Russell, 1998).

As presently structured, many social service programs for the disabled terminate health insurance or attendant care if recipients are employed. Vital services may not be covered by employer insurance programs because of preexisting condition clauses. People with disabilities often must remain unemployed in order to maintain health coverage for such necessities as assistive technology equipment, personal attendant services, and ongoing prescription medications. Furthermore, employment opportunities are closely connected to educational attainment. People with disabilities are less likely to complete high school, attend college, or pursue graduate study (Kaye, 1997). Many lack the education necessary to successfully compete in the job market. Lower education often means manual labor positions unsuitable for disabled job seekers.

The legal definition of *disability,* commonly defined as the inability to work, often serves to lock people into a cycle of dependency in which they lower or even abandon their employment aspirations. There is no middle ground for many beneficiaries of government disability programs; if earnings exceed a certain amount ($780 per month in 2002) *all* benefits cease, and the individual essentially declares him or herself able-bodied, according to Social Security Administration guidelines. The perception that people with disabilities require assistance lowers expectations for them and sends the message that they are not capable, often resulting in prolonged dependency. Many are unaware of various government programs to help them with career planning, job retraining, or vocational rehabilitation. Though government-funded vocational rehabilitation averages a 50% success rate for full-time, competitive job placement, only 10% of new Social Security Disability Insurance (SSDI) or Supplemental Security Insurance (SSI) beneficiaries are offered these services (Kaye, 1997).

Societal Attitudes and Expectations

People with disabilities have a history of stigma and marginalization, often serving as examples and reminders of the delicacy of life and the scope of human vulnerability. People with disabilities often acquire reduced status representing pity, failure, frailty, and emasculation; a counterpoint to normality; a figure whose very humanity is questionable (Gliedman & Roth, 1979). Disability raises fear in others that impairment could happen to them and guilt among friends and family that it hasn't (Murphy, 1987). The stigma and rejection that often accompany disability can create a sense of shame over who one is, as well as a sense of responsibility and guilt for the rejection itself (Olkin, 1999).

This marginalization and stigma also create other challenges, most notably pity and loss of privacy. People with disabilities share several common experiences. Total strangers ask them intimate questions concerning their condition ("What happened to you?"). They speak to them as though their physical condition constitutes an intellectual deficit. The disabled experience unwarranted touching of their bodies, equipment, or guide animals, and often receive unrequested and unneeded assistance.

Even compliments such as "You're such an inspiration" or "I don't think I could ever live like that" essentially distance and objectify the individual (Shapiro, 2001) and result in a life at once highly visible and lived on the sidelines, a life in which it is nearly impossible to be treated as an ordinary person (Mairs, 1997).

Though the common belief may be that life with a disability is quite difficult, the expectation of the general public and many health professionals is that any suffering be done in silence. This speaks to several "requirements" or expectations for the disabled, among them the assumption of grief and mourning, the prohibition and pathologizing of anger, and the requirements of cheerfulness and positive attitude (Olkin, 1999). Many mental health professionals suggest that disability is a loss that must be mourned during a period of depression, after which individuals will hopefully emerge "adjusted," in the fashion of the Kübler-Ross model. Despite evidence that many experience negligible depression following onset of disability (Wright, 1983; Eliot & Umlauf, 1991), the absence of mourning, displays of anger, and less than constant cheerfulness are often interpreted as being stuck in an adjustment stage or lacking in social skills, thus implying pathology.

Isolation

Poverty, chronic unemployment, negative societal attitudes, and rigid expectations result in substantial social isolation for individuals with disabilities, most notably in close friendships and intimate relationships (Asch, 1984; Schneider & Anderson, 1980; Tringo, 1970; Wright, 1983). As relationships with disabled individuals grow more intimate, the comfort level of the nondisabled tends to decrease. A Harris Poll indicated that those who "personally knew" someone with a disability were more comfortable with them as acquaintances than as close friends. Most indicated that they would not marry a person with a disability (Olkin & Howson, 1994; DeLoach, 1994). People with disabilities have a lower marriage rate, a higher divorce rate, and in general are single longer and in greater numbers. Friends often fade away following the onset of disability, out of discomfort, awkwardness, or fear. The resulting isolation is similar to that experienced by those recently divorced or diagnosed with serious or terminal illnesses—akin to having a contagious disease. After the onset of their disabilities, both Dennis and Nancy experienced difficulty with relationships. Dennis found it difficult to make friends at college; Nancy lost touch with her closest relatives, her sons.

Lack of transportation also results in isolation. Poverty, insufficient rehabilitation, and lack of social skills result in poor information about public transportation and the assertiveness necessary to use it (especially for the sight or hearing impaired). Wheelchair users must rely on other people and spotty and unreliable lift-assisted public transportation, or spend up to $50,000 for a modified van. Dealing with disability can be exhausting and time consuming, with unpredictable and disabling pain a constant companion and isolating feature of many conditions. People with disabilities often strive to "overcome" pain and fatigue much the same way they strive to overcome other aspects of their disability, the result being more pain, more fatigue, and even more isolation.

Decreased Sense of Community and Lack of Role Models

People with disabilities frequently miss the validation of shared experience and a sense of community and culture with their peers. Because of the stigma attached to disability and the fact that most people undergo rehabilitation without exposure and contact with others with disabilities, the resultant isolation supports internalized negative cultural messages regarding disability. In addition, few role models exist for people with disabilities, either in the popular electronic or print media, or in the written, visual, or performing arts, which exist to reflect and help explain the human condition. Such absence fosters further misunderstanding and misrepresentation and denies individuals a mirror of what is possible for them. If people with disabilities see only pity, loss, anger, and limitation, they may easily mistake that for truth and reality, lending credibility to lowered expectations and the impossibility of a normal life.

Anger and Depression

Though anger and depression often accompany disability, neither is inevitable. Anger is common shortly after onset of disability, often in relationship to loss of control—of body function, finances, power, position, images, and friends. People commonly ask the question "Why me?" As many as 30% of people with disabilities experience depression (Turner & McLean, 1989) as either a primary or secondary condition. Depression can complicate recovery or rehabilitation, but attributing negative mood solely to the disability can cloud a diagnosis. Likewise, secondary symptoms of disability, such as pain, sleep difficulties, appetite change, or fatigue can complicate treatment.

Higher Rates of Substance Abuse

People with disabilities experience a significantly higher rate of substance abuse than the population at large, due to the stresses of dealing with disability; an enabling environment of family and friends unwilling to confront inappropriate use; much higher use of prescribed drugs to manage the condition; higher levels of unemployment, isolation, low self-esteem; higher rates of chronic pain; and higher levels of predisability abuse. Rehabilitation programs have traditionally failed to identify substance abuse or offer treatment. In addition, and reflective of society in general, many substance-abuse treatment programs are either physically or attitudinally inaccessible. Clients may be unable, literally, to get in the door; others may require daily assistance not offered by the facility. Most programs demand that clients be totally substance free, an impossibility for many potential clients who need prescription drugs to manage their conditions (Helwig & Holicky, 1994).

Using Medical and Social Service Delivery Systems

While most disabilities are conditions, as opposed to illnesses, they are rarely static and normally require at least some regular monitoring. Being medical anomalies, people with disabilities often fall outside the medical mainstream. Few physicians choose to enter the field of rehabilitation medicine, and many others choose not to treat people with disabilities (Putnam et al., in press).

People with disabilities become experts in identifying the many subtle symptoms that manifest as aches, pains, and levels of spasticity—as well as the appropriate interventions for them. Professionals often discount this expertise, leaving symptoms ignored and problems untreated. HMOs and insurance carriers deal primarily with treatable and curable medical conditions rather than various disabling conditions, resulting in frequent denials of necessary treatment or equipment. High rates of poverty and dependence on government health care programs further constrict choice of physicians.

Economic conditions also drive people into various other government support programs, such as SSDI and SSI (welfare), adding the stigma of dependence in a country priding itself on self-reliance. As evident in Nancy's case, interacting with these bureaucracies can be daunting and confusing. Necessary medical treatment or poverty-level benefits are subject to denial or revocation, often through no fault of the client.

SUGGESTIONS FOR ENHANCING COUNSELOR EFFECTIVENESS

In order to work effectively, clinicians should assess the *meaning* of disability for both their clients and themselves by examining feelings regarding dependency, body image, and general physical function. One way to confront one's deep-seated feelings and beliefs is through close and prolonged contact with individuals with disabilities, especially with disabled peers. Doing so allows the clinician to become more accustomed to behaviors such as altered speech, drooling, grimacing, twitches, spasms, or constant movement. Therapists must be open to accomplishing tasks in a slower, more deliberate fashion as well as the possibility that disability is much more of an issue for them than it is for the client. Following are some additional suggestions and questions for consideration.

The process of a self-examination and personal inventory should include a ruthlessly honest assessment of feelings and beliefs, including: Am I frightened by or uncomfortable in the presence of a person with a disability? What is the first emotion that comes to mind when I see a person with a disability in a public place? How many people with disabilities do I know? How many of them do I consider to be good friends or peers? What personal experience do I have with disability over my lifetime? What portrayals of disability in the arts (literature, film, television, theater) can I recall? What was the message of those portrayals? (See the Experiential Activities at the end of this chapter for additional assessment questions.)

Holding professional credentials provides no exemption from countertransference and projection. Just as men can only imagine the process of giving birth, imagining what it is like to be paralyzed or sight impaired or to live with chronic pain is not the same as living with these conditions. Mental health professionals should familiarize themselves with the social construct of the minority model. As described earlier in this chapter, disability has been viewed as either a personal shortcoming or weakness (moral model) or as strictly a medical condition (medical model). These views pathologize the client and place any dysfunction within her or him. Employing the minority model presents many issues in the context of civil rights and social inequities, rather than moral or medical problems. Using the minority model does not place the client in the role of victim, but rather relieves her or him of responsibility for social inequity and inequality. Doing so provides a context for disability and reduces the assumption that the disability per se always creates problems and tensions.

Although physical disability can profoundly affect one's life, clinicians should not assume that it is the defining aspect of an individual or that all problems she or he faces stem from it. Better to honor the client's assessment of the presenting problem and proceed from there than to assume that the disability is the presenting problem. Counselors also do clients a disservice by allowing them to assign responsibility for all ills to the disability. The challenge for both therapist and client is to place disability in context and perspective without trivializing its potentially profound effects.

Clinicians should allow the client to be an expert and the teacher concerning disability. Able-bodied therapists, regardless of their exposure to and familiarity with disability, would do well to learn as much as possible regarding both specific conditions and general issues related to disabilities by reading disability literature in the form of texts, memoirs, anthologies, or periodicals; visiting and acquainting themselves with local independent living centers and advocacy groups; attending disability-related events and activities; and seeking information from rehabilitation specialists.

Clinicians should observe a code of etiquette, rather than political correctness, when interacting with people who are disabled. As in any cross-cultural communication and interaction, polite and civil behavior is appropriate.

Clinicians should consider their reactions the first "test" of their credibility as professionals. Avoid staring or otherwise being consumed or distracted by various movements or pieces of equipment connected with disability. Like any other client, one with a disability should feel comfortable, rather than having to explain aspects of his disability that have little or no bearing on his treatment.

View assistive devices (wheelchairs, crutches, voice computers, etc.) as extensions of the person. Such devices are neither conversation pieces nor toys to be touched, handled, or closely examined; doing so is quite similar to touching the person.

Honor the client's independence and look to her for both guidance and requests regarding assistance. Be mindful of the client's individual space. Do not push a wheelchair or take an arm without request or suggestion. Take no action that implies that assistance is necessary or required. The general layout of your office and its accessibility is a reflection of your sensitivity and disability awareness. Barrier-free office design serves to foster better understanding, familiarity, and openness to disability issues.

Disability can change significantly the meaning of body language and other nonverbal cues. For example, when individuals in wheelchairs sit with their arms crossed, they often do so to maintain balance or to deal with fatigue or pain rather than to close themselves off. Experience is the best teacher in familiarizing oneself with the meaning of various movements and general body language.

The meanings of such idioms such as "Do you see what I mean?" or "Take a walk" remain the same for individuals who are visually or mobility impaired; there is no need to be overly concerned about word choices. Exercise vigilance and awareness, however, regarding the use of loaded terms such as *crippled, wheelchair-bound,* or *invalid,* which often reflect negative feelings and beliefs. If unsure, admit your inexperience and request guidance from the client or employees at an independent living center.

Clients pay good money for sessions and expect to be understood. The speech of a client with cerebral palsy may be difficult to understand; other clients may use specialized medical terms in the course of a session.

Rather than fake understanding, ask the client to repeat or clarify the meaning or significance of words or terms.

Separate personal curiosity from therapeutic relevance. Before asking how a client acquired a disability, how long they've dealt with it, or just what the manifestations of the disability are, clinicians should examine the motivation for asking such questions and their pertinence to treatment issues. Does a clinician need to know how a person who has been dealing with quadriplegia for twelve years acquired the condition? Is there therapeutic value in knowing how a disability was acquired? Conversely, counselors should not totally discount the possible contributions of disability to the presenting problem, just as they must follow hunches and inquire about alcohol use or physical abuse.

Refrain from sharing with the client how many relatives, friends, acquaintances, or clients with disabilities you have unless asked about it directly. Doing so is usually intended to enhance the comfort level and well-being of the speaker, in the same way that one might say, "Some of my best friends are Jews [or Blacks, gay, ex-convicts]."

Practice flexibility with regard to treatment goals, interventions, and issues of time and of session length and frequency. Viewing the client as bicultural and part of a minority group helps change the viewpoint of both client and clinician and assists the clinician in remaining open and flexible to new ways of understanding disability and its cultural implications. Chronic tardiness, last-minute cancelations, or seemingly rigid appointment requirements often reflect the hassles of managing disability rather than resistance, ambivalence, or control and offer treatment opportunities in addressing how to manage and accommodate such issues. Other opportunities exist for the client to learn more about the disability, connect with peers, or read about how others have dealt with similar challenges.

CONCLUDING REMARKS

According to the WHO (1980), impairment is a person's actual physical dysfunction at an organ level, whereas disability is an individual's ability to perform normal activities of daily living, and handicap defines how social conditions limit the fulfillment of ordinary societal roles. Impairment and disability both reside within the individual, while handicap is a social construct and phenomenon. Whatever the distinction, persons with disabilities as a group have a long history of persecution and discrimination, as evidenced by the moral and medical models for understanding disability. The minority model, on the other hand, considers social and environmental explanations for the economic, interpersonal, medical, and physical concerns of this population. Finally, it is incumbent upon counselors to examine their own attitudes and beliefs about disability and to ask their clients for assistance before presuming to counsel members of the population of persons with physical disabilities.

EXPERIENTIAL ACTIVITIES

Individual Activities

1. Answer the following questions thoughtfully and honestly.
   - What does disability mean to me? What do I think of when I hear that word? What images and feelings come to mind?
   - Am I frightened by or uncomfortable in the presence of a person with a disability?
   - What is the first emotion that comes to mind when I see a person with a disability in a public place?
   - How many people with disabilities do I know? How many of them do I consider to be good friends or peers?
   - What personal experience do I have with disability over my lifetime?
   - When was the last time I had contact with any person with a disability?
2. What past experience do I have with disability? (List personal and family history with physical disability.)
3. When you have seen people with disabilities:
   - What did you think?
   - What were you taught?
   - How were you expected to act?
   - How did you see others react?
   - What expectations did you have of them? Of yourself in relation to them?

4. Recall the first three nonrelatives with physical disabilities with whom you interacted. List your impressions and reactions, then and now. (These could be friends, associates, schoolmates, classmates.) Do you presently have any regular contact/interaction with a person with a disability? Is this person a relative stranger, a neighbor, work associate, classmate, teacher, mentor, friend?

Group Activities

1. Recall the last three times you came across references to disability in the arts (literature, television, music, film, theater, etc.). Was the person with a disability treated with scorn, fear, or pity, or with sympathy and sensitivity? Was the disability treated as something to be feared? Elaborate.
2. What do the following terms bring to mind? *Cripple, invalid, blind, paralyzed, AIDS, deaf, chronic pain.* What do the following names bring to mind? *Helen Keller, Franklin Roosevelt, Christopher Reeve, Stephen Hawking.*
3. Spend some time at a local independent living center to gain some familiarity with issues, conditions, behaviors, and mannerisms of people with disabilities. Take notes and report back on the following:
   - Types of problems (finances, insurance, housing, transportation) for which people sought help.
   - Types of disabilities for which people sought help.
   - Conditions, behaviors, or mannerisms that caused you discomfort.
   - Overall impression of the atmosphere and attitude within the center. Were the people angry, happy, energized, depressed? What was the general mood?
4. From the information provided about Dennis, which model(s) of disability does he fit? Use examples from the case example to support your answer. Identify and categorize Dennis's concerns using the WHO model of disablement—that is, impairment, disability, handicap. Use the same procedure to assess Nancy's case.

REFERENCES

Asch, A. (1984). The experience of disability: A challenge for psychology. *American Psychologist, 39,* 529–536.

DeLoach, C.P. (1994). Attitudes toward disability: Impact on sexual development and forging of intimate relationships. *Journal of Applied Rehabilitation Counseling, 25,* 18–25.

Eliot, T.R., & Umlauf, R.L. (1991). Measurement of personality and psychopathology following acquired physical disability. In L.A. Cushman & M. Scherer (Eds.), *Psychological assessment in medical rehabilitation.* Hyattsville, MD: American Psychological Association.

Florian, V. (1982). Cross-cultural differences in attitudes towards disabled persons: A study of Jewish and Arab youth in Israel. *International Journal of Intercultural Relations, 6,* 291–299.

Fuhrer, M. (1996). The subjective well-being of people with spinal cord injury: Relationships to impairment, disability, and handicap. *Topics in Spinal Cord Rehabilitation, 1* (4), 56–71.

Gliedman, J., & Roth, W. (1979). *The unexpected minority: Handicapped children in America.* New York: Harcourt Brace Jovanovich.

Helwig, A.A., & Holicky, R. (1994). Substance abuse in persons with disabilities: Treatment considerations. *Journal of Counseling and Development, 72* (January–February), 227–233.

The invalids. (2001, November 3). *Denver Post,* p. 4F.

Kaye, H.S. (1997). *Disability watch.* Volcano, CA: Volcano Press.

Mairs, N. (1997). *Waist high in the world: A life among the non-disabled.* New York: Beacon Press.

Murphy, R. (1987). *The body silent.* New York: Norton.

Norden, M. (1994). *The cinema of isolation: A history of physical disability in the movies.* New Brunswick, NJ: Rutgers University Press.

Olkin, R. (1999). *What psychotherapists should know about disability.* New York: Guilford.

Olkin, R., & Howlson, L. (1994). Attitudes toward and images of physical disability. *Journal of Social Behavior and Personality, 9,* 81–96.

Putnam, M., Geenen, S., Powers, L., Saxton, M., & Finney, S. (In press). Health warriors: People with disabilities discuss definitions of, and facilitators and barriers to, being healthy and well. *Journal of Rehabilitation.*

Russell, M. (1998). *Beyond ramps: Disability at the end of the social contract.* Monroe, ME: Common Courage Press.

Schneider, C., & Anderson, W. (1980). Attitudes toward the stigmatized: Some insights from recent research. *Rehabilitation Counseling Bulletin, 23,* 299–313.

Shapiro, J. (1993). *No pity.* New York: Time Books.

Shapiro, J. (2001). Eyes wide shut: Teaching medical students about people with disabilities. *Kaleidoscope, 42,* 36–42.

Tringo, J.L. (1970). The hierarchy of preference toward disability groups. *Journal of Special Education, 4,* 295–305.

Turner, R.J., & McClean, P.D. (1989). Physical disability and distress. *Rehabilitation Psychology, 34,* 225–242.

U.S. Bureau of the Census. (2001). *11th anniversary of Americans with Disabilities Act.* Washington, DC: U.S. Government Printing Office.

Wolfe, K. (1993). Springtime for Hitler. In B. Shaw (Ed.), *The ragged edge: The disability experience.* Louisville, KY: Avocado Press.

World Health Organization. (1980). *International classification of impairments, disabilities, and handicaps.* Geneva: World Health Organization.

Wright, B.A. (1983). *Physical disability: A psychological approach* (2nd Ed.) New York: Harper and Row.

CHAPTER 12

Counseling Sexual-Minority Clients

Donnie G. Conner

Donnie G. Conner, Ed.D., is a private practice licensed professional counselor in Richmond, Virginia, who specializes in providing mental health services to gay, lesbian, bisexual, and transgender clients. He also serves as an adjunct faculty member to the Medical College of Virginia's Graduate Program in Health Administration. Dr. Conner has published research on chemical dependent treatment in the *Journal for Specialists in Group Work,* wrote the chapter on AIDS and the family for the *National Institute on Drug Abuse's Pilot Training Manual,* and edited a special edition on AIDS for the *Virginia Counselors Journal.* He collaborated with Dr. Elisabeth Kübler Ross on a national counselor training project on HIV for the American Mental Health Counselors Association. For his extensive work with AIDS clients, Dr. Conner has been recognized with awards from the American Counseling Association, Virginia Commonwealth University, and the American Mental Health Counselors Association.

AWARENESS INDEX

Please test your knowledge by marking the following statements true or false before proceeding to the text in this chapter. Compute your score from the scoring guide at the end of the Awareness Index.

1. T F Scientists believe that sexual orientation is shaped during adolescence.

2. T F Research evidence indicates that reparative therapy is effective in changing sexual orientation.

3. T F Children are at greater risk to be molested by lesbian/gay people.

4. T F Violent crimes against gay Americans are increasing.

5. T F Gay/lesbian youth are at greater risk for suicide attempts.

6. T F Despite social progress, homosexuality remains on the American Psychiatric Association's list of mental disorders.

7. T F New HIV infection rates among gay and bisexual men continue to be a public health concern.

8. T F Bisexuality is more common in women than in men.

9. T F Gallup poll data reveal that currently 50% of the American public believe that homosexuality is the result of genetic causes.

10. T F Substance abuse occurs with greater frequency in the gay/lesbian population.

11. T F Marriage between persons of the same gender is prohibited in all fifty states.

12. T F Children who grow up with same-gender parents are more likely to be gay themselves.

Scoring guide: **1.** F; **2.** F; **3.** F; **4.** T; **5.** T; **6.** F; **7.** T; **8.** T; **9.** T; **10.** T; **11.** T; **12.** F.

INTRODUCTION

In the United States, people who identify as gay, lesbian, bisexual, or transgender face a tremendous challenge developing into healthy, fulfilled individuals. While all people in our complex culture struggle to achieve mental, emotional, physical, spiritual, and social balance, this journey is especially daunting for a population historically oppressed and maligned. This chapter identifies special issues that confront persons whose primary sexual and affectional orientation is not heterosexual. Suggestions to mental health professionals regarding client assessment and appropriate interventions with sexual minority persons are offered.

CASE EXAMPLE

Isaac, age 33, indicated in his initial telephone contact that he called our particular practice because he understood that we specialized in providing mental health services to the gay and lesbian community. When this information was confirmed, he expressed relief and scheduled an appointment. In the first interview Isaac appeared extremely depressed and moderately anxious. He openly expressed his confusion, guilt, and sadness. Isaac described his ten years of marriage and his two well-adjusted children. He explained his struggle with obesity and compulsive overeating since the beginning of the marriage. During the past year, Isaac reduced his weight by more than one hundred pounds and was running as a regular form of exercise. Although he felt good about this physical change, Isaac explained that the factor motivating the weight loss was the cause of distress. In his work as a church musician he had met Jeffrey, a member of Isaac's congregation who was also married, had a passion for music, and was an accomplished singer. Jeffrey began to take private lessons with Isaac and over time a friendship developed. Isaac stated that at the beginning of this relationship he was aware of some vague attraction to Jeffrey but felt "safe," as Jeff was married and "straight." As their professional and personal relationship deepened, Isaac became aware of intensifying sexual and romantic feelings toward Jeffrey. Isaac kept these feelings to himself, since he believed that such emotions were immoral. About three months prior to the first counseling appointment, Jeffrey revealed to Isaac that he shared feelings of attraction, and a sexual and romantic involvement between the two men ensued. During the initial session, Isaac tearfully explained that he felt "in love" for the first time in his life but was very frightened and conflicted, as he did not want to hurt his wife or children, for whom he expressed deep caring and commitment. The goals of the first session were to establish a safe context for Isaac to externalize his repressed emotions and to commit to the counseling process.

During the course of treatment with Isaac, I employed a "whole person" model that addressed his mental, emotional, social, spiritual, and physical needs. The early phases of the counseling process focused on Isaac's relationship with himself. He reported a long history of negative self-image beginning early in his childhood when he felt "different" from his older brothers regarding interests and behavior. These negative feelings were exacerbated as Isaac became aware of having sexual feelings for other boys during his early adolescence. He did not act upon these feelings, as he felt they were wrong. Isaac shared also that he had struggled all his life to be "normal." During this part of the counseling, I used cognitive techniques to confront Isaac's negative self-image and internalized homophobia. In the physical area, Isaac met with a personal trainer, attended Overeater's Anonymous, and consulted a psychiatrist, who prescribed an antidepressant. To address his religious/spiritual concerns, Isaac joined a support group for lesbian and gay Catholics and began a daily process of meditation and reflection. In the social area, Isaac participated in a support group for gay fathers, where he met other gay men who understood and empathized with his personal struggle. Finally, he was able to identify, confront, and relieve long held feelings of shame and to release feelings of anger and sadness associated with the many losses and hurts he had experienced in his life.

Isaac responded positively to counseling. As a result of his personal work, he was able to come out to his wife and children. The couple eventually divorced and, although painful for all family members, they eventually reestablished positive relationships. Isaac continued to actively parent his children. His depression was lessened, medication was no longer needed, and his weight stabilized. Isaac now has a positive identification as a gay man and is out to his family of origin, at his place of employment, and in his faith community. He established a large social network of support and a smaller circle of intimate friends. Isaac discontinued the relationship with Jeffrey, as Jeffrey wanted to keep his relationship with Isaac secret and continue in his marriage. At the conclusion of therapy, Isaac was dating and expressed interest in developing a committed relationship with another man. Isaac's case illustrates how participation in the counseling process with an affirming, supportive mental health professional can help sexual-minority clients achieve fulfilling and purposeful lives despite the external challenges of a nonunderstanding cultural context.

A HISTORICAL OVERVIEW

Homosexuality is referred to as "the love that dare not speak its name" (Kaiser, 1997) and "the love that will not shut up." This contradiction reflects both our culture's ambivalence toward lesbian and gay people and the reality that homosexuality is an intensely polarizing issue that continues to challenge professionals in law, religion, politics, medicine, and mental health. Historically in our country, sexual-minority people have been oppressed by religious organizations that labeled them "immoral," by civil authorities who identified them as "criminals," and by the medical establishment that diagnosed them as "sick." There are professionals who would argue the validity of including this chapter in this book. Their position is based upon a belief that, unlike other "legitimate" minorities, gay and lesbian people choose their lifestyle and therefore are not truly oppressed. This widely held belief is challenged by the American Psychological Association's research that indicates that homosexual orientation begins very early in life, possibly before birth (Presbyterian Church, 2001, p. 10). The myth of choice is only one of many false beliefs used to justify continued discrimination against this particular group of people.

Until the early 1970s, it was extremely risky to identify oneself as homosexual in the United States. Indeed, it was necessary to remain silent and hidden in order to function safely in society. Subsequent to the Stonewall riots in New York City in June 1969, increasingly courageous and defiant gay and lesbian people began to "come out" and speak out against the mistreatment of members of their community. The mantra of the '70s became "Gay Is Good" as sexual minority persons began to protest institutionalized oppression. The gay civil rights movement accomplished a great deal over the next thirty years. For example, The *Advocate,* a national lesbian and gay magazine, reported that in 2001 50% of the American public believed that homosexuality was the result of genetic causes rather than a lifestyle choice. Additionally, the same Gallup poll survey revealed that 52% of respondents considered homosexuality acceptable and 54% agreed that sexual relations between consenting adults of the same genders should be legal. These statistics indicate significant progress toward tolerance of gay people when compared to a similar survey conducted in 1977 (Dahir, 2001). Gay political activists believe that a crucial factor in these social gains for lesbian and gay persons is increased visibility as more sexual minority persons are open regarding their sexual orientation. The 2000 U.S. census is the first in our nation's history in which gay Americans were specifically considered. The September 25, 2001, issue of the *Advocate* reports that gay and lesbian citizens are living in 99.3% of all counties in the United States. Additionally, the number of people reporting themselves to be in same-sex partnerships increased 314% from the previous census. The latest census does not include single gays and lesbians. However, exit polls by the Voter News Service in the last three elections registered the gay vote at between 4% and 5%. If 5% of the total U.S. adult population is gay, then at least 10.4 million residents of our country are sexual-minority persons (Dahir, 2001). It is difficult to assess an accurate count of sexual minority persons, since lack of legal protection or concern for privacy may prevent individuals from identifying themselves as gay, lesbian, bisexual, or transgender. Despite these considerable gains in social acceptance, sexual-minority persons continue their struggle for civil rights protection and equality. Today, lesbian and gay people are correctly identified as the only minority whose overt and covert discrimination are officially sanctioned.

The mental health profession's history in regard to its treatment of sexual-minority persons parallels our culture's ongoing ambivalence. Members of the helping services community have been instruments of abuse and pioneers of positive change. Beginning in the mid-nineteenth century in the United States any form of nonprocreative sex was considered by the medical profession as a concern and, in the case of homosexuality, a mental illness. As a result, homosexuality was seen as a sign of pathology, immaturity, or arrested development and, therefore, in need of treatment in order to assist the patient in becoming heterosexual. Treatment approaches ran the spectrum from well intentioned and relatively humane to emotionally and physically abusive aversion therapy techniques such as electroshock. Dr. Evelyn Hooker, whose seminal study in this area was presented to the American Psychological Association in

1956, was the first to seriously question such methods (Kaiser, 1997). Using matched groups of gay and nongay men, Hooker's investigation revealed that gay men were as well adjusted as nongay men. The study stated unequivocally that there was no demonstrable pathology differentiating homosexuals from heterosexuals. Members of her profession labeled Hooker's study as flawed, and she was ridiculed as "crazy." Despite the considerable negative reaction to Hooker's findings, her groundbreaking study began a seventeen-year struggle that resulted in a December 1973 ruling by the Board of the American Psychiatric Association removing homosexuality from its list of mental disorders (Isensee, 1991).

During the 1970s, lesbian and gay people began to establish self-help groups in their community centers as alternatives to traditional mental health methods that had heretofore pathologized sexual minorities. These groups promoted homosexuality as an acceptable "alternative" lifestyle. George Weinberg's *Society and the Healthy Homosexual* (1972) was considered by many the first mental health book about gay people to have a positive perspective. Currently, the position taken by major mental health and medical professional organizations can be summarized by this official statement from the American Medical Association: Most of the emotional disturbance experienced by gay men and lesbians around their sexual identity is not based on physiological causes but rather is due more to a sense of alienation in an unaccepting environment (Presbyterian Church, 2001, p. 13). While it is clear that there is now more understanding, compassion, and humane treatment in the helping professions, professional debate continues over the efficacy and ethics of approaches such as reparative therapy, which is aimed at "curing" homosexuals. Gay and lesbian clients are encouraged to choose professional helpers carefully, as subtle and blatant mistreatment of sexual minority clients persists in both the medical and mental health fields.

CURRENT ISSUES

The American Psychological Association defines sexual orientation as an enduring emotional, romantic, sexual, and/or affectional attraction to persons of a particular gender (Presbyterian Church, 2001, p. 64). Sexual-minority persons grow up in a nonaffirming culture that causes them to experience particular challenges and difficulties. Although each client is a unique human being, certain general themes can be identified as common concerns for lesbian, gay, bisexual, and transgender persons. Many clients who initiate counseling are struggling with their identities, a process often referred to as "coming out." During this time, an individual acknowledges emotional and physical attraction to a particular gender. In the initial phases of the counseling process, as was the case with Isaac in the example presented previously, the counselor usually assists the client in coming out to him or herself, an effort involving acknowledging, affirming, embracing, and eventually celebrating the sexual aspects of the client's personhood. This frequently involves supportive confrontation of the client's internalized negative beliefs regarding sexual minority people and consequent shame. Claudia Black, in her book *Double Duty* distinguishes guilt from shame: "guilt is feeling bad about something that I've done, while shame is feeling bad about who I am" (p. 29). Again, counseling concerns are illustrated by Isaac's circumstances as he described his longing be "normal" and characterized his feelings of same-gender attraction as immoral and wrong. In addition to addressing these issues in the counseling sessions, exposing the client to reading containing accurate information and affirming ways of thinking regarding sexual-minority people can be relieving and stabilizing.

As the counseling progresses, clients begin the process of coming out to others. Initially, it is recommended that this be done with persons that the client feels will likely be accepting and supportive. When the client is more secure in her or his identity, sharing with additional persons, including family members, is considered. It is important to assess with clients their readiness to deal with reactions, including unexpected or intensely negative ones. This is especially important when dealing with family members, in whom the client's emotional investment is usually high. In the case example, Isaac did not disclose his sexual orientation to his wife or children until he had positively integrated this aspect of his identity. While some families are supportive, as, fortunately, was Isaac's, many are shocked and angry when this disclosure is made. Often the revelation confronts the family's denial, activates their negative feelings about gay people, and initiates a process of grief and loss (Presbyterian Church, 2001, p. 37). Clients who are not properly prepared for this kind of reaction may become extremely angry or depressed, especially if internal and external support systems are not established. The need for these support systems involves coming out by the client in a variety of settings including work, church, and community. Again it is essential to assist the client by identifying gay-affirming resources. Also, coming out in certain arenas, such as places of employment, can be very risky if discrimination policies do not cover sexual-minority people. As the client becomes more comfortable with self-identity and management of personal disclosure, common symptoms such as shame, guilt, confusion, sadness, and anger diminish. It is essential to note, however, that coming out is an ongoing process that sexual-minority persons face on a daily basis, since there is often a presumption of heterosexuality.

In addition to coming-out concerns, lesbian and gay persons typically begin to explore and express their sexuality (Isensee, 1990). Feelings of uncertainty, ambivalence, guilt, and fear coexist with ones of excitement and anticipation. It is important to explore with clients their personal values regarding the expression of sexual feelings. The goal is that behaviors be congruent with these values. For example, many clients believe in sexual expression only within a monogamous committed relationship. Being comfortable in discussing sexual specifics becomes particularly important in work with gay and bisexual men, since this is a client population that continues to be at considerable risk for exposure to the human immunodeficiency virus (HIV) (O'Bryan, 2001). It is important, however, that HIV assessment be related to the client's behaviors rather than sexual orientation. An assumption that all gay people have HIV is inaccurate, insensitive, and potentially disruptive to the counseling process. It is common that adult sexual-minority persons have a need to experience a form of adolescence, since this developmental phase is often denied them. Long-held feelings of guilt and shame may express themselves as an avoidance of sexual contact or may take the form of compulsive or anonymous sexuality. A goal of counseling is to assist clients with the creation of healthy attitudes, positive beliefs, and safe expression of sexual feelings.

As clients explore their sexual feelings, they tend to examine their affectional ones. It is important to confront the myth that lesbian and gay relationships do not last and that sexual-minority persons are doomed to a life of isolation and loneliness. In assisting clients with the development of intimate relationships, many of the issues considered with heterosexual clients apply. However, there are particular concerns that are helpful to address with this special population. For example, gay men, as is true with other males in this culture, are socialized to be sexual and to avoid emotional intimacy. Males are encouraged to control their emotions and to mask emotional vulnerability. Boys, for instance, may be severely ridiculed for crying, seeking comfort, or showing fear. In fact the one emotion that is acceptable for males to demonstrate is anger (Isensee, 1990). Since men are discouraged from expressing tenderness and displaying other vulnerable emotions, it can be especially challenging to integrate physical and emotional attraction. Men in our society are also taught to compete with other males, which also poses a challenge, as a primary relationship requires cooperation and compromise.

Female couples also experience issues that are particular to them. In the women's community, "lesbian fusion" is a concept frequently considered. This issue identifies how female couples struggle to balance the identity of the couple with that of the individual. For example, members of lesbian couples may need to develop separate friends, experience individual time, and participate in separate activities in order to avoid overburdening the relationship. Gay and lesbian couples often do not have positive same-gender role models available to them. The counselor can serve as a resource by identifying social contexts in which same-gender relationships are affirmed. Also, resources such as Permanent Partners (Berzon, 1988), a relationship guide for gay and lesbian couples, can be an excellent adjunct to couples therapy with same-gender clients. Some couples are concerned that when they commit to a long-term relationship, they increase their visibility as lesbian or gay people. This is a legitimate concern and illustrates how coming out is a process rather than an event. Finally, despite such advances as Vermont's civil union law and the provision of Holy Union Ceremonies by gay-affirming churches such as Metropolitan Community, same-gender couples cannot legally marry in our country. Lesbian and gay partners may want, therefore, to consider consultation with a knowledgeable and gay-friendly attorney. Legal devices such as a partnership agreement, a will, or a medical power of attorney can provide alternatives to the protection afforded by formal marriage (Hertz, 1998).

Another typical area of concern for many gay and lesbian clients is in the area of religion and spirituality. It is not uncommon for clients to have backgrounds in which homosexuality was viewed as immoral, sinful, or even evil (Helminiak, 2000). Many clients experience shame, pain, and ambivalence in this area of their lives. It is a myth that gay people are anti-church or anti-Christian. More commonly, lesbian and gay people have been wounded by their faith communities and are in search of a spiritual context in which they can be affirmed. Again the counselor can assist in this area by helping to externalize anger and sadness and by identifying resources that minister to sexual-minority clients. The helpfulness of this intervention was seen in the case example. Isaac found considerable comfort by participating in his church's support group for lesbian and gay Catholics. Currently, the Metropolitan Community Church, founded by the Reverend Troy Perry, is a worldwide Christian denomination with special ministry to lesbian, gay, bisexual, and transgender persons. A number of established religions including Judaism and Buddhism as well as Christian faith communities welcome openly gay members. Participation in these supportive religious or spiritual contexts is a healing experience for many sexual-minority clients.

Healthy individuals, including gay and lesbian people, are persons who feel fulfilled in all aspects of their lives. This includes a work life that provides financial security and an opportunity to contribute to our society. In the area of employment, sexual-minority people have historically experienced discrimination. For the counselor who is dealing with a gay client's work life, many of the potential concerns are the same as for heterosexual clients. Career counseling theories and approaches advanced by John Holland, Donald Super, and others are appropriate and are likely to be useful to sexual-minority clients. There are special concerns, however, when providing career counseling services to lesbian and gay persons. Some state and local governments or private companies have nondiscrimination employment policies, but many do not. Currently there is no federal law protecting sexual-minority people from discrimination with regard to hiring and firing practices. This reality has affected gay people in their process of career selection. For example, certain careers, such as professional sports, are regarded as anti-gay and may be eliminated as an option despite interest in that particular vocational field.

Other clients may choose jobs, like military or law enforcement positions, in which it is necessary to conceal their sexual orientation. Some lesbian and gay people choose to come out and to challenge unfair treatment and, therefore, face additional risks. Finally, clients may choose to identify career clusters and particular organizations that have a history of being gay friendly. Again, the counselor can assist with career concerns by using traditional assessment methods and by being sensitive to particular issues faced by this client population. It is essential that any mental health professional working with lesbian and gay clients, involving personal or vocational concerns, know what community resources are available to assist these minority persons in achieving meaningful and complete lives.

The issues and concerns previously presented are matters of importance to many sexual-minority clients who seek counseling services. Within this special population of people exist subgroups whose challenges require mental health professionals to have further knowledge and additional skills. Gay youths, for example, frequently suffer from serious depression and are often isolated and hidden even within their own families. Currently, however, many gay, lesbian, bisexual, and transgender adolescents are coming out at a much younger age, with the average now being fifteen years old (Presbyterian Church, 2001). It is estimated that sexual-minority youths, at this vulnerable developmental period, are two to three times more likely to attempt suicide. Of completed adolescent suicides, 30% are committed by sexual-minority youth (Presbyterian Church, 2001).

Lesbian and gay teens who seek counseling who are not "out" may not disclose their sexual orientation to the therapist for fear of rejection by the counselor or their families. Sexual-minority youths often do not feel safe in their homes, churches, schools, or communities. In schools, for example, lesbian and gay youths are frequently the victims of verbal and physical abuse. One study revealed that among second graders the second most commonly heard insult was "that's so gay" (Presbyterian Church, 2001). Additionally, while FBI crime statistics indicate that violent crimes are decreasing in the United States, physical assaults on gay-identified persons are increasing (Presbyterian Church, 2001). Research compiled by a study group for the Presbyterian Church indicates that 13% of sexual-minority young people have suffered physical attack. Discrimination against gay youths in their communities is practiced by such groups as the Boy Scouts of America, which openly bars gay youths from membership (Freiberg, 2001). The counselor's office is a potential and frequently needed haven in this emotional storm. It is important for mental health professionals to be aware of community resources, as increasingly there are support groups for young people who are struggling with sexual identity matters.

A second subgroup within the sexual-minority community is persons who are living with AIDS (acquired immune deficiency syndrome). Men who have sex with other men are currently most at risk for HIV infection (O'Bryan, 2001). HIV is widely recognized by the medical community as the agent that causes the development of AIDS-related conditions. O'Bryan's report further indicates that young gay and bisexual men may not know "safe sex" practices or are likely to minimize the possibility of infection. For counselors who work with gay male adolescents this is particularly disturbing, as 95% of this client population identified sexual encounters as their initial form of contact with the gay community (Kus, 1990). In addition to coping with the reality of a life-threatening disease, clients who are HIV infected face multiple emotional challenges. For a number of men, the HIV diagnosis discloses their sexual orientation, which can trigger feelings of emotional vulnerability and shame. Additionally, as this debilitating disorder progresses, accompanying symptoms of depression and anxiety are common. Frequent episodes of illness and steadily diminishing physical capability and appearance often exacerbate emotional distress. For a significant number of AIDS patients, the effects of this disease culminate in an inability to work. For males this loss may be especially devastating, as self-identity for many men is defined by their work. The lack of employment and the extremely high cost of prescription medications and other medical expenses create additional concerns and stress for people living with AIDS. Additionally, as physical and financial resources decline, HIV patients are at risk of social isolation and emotional withdrawal. Therefore, a nonjudgmental counselor, a knowledgeable physician, and access to AIDS support services can be invaluable to clients challenged with this as yet incurable disease.

Gay and lesbian parents are a third subpopulation facing real and unique challenges. As a group, sexual-minority persons are often portrayed as being anti-family. The available research does not support this depiction and exposes still another myth regarding lesbian and gay people. Bozett (1987), in his study of sexual-minority parents, reports that one-fifth of gay men and one-third of lesbians in the United States are biological parents, a large majority of whom are actively and positively involved in caring for their children. Bozett refutes the assertion that youths reared by lesbian and gay parents are more likely to be homosexual themselves and cites no significant differences in sexual orientation between children raised by same-gender parents and those raised by different-gender parents. The myth of child molestation is often introduced as evidence of the unsuitability of gay or lesbian parents in legal custody situations. On the contrary, 95% of all molestation is committed by heterosexual males (Presbyterian Church, 2001, p. 66). Gay and lesbian parents may be discouraged from utilizing community support services, as they are concerned that increased visibility may put their parental rights at risk. In many states, the identification of a parent as lesbian or gay is sufficient grounds for case review and, in some instances, removal of custody or termination of visitation rights. As a result, many gay parents feel isolated and fearful. This situation was eased for Isaac, the client described in the case example, as he was referred to a monthly gay father's support meeting, which he found informative and affirming. Confidentiality, always an important issue in the helping process, obviously takes on particular significance in these circumstances.

Older lesbian and gay persons are also a segment of the sexual minority community who are often unfairly and inaccurately portrayed as growing old alone and lonely (Kus, 1990). In addition to being largely untrue, this image is potentially troubling for younger persons who are struggling with coming out. The reality is that most older gays and lesbians adjust quite well to the natural process of aging and are not overly concerned with the challenges of the later stages of life. These persons, on the contrary, most often report stable self-images, greater comfort with disclosure, and a strong social network of support (Kus, 1990).

Persons of color who also identify as sexual-minority individuals face the double challenge of trying to bridge two communities and integrate two identities. Homophobia is an issue in racial-minority communities, and racism is an issue in the gay, lesbian, bisexual, and transgender communities. The counselor assisting these clients must be sensitive to both issues and use resources that are available to assist with these special challenges.

Bisexual persons, like sexual-minority persons of color, encounter complex social challenges. Bisexuality is a phenomenon in which people experience significant feelings of attraction to members of both genders (Bettinger, 2001). Frequently, it elicits negative reaction from both heterosexual and homosexual communities. Often bisexuality is seen as denial, intense homophobia, or simply as a transition period for a lesbian or gay person who is struggling with coming out. This is an especially challenging issue for the counselor, since this assertion is sometimes valid. As the person progresses in therapy, it is not uncommon for this identification to alter (Bettinger, 2001). Bisexuality, while more common in females, does occur in both men and women (Burr, 1996). The counselor must be cognizant of assisting the client in discovering his or her personal truth and assist also with the creation of a life that is congruent with the client's identity.

Perhaps the group of people within this client population who are least understood are transgender persons, men and women whose psychological and emotional gender identification is the opposite of their physical gender form (Bettinger, 2001). Michael Bettinger notes that in his counseling sessions with transgender clients phrases such as "I am a man trapped in a woman's body" or "I am a woman trapped in a man's body" are common. When providing services to transgender clients, it is essential that sensitive medical professionals, specifically psychiatrists, are involved. This is particularly true if the client intends to pursue gender reassignment surgery, which is a complicated medical procedure that causes the body to look like that of the other gender. Reactions to transgender persons can be intensely negative, even from professionals. Transgender people are frequently the victims of verbal and physical violence. Fortunately, in many communities, support groups are emerging for clients who are facing this particularly complex psychological and medical issue.

Finally, counselors who work with lesbian and gay clients need to know how to assess and intervene with clients who are abusing alcohol or other substances. Research indicates that chemical abuse and dependency is significantly higher in the sexual-minority community than in the general population (Kus, 1990). Although the reasons for this are unclear, it is logical that clients who suffer depression, anxiety, and guilt as a result of being oppressed may turn to unhealthy methods of relief. Substance abuse has a devastating effect on both personal and professional relationships. Chemical dependency, if not arrested, is a progressive and potentially fatal disorder. For men who are exploring sexuality with other men, using substances can affect judgment and place them at greater risk for HIV infection. In short, assessment of gay and lesbian clients' use of substances is an essential component of the helping process and may need to be an integral component of treatment planning.

SUGGESTIONS FOR ENHANCING COUNSELOR EFFECTIVENESS

Well-intentioned mental health professionals who are not properly educated and trained to work specifically with sexual-minority clients may do unintentional harm. Counselors who have not resolved their own issues regarding homophobia may be overtly or subtly judgmental. An important first step for improving professional effectiveness is investigating published research regarding this client population. Efforts at changing sexual orientation are unsuccessful, unethical, and may damage clients by exacerbating depression, shame, and anxiety (Presbyterian Church, 2001, p. 12). Through clinical supervision or psychotherapy, counselors can address their own homophobic feelings that are a natural consequence of growing up in our culture. Self-reflection regarding the counselor's personal values and beliefs is necessary to avoid countertransference issues when working with sexual-minority clients. If a counselor feels that personal beliefs prevent the affirmation of lesbian and gay clients, then referral to another professional is an ethical requirement. Perhaps what is most important in being effective with this population is to know and have experience with lesbian and gay people. Direct contact dispels the false and hurtful myths that are assigned to sexual-minority people and encourages viewing them with the unconditional positive regard and support that all individuals deserve.

In addition to increased awareness and affirming attitudes toward sexual-minority clients, practical operational changes can positively affect levels of comfort and trust for gay, lesbian, bisexual, and transgender clients who are seeking or receiving mental health services. For example, the counselor's intake form should use gay-sensitive language such as *life partner, coupled, significant other,* and *sexual orientation.* Mental health professionals may openly display gay resource materials such as books, pamphlets, or a referral list to gay-sensitive medical and other service providers. The waiting area could have available periodicals, such as the *Advocate,* which focus on topics of interest to sexual-minority persons. A bulletin board that includes community resources and events could communicate sensitivity to gay-related concerns. Finally, the counseling practice could advertise in local gay newspapers or other publications indicating expertise in assisting with sexual-minority issues. In the case study, for example, Isaac's location of a practice that openly marketed itself to the lesbian and gay community was extremely relieving for him.

CONCLUDING REMARKS

Sexual-minority people historically have been oppressed by a culture that justifies this abuse largely through the use of myths and the distortion of truth. As more lesbian, gay, bisexual, and transgender persons have had the courage to "come out," we discover them to be our sons, daughters, physicians, firefighters, attorneys, therapists, carpenters, and ministers as well as occupying other important places in our lives and hearts. Nevertheless, such persons continue to face individual prejudice, institutionalized discrimination, and internalized homophobia (Isensee, 1991). Lack of experience with gay and lesbian persons perpetuates stereotypes characterizing them as promiscuous, child molesters, and a threat to valued institutions like marriage and family. Discrimination against sexual-minority persons is openly practiced by vocational, governmental, religious, and educational organizations. Lesbian and gay individuals who grow up in this hostile environment often feel isolated, suffer low self-esteem, and experience intense feelings of guilt and shame. Until recently, this group had few role models and community resources that could assist with positive identity development. Clearly, mental health professionals who are properly trained and experienced can provide valuable services to sexual-minority clients. Additionally, counselors can demonstrate through their personal and professional lives acceptance and affirmation of this disen-franchised group. Human service providers need the vision to see all peo-ple regardless of race, religion, ethnicity, gender, class, physical challenge, or sexual orientation as unique individuals who deserve caring, respect, support, and assistance in developing to their full potential as valuable, capable, and evolving human beings.

EXPERIENTIAL ACTIVITIES

Taking a Stand (Group Awareness Activity)

Directions to facilitator.   The group leader will direct participants to move to the center of the room as a group. Each corner of the room is designated with an individual sign that is marked: (1) Strongly Agree, (2) Agree, (3) Disagree, and (4) Strongly Disagree. The facilitator will select and read from the suggested sentences that follow. As each sentence is shared, group members will move to the corner that best expresses their beliefs/opinions regarding the statement. The experience leader will take note of both verbal and nonverbal behaviors. The facilitator will invite and encourage discussion among the subgroups that have taken different positions ("stands") on these issues. The process is most effective, of course, when one sentence is considered at a time.

Purpose of activity.   This activity may be used as a way of reviewing responses to the pretest. It also expands the pretest by discussing personal and professional values and beliefs. It provides an opportunity to provide feedback either in a group or individually to participants as to potential problem areas for counselors training to provide mental health services to gay, lesbian, bisexual, or transgender clients.

Suggested statements for consideration.

1. Gay people in our country should be given the right to marry.
2. It is unethical for Christian counselors to provide mental health services to gay clients.
3. The military's policy of "Don't ask, don't tell" is a sound and fair compromise position.

4. Gay people who are Republican are suffering from internalized homophobia.
5. Adolescents are too young to understand whether they are gay or not.
6. Sexual-minority people should not be permitted to teach in elementary schools.
7. Everybody knows someone who is lesbian/gay.
8. It is impossible to be both gay and Christian.
9. Gay people are anti-family.
10. Gay relationships don't last.
11. Most lesbian/gay people "pass" as straight.
12. Heterosexuals have a life. Gay people have a lifestyle.
13. About 10% of our population is composed of gay, lesbian, bisexual, and transgender people.
14. Homophobia is the last socially acceptable prejudice.
15. Crimes against gay people should be included in hate-crime legislation.
16. In custody cases, gay/lesbian parents should be evaluated on their ability to provide a stable home rather than their sexual orientation.
17. Gay rights organizations are seeking special rights for sexual-minority people.
18. Most families are accepting of members who come out as lesbian/gay.
19. Sexual orientation is a choice; therefore, lesbian/gay people are not a true minority.
20. Being heterosexual is preferable to being homosexual.

Follow-up to activity.   Once participants have had an opportunity to discuss the issues presented, a helpful method of processing the experience is to have them form a circle, then have each person mentally and then verbally share the following: "What I learned about myself from this experience is _____, and something new that I learned about lesbian/gay people is _____." The facilitator can use this time to share observations about the group and provide individual feedback as appropriate.

Making a Visit (Group Awareness Activity)

Directions to facilitator.   The group leader will request that participants visit one of the following community resources for sexual-minority persons:

1. An open twelve-step recovery meeting for lesbian/gay alcoholics.
2. A Sunday-morning worship service at a Metropolitan Community Church.
3. A PFLAG meeting.
4. A support group for sexual-minority youth.

Participants will prepare a brief paper that summarizes their experiences using the following questions:

1. What expectations of this experience were confirmed?
2. What surprised you?
3. What stereotypes were reinforced? Which ones were challenged?
4. What positive observations did you make?
5. Did you experience discomfort? If so, describe it.

In addition to the written self-reflection, participants will share observations verbally by forming subgroups with others who visited the same resource. Each subgroup will report to all participants how individuals' experiences compared. The facilitator will process, placing particular emphasis on bias, conflict of values, and potential countertransference issues. Note: in some communities, these resources may not be available. If they are not, have participants view at least three episodes of Showtime's *Queer as Folk* series (including the first and last episodes). Use the same questions and process as described for the Making a Visit activity.

REFERENCES

Berzon, B. (1988). *Permanent partners: Building gay and lesbian relationships that last.* New York: Dutton/Plume.

Bettinger, M. (2001). *It's your hour.* Los Angeles, CA: Alyson Books.

Black, C. (1992). *Double duty: Dual identity.* Denver, CO: Claudia.

Bozett, F.W. (1987). *Gay and lesbian parents.* New York: Praeger.

Burr, C. (1996). *A separate creation: The search for the biological origins of sexual orientation.* New York: Hyperion.

Dahir, M. (2001, July 17). Why are we gay? *The Advocate,* 30–39.

Freiberg, P. (2001, June 22). Justice for all? *Washington Blade,* A1, A19.

Helminiak, D.A. (2000). *What the bible really says about homosexuality.* Tajique, NM: Alamo Square Press.

Hertz, F.C. (1998). *Legal affairs: Essential advice for same-sex couples.* New York: Henry Holt.

Isensee, R. (1990). *Love between men: Enhancing intimacy and keeping your relationship alive.* Englewood Cliffs, NJ: Prentice Hall.

Isensee, R. (1991). *Growing up gay in a dysfunctional family: A guide for gay men reclaiming their lives.* New York: Prentice Hall.

Kaiser, C. (1997). *The gay metropolis.* New York: Harcourt Brace and Company.

Kus, R.J. (1990). *Keys to caring: Assisting your gay and lesbian clients.* Boston: Alyson Publications.

O'Bryan, W. (2001, June 1). HIV infections increase among young gay men. *Washington Blade* A1, A23.

Presbyterian Church. (2001). *What We Wish We Had Known.* Available at: www.mkpc.org/Blue__Book__2001.pdf.

Weinberg, G. (1972). *Society and the healthy homosexual.* New York: St. Martin's Press.

CHAPTER 13

Counseling Older Persons

Andrea Dixon Rayle
Jane E. Myers

Andrea Dixon Rayle, Ph.D., NCC, is an assistant professor of counseling psychology and counselor education at Arizona State University. She received her graduate training in counselor education at the University of North Carolina, Greensboro. She has worked as a school counselor and a private practice counselor and has counseled persons aged four through ninety.

Jane E. Myers, Ph.D., LPC, NCC, NCGC, is professor of counselor education at the University of North Carolina, Greensboro. She received her graduate training in counselor education with a specialization in gerontological counseling at the University of Florida. She has worked as a rehabilitation counselor, an administrator of aging programs, and a rehabilitation and counselor educator. She also has directed five national curriculum development and training projects in gerontological counseling. Dr. Myers has written and lectured extensively in the field of gerontological counseling and was the founding president of the Association for Adult Development and Aging.

OLD OR NOT?

Age is a quality of mind. If you have left your dreams behind,
If hope is cold, If you no longer look ahead
If your ambition fires are dead,
Then you are old

But if from life you take the best,
and if in life you keep the just,
If love you hold;
No matter how the years go by
No matter how the birthdays fly,
You are not old.

—Author unknown

AWARENESS INDEX

Please test your knowledge by marking the following statements true or false before proceeding to the text in this chapter. Compute your score from the scoring guide at the end of the Awareness Index.

1. T F An older person is one who has attained fifty-five years of age.

2. T F Older persons are very much alike.

3. T F The number of older persons is increasing rapidly.

4. T F Over 21% of all older persons have incomes below or near the poverty level.

5. T F Physical impairment is largely limited to those who are sixty-five years of age and above.

6. T F Stereotypes of older persons often become self-fulfilling prophecies.

7. T F Counselors are likely to have some degree of prejudice against older persons.

8. T F Self-acceptance is an important counseling need of older persons.

9. T F Older adults are likely to be considered unproductive citizens in the U.S. workforce.

10. T F Sexual desire and activity become obsolete among older adults after the age of sixty-five.

11. T F Older adults struggle with feelings of loneliness, worthlessness, and depression.

12. T F Older adults make up a large proportion of counselors'
active clientele.

Scoring guide: **1.** F; **2.** F; **3.** T; **4.** T; **5.** F; **6.** T; **7.** T; **8.** T; **9.** T; **10.** F;
11. T; **12.** F.

INTRODUCTION

Older individuals, those persons aged sixty-five and older, comprise more
than 35 million persons in the United States (U.S. Bureau of the Census,
2000). They share many characteristics in common with persons of other
ages as well as unique characteristics as a result of their longer lives, developmental tasks, and the situational challenges of later life. In fact, the
diversity within the older population, the focus of this chapter, may be
greater than that between older and younger adults. Counselors in training increasingly will encounter older persons as clients, or families in
which older persons are significant members. Thus, we believe that all
counselors need to be familiar with the concerns of later life and strategies for helping older persons address these concerns.

In this chapter, a historical perspective on the older adult population
will be presented. Selected demographic indices will be described as a
basis for discussing current and unique issues in counseling older persons, and the case examples will be mentioned in reference to these issues. These issues include the need to consider prevalent negative myths
and misconceptions about older adults, the counseling needs of older persons, and the Aging Network, a national network of services and programs designed to provide services to persons in later life. The chapter
concludes with a discussion of strategies for enhancing counseling effectiveness in work with older persons. Two case examples are presented and
discussed to underscore the heterogeneity of the older population.

CASE EXAMPLES

An older female and an older male illustrate the range of differences
among older persons. Across ethnicity, age, gender, socioeconomic status, and geographical location, the diversity of older adults is even greater
than demonstrated in these examples. The case examples will be referred
to throughout the chapter.

Mrs. G.

Mrs. G. is seventy-two years of age and lives alone in a northeastern college town where her husband was a member of the faculty at the local university before his sudden and unexpected death. She is Caucasian and from a professional, middle-class family. Today, she remains financially comfortable. Mrs. G. usually attempts to keep busy, primarily with other women who are about her age. Together, they help others through a number of local community agencies. She finds that age has brought new opportunities. Mrs. G. has lived through her grief over the loss of her husband and has joined a small group of widows who, after a short training period, are active in assisting older, recently widowed women to work through their sense of loss and fear of the future. Mrs. G. enjoys a close relationship with a son and his family who live in the same town. She has a number of friends in other surrounding communities, and maintains an active correspondence through phone calls and E-mail. Mrs. G. is a vigorous person who finds happiness and support in her family, friends, social encounters, and service for others.

Mr. C.

In another area of the country, Mr. C. is an African American male in his mid-eighties who represents a very different segment of the U.S. population. After his wife's early death, and up until his retirement from the railroad system, Mr. C. helped to raise his grandchildren and great-grandchildren. He now lives with his daughter, who is in her sixties, two grandchildren, and five great-grandchildren. Mr. C. is financially dependent upon his daughter's family and a small supplemental social security income provided by the federal government. Although living in crowded conditions with insufficient income, the family is strong and able to provide support to its members.

Currently Mr. C. is not in good health and spends a great deal of time in bed watching television. The only time he leaves the family home is for church or a doctor visit. Also, Mr. C. has lost all of his hearing in his left ear and is hard of hearing in his right. He has severe arthritis in his hands and therefore cannot work carving wood, a hobby that he has always loved. For thirty years Mr. C. worked for the railroad system, where he made many close friends and acquaintances. Since his retirement and the onset of health problems he has lost all connection with these friends. Due to the fact that he has difficulty hearing and cannot engage in extensive conversations with his family, he has become withdrawn and depressed.

A HISTORICAL OVERVIEW

In 2000 the population of people sixty-five and older was approximately 35 million, or 12.4% of the U.S. population, and the estimate for 2030 is almost 70 million, a growth of about 50% (U.S. Bureau of the Census, 2000). Of particular interest is the increase in the numbers of older persons by age groups. Between 1900 and 1999, the sixty-five to seventy-four age group grew by a factor of eight, the seventy-five to eighty-four group increased by a factor of sixteen, and the eighty-five-plus group by a factor of thirty-four. Overall, during the same time period the total number of older Americans grew by 10.6%. Within the population of older adults there is tremendous heterogeneity. Selected subpopulations, however, share characteristics that result in stress and significant needs for coping strategies. In this section we will overview these subpopulations and their challenges in terms of race, gender, marital status, educational status, financial issues, employment, and health.

CURRENT ISSUES

Race, Gender, and Marital Status

On the basis of race, approximately 84% of persons sixty-five years of age and over are White, 8% are Black, 5.3% persons are of Hispanic origin, and 3% are of other racial origin. Females represent 58.5% of the total percentage of older adults, with a gender ratio of 141 women for every 100 men. In 1999, almost half of all older women were widows (45%) and one-sixth of older men were widowers. Only 43% of older women were married compared to 77% of older men; 8% of all older persons were divorced or separated (American Association of Retired Persons [AARP], 2000).

Education

Older persons have substantially less formal education than do those under sixty-five years of age; however, steady growth in the educational level of older persons has resulted in a rise in the number of years of schooling from 8.7 to 12.8 years in the period from 1970 to 1999. Between 1970 and 1999, the percentage of older people who completed high school rose from 28% to 68%, with 15% of older persons having four or more years of college. The number of years completed varies considerably by ethnic origin. In 1998, the percentage that completed high school was 71.6% for Caucasians, 47% for Asian Americans, 43.7% for African Americans, and 29.4% for Hispanic Americans (AARP, 2000).

Financial Issues

An appalling fact about the aging population is the sizeable number who live at or below the poverty level. As of 2000, approximately 10.6% lived below the poverty level, described as an annual income of $8,590 for an older person living alone or $11,610 for an older couple (U.S. Department of Health and Human Services [HHS], 2001). Although the poverty rate has dropped for persons over the age of sixty-five, over 20% of the older population is poor or near poor (Administration on Aging [AoA], 2000). In an inflationary period characterized by rising costs and declining value of fixed incomes, older persons are especially vulnerable to financial difficulties. It is unrealistic to assume that any person can maintain a decent standard of living on $8,590 a year, or $165 per week. Financial concerns are an area that counselors may consider exploring with, as well as advocating for, older adult clients. In our experience, older clients may require help locating resources for financial assistance. Federal organizations that offer financial assistance to older persons exist, and counselors should become familiar with these. Several of these organizations will be discussed later in the chapter.

Employment

Considering the rapidly growing number of older adults in the United States, it is noteworthy that the percentage of employed older persons is dropping steadily. In 1900, 63.1% of men over sixty-five were employed;

by 1989 this percentage had fallen to 16.6%; by 1992 it was 15.8% (AoA, 2000); and by 1999 it had fallen to only 12%. Older adults comprise 12.7% of the total population but only 2.9% of the American workforce. Among the factors precipitating a decline in the number of older workers are pension plans permitting early retirement in order to open up employment and promotion opportunities for younger workers, and federal early retirement plans. Additionally, the inability to find or keep regular work has led some older workers to use their retirement options earlier.

Currently, efforts are being made to encourage older persons to continue working if they have the interest and capability to do so. With the passage of the federal Age Discrimination in Employment Act (ADEA) in 1967, the government began a campaign to support the hiring of older adults and to combat age discrimination, stereotypes, and prejudices in the workplace. The ADEA states that ability, not age, should be the deciding factor in older adults' retirement and/or other employment decisions.

Trends toward earlier retirement apparently do not reflect the preferences of a substantial proportion of workers and retirees. According to a 1994 Harris study, 66% of surveyed employees expressed a preference to keep working rather than to retire; 53% in the fifty to sixty-four age group preferred to keep working after age sixty-five; and 68% of the retired group wished they had not stopped working.

The emotional and financial concerns surrounding employment, and lack thereof, is another area within which counselors may consider working with and advocating for older adults. The case involving Mrs. G. is an example of an older person remaining involved in her community; counselors may encounter other older adults who want that connection but are unsure of how to go about making it. Often, older clients who want to work and are able to work feel discriminated against and may require assistance locating resources.

Health

According to the AoA (2000), 80% of older persons report one or more chronic diseases that limit their daily activities. This age group accounts for about 25% of our country's health costs and purchases as much as 25% of all pharmaceutical drugs. At the same time, only 27% report their health as fair or poor. The most commonly stated conditions were arthritis (49%), high blood pressure (36%), hearing impairment (30%), heart disease (27%), cataracts (17%), orthopedic impairment (18%), visual impairment (14%), arteriosclerosis (12%), and diabetes (10%). Brewi and Brennan (1999) estimate that 72% of individuals in the forty-five to sixty-four age group have one or more of these chronic diseases. In fact, statistics concerning functionally disabled persons indicate that one-third are below age sixteen, one-third are aged sixteen to sixty-four, and one-third are aged sixty-five or older (AoA, 2000). Many individuals remain generally active and independent well into older age. At least 85% live in their own communities, independent assisted living communities, or with family; only about 7% live in institutions such as nursing homes. In the past, aging and disease were regarded as part of the same process. More recently, medical and mental health professionals have recognized the importance of distinguishing among changes resulting from aging, disease, and social-psychological factors. For example, Butler, Lewis, and Sunderland (1998) concluded that, in general, physical changes are not as significant to the aging process as are the psychological and emotional reactions to sociogenic factors. Sociogenic factors are those imposed on individuals by the negative stereotypes about aging maintained through the culture of which they are a part. For example, in American society many believe that with age come declining mental alertness and ability; therefore, older adults may experience negative reactions to these stereotypes. The authors have witnessed this become somewhat self-fulfilling as older persons give less attention to their mental capacities and preparedness.

The case involving Mr. C. is an example of an older person experiencing declining physical health, emotional depression, and loss of connection with friends. Counselors will encounter older adults whose declining physical health is similar to the stereotypes many people have of them. If aging is to some extent socially imposed, the knowledge of current issues and concerns in counseling older persons and awareness of the need for changes in negative stereotypes, should receive high priority.

Discrimination

Discrimination is a basic problem experienced either directly or indirectly by older Americans. Younger persons often consider older people inferior to themselves (McFadden, 1996). This kind of discrimination enables younger persons to deny the possibility of their own aging. Butler et al. (1998) have defined this prejudice against older persons as ageism. Examples of ageism may include older persons not being hired due to their advancing age or not being allowed to participate in certain activities, such as driving or living alone, after a certain age. The effects of ageism include the negative stereotypes attributed to older persons. In practice, we have witnessed the consequences of older persons accepting and believing in the inferiority and weaknesses attributed to them. Perceived inferiority involves older individuals acknowledging and believing they are weaker or not able to perform as well as younger persons; these negative beliefs can be detrimental to older persons' self-concepts as they grow older, and can become self-fulfilling prophecies.

The lead author worked with an older client, Anne, who felt this pressure from younger coworkers at her part-time workplace and consequently began to believe that she was not efficient at her work. Anne became convinced she was a hindrance to the small company where she had worked for seven years, and left the position without acknowledging her feelings or beliefs until her physician referred her for counseling for depression. The age discrimination she experienced firsthand at her workplace is only one of the stereotypes she began to believe about herself, only because she was in her late seventies. More of the popular myths and stereotypes ascribed to older individuals are described below, followed by a discussion of the counseling needs of persons in later life.

Common Myths and Stereotypes

There is an abundance of myths and stereotypes attributed to older persons in American society. These myths may vary in some forms; however, all often involve negative beliefs of aging individuals and provide a systematic manner for ageism to occur (Scrutton, 1996). They may be related to the mental, emotional, or physical aspects of older persons' lives. In addition, personal and family history and geographical location may affect the various myths and stereotypes (Morgan & Kunkel, 2001). For purposes of better understanding older adults, and the ideas people may share about them, knowledge and awareness of some of the popular myths and stereotypes is required (Scrutton, 1996).

Myth of unproductiveness.   Anne's situation illustrates one persistent myth about older persons: they become unproductive and, hence, useless, a point of view long supported by the concept of mandatory retirement. Given the opportunity, however, many older persons continue to be productive and actively involved in work and community life—such as in the case example of Mrs. G. Contrary to popular belief, older workers are as effective as younger workers, except perhaps in jobs requiring prolonged physical exertion or rapid response behaviors. Older workers are dependable, maintain excellent attendance and safety records, and require minimum supervision after job requirements are learned (Uhlenberg, 1992). In terms of creativity, some persons remain active in their eighties and nineties. Examples include Pope John Paul working at church reform; Michelangelo completing St. Peter's Cathedral in Rome; Mother Teresa working with the less fortunate in India; current Supreme Court justices John Paul Stevens and William Rehnquist; and older actors and actresses such as Sean Connery and Katharine Hepburn, who received three of her Oscars after the age of sixty.

Myth of disengagement.   One explanation of the behavior of older persons is that they gradually withdraw from customary life activities and become more concerned with self. Such withdrawal is selective: relationships are retained with some persons, but the emphasis is on less interaction with others and on living with memories of the past. While this theory of disengagement may explain the behavior of some older persons, and their withdrawal from active life (such as in the case of Mr. C.), it by no means has application to all. The fact is that many older persons are very much involved in the life of their communities. Therefore, the benefit of older individuals' remaining active should be researched and is encouraged (AARP, 2000).

Others suggest that it is in society's best interest for its older members to disengage from their roles and relationships (Fry, 1992). In other words, in order for older persons to adapt to later life, it is inherent that they begin by reducing their emotional investment in persons and their environment, and members of society must react in the same manner. Yet another explanation of the disengagement process focuses on the idea that old age is to be a privileged time economically, socially, and psychologically (Fry, 1992). Adherence to this particular idea may not allow for understanding of the many struggles some older persons must endure, especially if they disengage from others in their lives.

Myth of inflexibility.   Another stereotype is that older persons are set in their ways. This stereotype involves older individuals' following specific patterns of behavior and being unwilling to consider change. At least two factors may be involved in this stereotype. First, older individuals often have a preference for what is familiar and customary, such as the ways in which they have experienced transportation and purchased goods and services during their lifetimes. Second is older adults' fear resulting from awareness of a slowdown in personal reaction time coupled with acceleration in the tempo of life in the world around them. Many healthy older people, however, do respond positively to change, remaining open to new points of view and alternate lifestyles as part of their continued personal growth. This is true with older clients we have worked with who actively pursue learning to work with computers and become "connected" with the world through the use of the Internet, and also with a few older female clients who have learned to drive in their late sixties. The ability to change and adapt seems to be related more to lifelong behavior patterns than to age (Grob, Krings, & Bangerter, 2001). Older adults already have experienced many situations requiring change and adaptation. Overall, the stereotype of older persons' inflexibility has more to do with the individual's ability to adapt than with their chronological age or phase in the lifespan.

Myth of declining ability to learn.   The popular saying "You can't teach an old dog new tricks" expresses the notion that persons can no longer learn when they grow older. Although many believe that intelligence slides downward from adult years through old age, healthy older persons actually increase their ability to organize their thinking and can successfully complete training and college degree programs with notable efficiency. Decreases in reaction time, which universally occur in later life, are unrelated to intelligence; however, slower reaction time does contribute to slower learning rates. Ultimately, older people learn as well as younger ones, if given more time to master new tasks (Fisk & Warr, 1998). Again, we have been witness to older clients actively wanting to learn new tasks and skills (such as Internet use and learning to play instruments), mastering them in a short amount of time, and finding ways to share their newly acquired knowledge and talents with others.

Myth of senility.   Historically, the term *senile* was used loosely and inaccurately to describe any forgetful, confused, or inattentive older person. In actuality, senility is the physical and mental infirmity of old age involving the loss of intellectual and social abilities severe enough to interfere with daily functioning (Crose et al., 1997). Older individuals often are stereotyped as being senile with no real evidence to support this contention. Contrary to this popular stereotype, senility is not a normal part of aging or inevitable. Most studies estimate that approximately 2 to 3% of adults in their seventies experience some form of senility, as opposed to 5 to 10 percent of adults in their eighties, and as many as 20 to 30% of adults in their nineties (Miller & Dodder, 1980). In many instances, behavior caused by medication, inappropriate drug use, or malnutrition may inaccurately be labeled as senile. When promptly diagnosed, physicians may be able to aid older persons in living happy, healthy lives without the repercussions of this senility stereotype.

Although both older and younger persons experience anxiety, grief, and depression, when the former give evidence of these problems they are sometimes assumed to be senile. Additionally, the overuse of drugs, malnutrition, psychosocial stresses, and undiagnosed physical ailments may produce behavior labeled senile. For instance, Mr. C. may be considered senile by some due to the loss of his hearing and therefore his inability to communicate as effectively as he once could. This physical challenge may lead younger persons to believe that Mr. C. is senile, when in actuality his mental alertness may remain sharp for many years. Diagnosis and treatment of physical concerns generally relieve all symptoms for older individuals, and much of what is called senility can be successfully treated. When treatment for acute conditions is not provided, permanent brain damage other than that caused by physical injury, described as senility, may occur and become irreversible. Inadvertently, many of older adults' symptoms and diseases are in fact iatrogenic, or physician induced (Butler et al., 1998). In other words, by not receiving appropriate diagnosis and treatment or by being ignored for the unstated reason that older persons are sometimes regarded as dispensable, physicians may actually induce older adults' symptoms and conditions.

Alzheimer's disease, sometimes misrepresented as senility, is a chronic brain disease that results in severe, progressive mental deterioration over ten to as many as twenty years after diagnosis and before death. Its symptoms include loss of memory, inability of the person to make changes quickly, and destruction of minds and personalities. Eventually, total care is required. Certain drugs show promise for treating Alzheimer's disease, at least in the early stages, but a cure is not yet known.

Myth of declining interest in sexual activity. The stereotype of loss of sexuality in later life has two elements. The first is the belief that sexual relationships for persons over sixty-five years of age are improper (e.g., the typical description of older men involved in sexual activity as "dirty old men")—lustiness in younger men becomes lechery in older ones. The second element is the common impression that older men and women lose their physiological capacities for sexual activity. Actually, healthy older persons who have maintained some degree of continuity in their sex lives continue to enjoy sexual relationships throughout most of the life span (Powell & Carpenter, 2000). Physiological changes do occur, but they tend to be gradual, and the body usually accommodates to them.

Sexual activity provides feelings of well-being and positive self-regard. Recent studies indicate that about 80% of older persons are sexually active (Fredman, Daly, & Lazur, 1995). Although age does not place a time limit on sexuality or sexual capacity, older persons commonly fear impotence. This is a particularly common fear for older males. One of the authors worked with a male client who presented with serious anxiety due to his recurring belief that he was going to become impotent, although he had experienced no physical indications that it was occurring. Perhaps this fear was an effect of the myth of loss of physiological capacity and desire for sexual activity in later life.

Myth of serenity. Often the news media and popular literature portray untroubled serenity as the reward of those who grow old. Grandma and Grandpa ride bicycles contentedly on a sunny trail in the local park. The apparent conclusion is that the storms of active life are over. Actually, older persons often face more stressful conditions than other age groups and exhibit a remarkable ability to endure crises such as living through multiple friends' and family members' deaths and stressful personal health and financial situations. Their resilience suggests that living longer has prepared them, somehow, to handle new stress.

The youth-oriented society of this country has effectively segregated its older membership, perpetuating a host of false beliefs about aging. Stereotypes about aging in some ways undermine important personal qualities of self-confidence and self-worth. The social prejudice confronting older Americans implicitly denies the possibilities for continued personal growth, and social barriers such as ageism are explicitly imposed for those striving to develop their own capabilities. On the other hand, recent research suggests that, increasingly, older persons are "aging well" (Knight & Stones, 2000). Counselors can be active advocates for societal change to rewrite the negative stereotypes and empower individuals for positive growth and change in later adulthood. To be most effective, strategies for empowerment need to incorporate the broad range of counseling concerns of older people.

Counseling Needs of Older Persons

Counseling needs vary widely among older persons. These needs may be situational or acute, or they may be long-standing and chronic. They may be related to individuals, couples, families, or groups. For purposes of better understanding these needs, Myers (1979) developed a classification system for personal, interpersonal, activity, and environmental needs.

Personal concerns. Personal difficulties for those over sixty-five include psychological concerns related to death and dying, mental health and independence, physical concerns related to health, and psychological and/or physical concerns related to acceptance of the aging process and of oneself as an aging person. These concerns contribute to decreased self-esteem, increased difficulty in decision making, and difficulties with coping and adjustment.

Two major areas of counseling need are assistance in resolving personal problems and continuing or renewing progress toward self-fulfillment. Personal problems often grow out of the loss of a spouse, friends, job, health, or youth, and generalize to feelings of loneliness, worthlessness, and depression. The passage of time awakens older persons to the realization that youthful dreams remain unfulfilled and that death is inevitable, and they struggle with questions such as "Who am I?" and "Why am I here?" Specific counseling strategies such as reminiscence journaling and life review can aid in older adults' working with these concerns. Reminiscence and life review are especially important for counseling with older clients. Offering older clients the opportunity to "experience" and reminiscence about where they have been by journaling on specific topics, or by reviewing their life through photographs and other meaningful items, may offer them a sense of peace and hope for what they have now and what they have left to live.

As older persons find answers to these questions, additional needs arise revolving around the development or renewal of realistic, short-term goals for living. Of particular value is for counselors to provide training in decision-making skills to enable older persons to consider alternative courses of action and resolve practical and emotional issues. Changes that go along with the process of retirement or relocating to a retirement community, including finding purpose in life, may require a present focus as opposed to living in the past or dreading the future. Asking older clients thought-provoking questions such as "What is it that brings you meaning in your life right now?" or "How do you make a difference in this world right now?" can aid in the process of living a present-oriented life.

Interpersonal concerns. The interpersonal dimension of counseling the older adult involves understanding his or her relationships with significant others. Strong relational support networks are essential to the maintenance of self-esteem and morale (Hogan & Eggebeen, 1995). Life satisfaction correlates highly with marriage and frequent personal and telephone visits with friends and family. Group memberships in card-playing clubs or other organizations for older persons are important to psychosocial wellness because they serve to mitigate isolation and provide identification with peers in their age groups. The presence of at least one close relationship, usually with a spouse or children, is the most important factor in determining general satisfaction over the life span (Hogan & Eggebeen, 1995).

As counselors, it is important for us to remember to involve the people important to our older clients in counseling activities. This may mean visiting clients' family homes or inviting their spouses, friends, and/or family into the counseling environment. Counselors may learn about and gain great insight into their older clients when they are able to experience them through the eyes and ears of others close to them. By involving family and friends in counseling activities, counselors may observe relationship dynamics and model supportive behavior for the older client to the family members.

Some 67% of older persons lived in family settings in 1995, including 13% who lived with children, siblings, or other relatives (AARP, 2000). Family members who become caretakers for older persons may experience numerous stresses, which are intensified when the older person has a physical or emotional impairment. In some families, care-giving stress can lead to elder abuse, an increasingly common problem. An estimated 10 million older persons each year are victims of abuse (AARP, 2000). Older individuals tend to be most at risk for physical, psychological, and financial abuse. Participating in group activities such as attending spiritual or religious ceremonies together or participating in outside hobbies and interests often can relieve family members of the stress involved in caring for aging relatives and prevent abuse. Again, involving all members of the family in counseling can aid in creating alliances, and offers a safe environment to speak to issues of stress caused by change and adaptation.

Activity concerns. Within the third category of needs are concerns related to work, skill utilization, and leisure time. Many Americans view retirement from a full-time job as the beginning of the end of life. For some, this view plays out: they decline rapidly in associations with others, in activities, in interests, and in health. Why? High among the possible factors is loss of the sense of personal worth derived from having a career. In U.S. society, employment has long been the focal point for self-definition, association with others with similar interests, social contacts, and development of a personal value system. To deny employment to those who want to keep working and have the capability to do so is, in fact, to destroy a significant support for life itself. However, the decline in the availability of labor is leading business and industry to encourage employees to remain on the job rather than retire. In addition, inflation has added much to the cost of living; therefore, the income and benefits that employment can bring are becoming essential, especially for those older individuals who have not been able to save or plan for retirement. On the other hand, many companies are offering early retirement packages as a cost-cutting measure. For them it is less expensive in the long run to hire younger, cheaper workers than to retain the older worker who may be more expensive in terms of salary, vacation time, and health care.

For older individuals who have worked most of their lives, the free time they find themselves with after retirement brings about concerns as to how this time will be spent. If the time is not spent in activities with family or peers in their age groups or in hobbies or activities that they can enjoy, depression can become an issue. Many older persons are overwhelmed by the extra time they find themselves with and do not know how to go about connecting with others. Although the desire to engage in leisure time may exist, some older individuals may find themselves staying at home more than they would want and spending less and less time with others. Again, this absence of time spent in enjoyable activities can negatively affect the joy of living in the later years. More and more, older persons who are able are seeking part-time employment as a means for meeting some of their financially related environmental needs. Counselors specializing with this client population may act as a catalyst for connecting older clients with one another through open group counseling, support groups, and adventure-based counseling techniques, such as nature walks and low-intensity ropes courses for those who are physically able.

Environmental needs.   Environmental concerns are those that relate to independence. To live independently, some older persons may need government or private agency assistance, transportation, shopping assistance, help with meal preparation, and/or housekeeping or chore services. It may be that as they age and their physical and mental abilities change, or as they lose spouses and friends to declining health and death, older persons must depend more on their children or outside agencies for aid in meeting their basic day-to-day needs. Of the 9 million Americans over age sixty-five who live alone, 2 million say they have no one to turn to if they need help (AoA, 2000). Along with the need for services can come increased dependence and feelings of anxiety and depression.

Needs of older women.   Older women have some special problems. Because they live longer than men, 45% of women sixty-five years and over are widowed (AARP, 2000). Because society frowns on their dating and marrying younger men and because older men tend to choose younger wives when they remarry, older women have limited access to male partners. Hence many, if not most, older widows continue to live alone; 80% of those living alone are women and nearly half of persons aged eighty-five or older live alone. Many older women have never worked except as housewives; those who have worked usually have received low wages (Hibbard, 1995). Older women often live on limited incomes with few, if any, opportunities for social activities, particularly after the loss of the husband. Some older women, such as Mrs. G., remain involved in their communities and in organizations, and receive personal support from these affiliations. Mrs. G. was able to work with the grief she experienced when her husband died, and in turn helped other grieving older women. With support set up through group counseling, counselors offer opportunities for older women to connect with one another.

Older women, and minority elderly people have the lowest incomes on average among the older population. Often this severely limits their ability to purchase the health care, goods, services, and housing options that could help them to remain independent (AoA, 2000). Identity may develop as a central issue, and loneliness is a common problem. Relationships with sons or daughters may change, with conflicts arising from differences of opinion regarding degrees of responsibility for each other.

Older women are overrepresented in the 31% of noninstitutionalized older persons who live alone, some 41% of older women compared to only 17% of older men (AoA, 2000). When disabled, they are far more likely to receive institutional care, and are more likely to live in poverty. Congressional acts passed by the federal government lend voice to the protection and care of not only older women, but all older individuals in America.

The Aging Network

The principal vehicle for federal, state, and local government assistance to older persons is the Older Americans Act passed by Congress in 1965 and subsequently amended several times. This act defined a national policy for older persons and included these specific objectives: an adequate income; the best possible physical and mental health; suitable housing; full restorative services; opportunity for employment without age discrimination; retirement in health, honor, and dignity; pursuit of meaningful activity; efficient community services when needed; immediate benefit from proven research knowledge; and freedom, independence, and the free exercise of individual initiative (Butler, 1975, p. 329).

The Older Americans Act provided for the Administration on Aging, one of the major agencies now functioning under the auspices of the Department of Health and Human Services. Between 1966 and 1985, this act was amended, and funding for older Americans increased. For fiscal year 1969, appropriations amounted to $31.9 million; for 1973, $213 million; for 1978, $720.4 million; for 1985, $1.2 billion; and for 2002, the date of this writing, appropriations are estimated at approximately $2 billion (AoA, 2000; Ficke, 1990).

Current federal legislation places heavy emphasis on the physical needs of older persons. Considerably less attention is paid to mental and emotional needs; therefore, the emotional and psychological needs of older persons may be overlooked by various agencies and policies. The Aging Network, an organization that includes the U.S. Administration on Aging, the Agency on Aging, other state agencies on aging, focuses its efforts more toward the physical well-being of older persons and less toward their emotional and psychological health. Current public policy includes the following services: access services such as information and referral, outreach, case management, and escort and transportation; in-home services, which include chores, homemaker, personal care, home-delivered meals, and home repair and rehabilitation; community services, including senior centers, congregate meals, day care, nursing home ombudsmans, elder abuse prevention, legal services, employment counseling and referral, health promotion, and fitness programs; and caregiver services such as respite, counseling, and education programs. Additionally, AoA's Older Americans Act Eldercare Volunteer Corps uses the talents of a half million volunteers, many of them older persons, to assist in service programs supported under the act. These volunteers work at the community level to enhance the independence of older individuals.

Organizations to Benefit Older Adults

Many services provided to older persons by federal, state, and community agencies have two common objectives: to improve and expand quality of life and to extend personal independence, delaying or avoiding dependence on long-term institutional care. Holmes and Holmes's (1979) study of human services for older persons described in detail most of the services listed previously. In addition, hundreds of organizations working to benefit older persons compete for grants funded by public and private agencies. Many exert political pressure on elected representatives to support legislation favorable to their programs and concerns. A smaller number are engaged in multiple programs and activities. Knowledge of these organizations and the services they offer are critical for counselors working with older adults. Clients such as Mr. C. could benefit from aid offered by these organizations. If he and his family were interested, this type of aid could provide Mr. C. an opportunity to reconnect with others his age, and also offer him experiences outside of the home. It may be that without the involvement of a counselor, neither Mr. C. nor his family would know of these types of services.

The American Association of Retired Persons, with an approximate membership of 35 million, is the largest organization of its kind in the world (AARP, 2000). Dedicated to the well-being and activities of retired persons, AARP is built on a well-developed network of local, state, regional, and national units that maximize membership participation. In each state a joint legislative committee considers political issues affecting older persons and initiates specific recommendations for legislative action on both the state and federal level.

The Gerontological Society of America is another sizeable national organization that is actively involved in the development and dissemination of information regarding aging and older persons. Its three branches focus on biological sciences, clinical medicine, and behavioral sciences. Its two journals, the *Gerontologist* and the *Journal of Gerontology*, are useful resources in the field of aging. The American Society on Aging and the National Council on the Aging are two additional professional associations with similar purposes. A variety of regional and state professional associations affiliate with these groups. Within the American Counseling Association, the Association for Adult Development and Aging is the focal point for counseling older adults. For more information, these and related organizations and their Web sites are included in Table 13.1 below.

Table 13.1 Selected Agencies Currently Serving the Older Population in the United States

Agency	Web site Addresses
Active Living Coalition for Older Adults	www.alcoa.ca
American Association of Retired Persons (AARP)	www.aarp.org
The American Society on Aging	www.asaging.org
The Gerontological Society of America	www.geron.org
International Council for Caring Communities	www.international-iccc.org
National Council on the Aging	www.ncoa.org
Setting Priorities for Retirement Years Foundation (SPRY)	www.spry.org
U.S. Administration on Aging (AoA)	www.aoa.dhhs.gov

SUGGESTIONS FOR ENHANCING COUNSELOR EFFECTIVENESS

Counselors of older persons are, first and foremost, counselors. Thus, the generic skills required of all counselors are necessary for their repertoire. All counselors must have basic counseling and communication skills, knowledge of theories and techniques of counseling, familiarity with vocational development theories, methods of assessment, and group counseling strategies. Other counseling interventions geared to the specific needs of older persons and awareness of older clients' intact support systems are discussed in the following section.

Counseling Older Adults

Counseling may be defined as the process through which a trained counselor helps an individual or group to make responsible decisions concerning personal, educational, social, or vocational development. This definition makes the important points that counseling is a process involving a relationship, one or more decisions on the part of the counselee, and positive action that can result in the client's further development. Counseling older persons, known as gerontological counseling, is perhaps best identified as helping individuals to overcome losses, to establish new goals in the process of discovering that living is limited in quantity but not quality, and to reach decisions based on the importance of the present as well as opportunities of the future. Considering older persons as possible counselees opens a new area of opportunity for helping professionals. At the same time, problems quickly emerge.

For many reasons, older persons tend to be reluctant clients for counseling. Today's older persons were reared prior to the emergence of counseling as a profession and are unlikely to have had experience with counseling in their earlier years. For many older individuals, personal matters were not discussed outside the family and seeking professional help was considered a demonstration of inadequacy. Mental health care is equated with significant psychiatric illness for some older persons. To seek counseling, therefore, would be an admission of serious mental disturbance. This lends voice to the need for counselors' advocacy and education about what counseling is and how it can be a positive addition to older individuals' development. As the baby boomers age, however, new cohorts of older adults likely will be more receptive to counseling.

In some instances, stereotypes about the aging process have so influenced the behaviors of older persons that change is difficult if not impossible. Accepting, for example, the stereotype that older persons are inflexible, unpleasant, difficult, and hard to get along with, at a time when an older person is losing family members and friends, may leave that person believing that the family circle will shrink because of his or her behaviors. This conviction can become a self-fulfilling prophecy. As counselors, we must recognize and appraise the degree to which older persons have been influenced by these stereotypes.

In addition, counselors and other helpers may have prejudice against older persons, often unknowingly. For example, when older persons are confused, forgetful, or depressed, the helper may consider these behaviors typical or expected rather than acute responses to situational events. These conditions, however, may be of medical or situational origin and corrected with appropriate treatments. Likewise, the helper's reaction to the older person who is ill and unlikely to recover may be "Nothing I can do will make any difference." This attitude ignores the importance of the older person's emotional state in the immediate present. Approaches to the problem of counselors' tendencies toward ageism with older clients include expanding the helper's knowledge base, advocacy of older persons' abilities, increasing frequency of association, stimulating sensitivity to older persons as unique human beings, and maintaining personal awareness of the subtle existence of ageism. Despite the best intentions of counselors and other helpers, however, some degree of prejudice against older persons is inevitable because of the entrenched societal attitudes in the United States and the majority of persons' own fears of aging.

Often the mental health system itself prevents older persons from receiving the services they require. Therapists tend to hold negative views of older persons and their growth potential and are reluctant to use time and resources in counseling them (Butler et al., 1998). Current estimates are that more than 25% of older persons could benefit from mental health care for significant problems, yet only about 6% of persons seen in community mental health clinics are over age sixty-five (Burns & Taube, 1990). If this condition doesn't change, more than 80% of older persons needing mental health care will never receive it (Butler et al., 1998).

The case of Mr. C. is one illustration of an older adult who may better understand his depression and benefit from counseling services. However, due to the lack of knowledge of available resources and/or awareness of the process of counseling among older adults, Mr. C. may be one of the many within the 80% that will never receive existing services. We know of counselors specializing in the older adult population who have visited senior centers and assisted living communities to educate older persons and their family members on the federal, state, and local services available. Also, some counselors elect to provide pro bono individual and group counseling services at these types of facilities.

Gerontological counselors assume a variety of roles: information and referral counselors, counselors for independent living, counselors for personal growth in aging, preretirement counselors, employment counselors, financial counselors, leisure activities counselors, marital and family counselors, counselors for nursing home patients, counselors for the terminally ill, bereavement counselors, trainers for peer counselors, consultants, and advocates. As a result, the competencies required for gerontological counselors are extensive and diverse (Myers & Sweeney, 1990). To consider the numerous roles of gerontological counselors separately is to risk overlooking the fact that these roles are closely interrelated. The needs of older persons are interconnected, and counselors must work to understand and help them in a holistic manner as unique human beings.

Due to the prevalence of the medical model in health care and the social sciences, the point of view that older individuals are unique human beings with interrelated needs seldom prevails today. The physical needs of older persons are preeminent in this model, and their emotional concerns garner considerably less attention. A more balanced approach might include an assessment of emotional as well as physical needs (Myers, 1991), which would aid clients such as Mr. C., who are being treated only for their physical challenges. Knowledge of client support systems and clients' access to them is important for the helping professionals who work with older persons. When older persons are the clients, the helping professional's scope of information and interventions must indeed be broad.

Awareness of Support Systems

The support systems that exist in older individuals' lives play integral parts in their mental, physical, emotional, and psychological well-being. Counselors should be aware of these educational, social, and health support systems and educated in how these systems can affect older persons' needs for counseling. Throughout the life span, educational support systems such as public and private educational institutions function to explain the aging process to young people in order to combat the fear of growing old and the discrimination caused by the negative stereotyping of older persons. A second function is to develop lifelong educational programs that will enable older persons to keep abreast of social, economic, and political changes in the world. Through these endeavors, older Americans can develop and maintain a competence level that will make it possible for them to participate meaningfully in community life.

The importance of a strong social support system is universally recognized. Because this system tends to grow smaller as people grow older, efforts to replenish and revitalize it are necessary. One possibility is for counselors to encourage older persons to remain active in part-time employment, leisure activities, civic affairs, and educational programs. Another is to suggest that older persons move into housing programs or form small living groups that have membership responsibilities.

Health insurance and hospital care are basic elements of the health support system. Lifetime health care training and lifetime programs for physical exercise historically have been neglected and need further development. In addition, medical training should include greater attention to geriatric medicine and close working relationships with professional counselors so that physical and mental health care can be coordinated effectively. When counseling older clients who are referred by their physicians, we suggest that contact with the physician be consistent and thoughtful so as to provide the most effective holistic care for clients.

Social support systems include access services such as transportation; information and referral; in-home services such as home health aides, visiting, and telephone reassurance; legal services; nutrition services; multipurpose senior centers; and housing. Agencies must make additional efforts to coordinate these services in order to maximize their results for older persons. Congregate housing and community care programs represent positive steps in this direction. In addition, training of individuals specifically for gerontological counseling maximizes the benefits of counseling for older adults.

Training Gerontological Counselors

Gerontological counselors are schooled in the many issues and concerns of older persons and are trained to work specifically with this population in various settings. Along with the generic skills required of all counselors, many counselor preparation programs have gerontology specialty areas through which students can gain explicit knowledge, awareness, and skills for counseling older adults. Although current programs look somewhat different, there are basic tenets of older life that are especially ascribed to the development of gerontological counselors.

Through the integration of concepts about aging and the needs of older persons into each of the core counselor preparation areas defined by the Council for Accreditation of Counseling and Related Educational Programs (CACREP, 2001), counselors-in-training gain knowledge of the needs, concerns, and life situations of older persons. For example, theories of aging can become part of the curriculum in the core course on counseling theories, and assessment methods for older persons can be addressed in psychological testing courses. A good resource describing the many generic and specialty skills required of gerontological counselors is *Infusing Gerontological Counseling into Counselor Preparation* (Myers, 1989). These skills are reflected in the current CACREP standards for gerontological counseling programs (CACREP, 2001).

In the absence of integration of information about older persons into core courses, or perhaps in addition to such integration, specialty courses in preparation of gerontological counseling need to be developed. Currently, counselor education programs may seek specialty accreditation in gerontological counseling through CACREP. The current CACREP standards require that gerontological counseling programs include training in

> the history, philosophy, and trends in gerontological counseling; settings for the practice of gerontological counseling, including private and public agencies, recreational and residential settings; the roles and functions of gerontological counselors; the ethical and legal considerations specifically related to the practice of gerontological counseling (e.g., the *ACA Code of Ethics*); the policies, laws, and regulations relevant to gerontological counseling; professional organizations and preparation standards relevant to the practice of gerontological counseling; and the role of racial, ethnic, and cultural heritage, nationality, socioeconomic status, family structure, age, gender, sexual orientation, religious and spiritual beliefs, occupation, and physical and mental status, and equity issues in gerontological counseling. (CACREP, 2001)

The CACREP (2001) standards also recognize the need for gerontological counselors to be trained in

> normal and abnormal human development in later life; attitudes toward older persons and the individual and societal consequences of ageism; situational and contextual aspects of aging; relationship between physical and psychological aspects of aging and factors affecting physical and mental health in later life; career, retirement, and lifestyle options for older persons; advocacy for lifespan wellness and empowerment of older persons; the aging network service delivery system, including informal support networks and the continuum of community care options, including adult day care, senior centers, recreational and wellness programs, residential and long-term care; and the social service needs of older persons, including education, employment, and retirement.

Continuing education coursework is recommended for gerontological counselors to help them keep abreast of new developments in the field and apply these to their work.

As today's counselors-in-training plan for work with older clients, they may find few opportunities available to meet their needs. Creativity, coursework in departments other than counseling, and attendance at professional conferences help to overcome gaps in training. Counselor educators, even in the absence of available coursework, can assist trainees through individual coursework and practicum experiences to examine their attitudes toward older persons and motivation for wanting to work with this population.

CONCLUDING REMARKS

Just as gerontological counselors are first of all counselors, older persons are first of all persons. As illustrated through this case examples of Mrs. G. and Mr. C., there is great variation among older persons, and the circumstances of aging may present differences in degree and experience; however, ultimately older adult clients have many of the same needs and emotions as others. These two older individuals, as well as other clients mentioned in this chapter, are experiencing later life very differently, and yet all can benefit from the resources and aid of counselors. Expectedly, the counseling interventions and approaches used with older adults will vary as much as the clients themselves vary. Therefore, counselors of older clients must be aware of their attitudes toward the needs and potential of older clients; if counselors hold negative attitudes, they will communicate them to the older person and inhibit rapport. If one firmly believes that persons possess the potential for growth and change regardless of age, then he or she can be a successful counselor to older individuals.

EXPERIENTIAL ACTIVITIES

Individual Activities

1. Attend an Alzheimer's support group meeting. Write down your personal and professional observations. How do these fit with what you have learned about counseling older adults? What counseling interventions do you believe would fit best for working with this segment of the older adult population?

2. Spend a day at an adult day care facility. Interview several older adults. Questions could include: How is life different now from your younger years? How is it better? What are the most important people/things in your life at this point? How do you enjoy spending your time now? Observe interactions between the older adults and

the staff. As a professional counselor, how would you see yourself fitting into this environment? Write down your personal and professional observations, as well as the experiences they share with you.

Group Activity

Divide into groups of five or six people. Ask one person to be the leader and one person to be the recorder. List all the losses that individuals may experience in later life, then choose one loss and discuss how counselors can intervene to help older persons adjust and develop a satisfying lifestyle in spite of that loss. Have each group report its list and suggestions to the full group.

REFERENCES

Administration on Aging. (2000). *Facts and figures: Statistics on minority aging in the U.S.* Washington, DC: U.S. Government Printing Office.

American Association of Retired Persons. (2000). *A profile of older Americans: 2000.* Washington, DC: U.S. Government Printing Office.

Brewi, J., & Brennan, A. (1999). *Celebrate mid-life.* New York: Crossroad.

Burns, B.J., & Taube, C.A. (1990). Mental health services in general medical care and in nursing homes. In B.S. Fogel, A. Farina, & C. Gottlieb (Eds.), *Mental health policy for older Americans: Protecting minds at risk.* Washington, DC: American Psychiatric Association.

Butler, R. (1975). *Why survive? Being older in America.* New York: Harper and Row.

Butler, R.N., Lewis, M.I., & Sunderland, T. (1998). *Aging and mental health: Positive psychosocial and biomedical approaches* (5th Ed.). Boston: Allyn and Bacon.

Council for Accreditation of Counseling and Related Educational Programs (2001). *The 2001 Standards.* Alexandria, VA: Author.

Crose, R., Leventhal, E.A., Haug, M.R., & Burns, E.A. (1997). The challenges of aging. In S.J. Gallant & G.P. Keita (Eds.), *Health care for women: Psychological, social and behavioral influences.* Washington, DC: American Psychological Association, 221–234.

Ficke, S.C. (Ed.). (1990, July). *An orientation in the Older Americans Act* (Rev. ed.). Washington, DC: National Association of State Units on Aging.

Fisk, J.E., & Warr, P.B. (1998). Associative learning and short-term forgetting as a function of age, perceptual speed, and central executive functioning. *Journal of Gerontology: Psychological Sciences, 53,* 112–122.

Fredman, L., Daly, M., & Lazur, A.M. (1995). Burden among White and Black caregivers to elderly adults. *Journal of Gerontology: Psychological Sciences, 50B,* 110–118.

Fry, P.S. (1992). Major social theories for aging and their implications for counseling concepts and practices: A critical review. *Counseling Psychologist, 20,* 246–329.

Grob, A., Krings, F., & Bangerter, A. (2001). Life markers in biographical narratives of people from three cohorts: A life span perspective in its historical context. *Human Development, 44,* 171–191.

Hibbard, J.H. (1995). Women's employment history and their post-retirement health and resources. *Journal of Women and Aging, 7,* 43–55.

Hogan, D.P., & Eggebeen, D.J. (1995). Sources of emergency help and routine assistance in old age. *Social Forces, 73,* 917–927.

Holmes, M., & Holmes, D. (1979). *Handbook of human services for older persons.* New York: Human Sciences Press.

Knight, C.A., & Stones, M.J. (2000). Aging well: Secrets from role models of successful aging. *Gerontologist, 40,* 314–326.

McFadden, S.H. (1996). *Handbook of the psychology of aging* (4th ed.). San Diego, CA: Academic Press.

Miller, R.B., & Dodder, R.A. (1980). A revision of Palmores Facts on Aging Quiz. *Gerontologist, 20,* 673–679.

Morgan, L., & Kunkel, S. (2001) *Aging: The social context* (2nd ed.). Thousand Oaks, CA: Pine Forge Press.

Myers, J.E. (1979). The development of a scale to assess counseling needs of older persons. *Dissertation Abstracts International,* Vol. 39 (12-A) 7165. University of Florida: Gainesville, FL.

Myers, J.E. (1989). *Infusing gerontological counseling into counselor preparation: Curricular modules and resources.* Alexandria. VA: American Counseling Association.

Myers, J.E. (1991). *Empowerment for later life.* Ann Arbor, MI: ERIC/CAPS.

Myers, J.E., & Sweeney, T.J. (1990). *Gerontological competencies for counselor and human development specialists.* Alexandria, VA. American Counseling Association.

Powell, J., & Carpenter, B. (2000). Sexuality, life stage, and life story: A symposium on narrative approaches to sexual identity. *Gerontologist, 40,* 327–348.

Scrutton, S. (1996). Ageism: The foundation of age discrimination. In J. Quadragno & D. Street (Eds.), *Aging for the twenty-first century.* New York: St. Martin's Press.

Uhlenberg, P. (1992). Population aging and social policy. *Annual Review of Sociology, 18,* 449–475.

U.S. Bureau of the Census. (2000). *2000 census counts of the elderly.* Washington, DC: U.S. Bureau of the Census.

U.S. Department of Health and Human Services (2001). *The 2001 HHS poverty guidelines.* Washington, DC: U.S. Department of Health and Human Services.

CHAPTER 14

Counseling Incarcerated Clients

Neresa B. Minatrea
Jered B. Kolbert

Neresa B. Minatrea, Ph.D., is an associate professor of counseling programs at Western Kentucky University. She earned her doctorate in counseling education at the University of South Carolina. She has experience in program development, supervision, training, and direct client services in many clinical settings, including as a social worker in the South Carolina correctional system. She has written and lectured in the field of addictions and working with high-risk populations.

Jered B. Kolbert, Ph.D., is an assistant professor in the Department of Counseling and Educational Psychology at Slippery Rock University. He obtained his doctorate in counseling from the College of William and Mary. He has worked as a substance abuse counselor, marriage and family counselor, and school counselor. His primary research interests include promoting cognitive and moral development and bullying prevention.

AWARENESS INDEX

Please test your knowledge by marking to the following statements true or false before proceeding to the text in this chapter. Compute your score from the scoring guide at the end of the Awareness Index.

   1. T F The prison population has increased by over 50% in the past twenty years.

2. T F Latinos and African Americans have higher incarceration rates than do Caucasians.

3. T F Most inmates meet the criteria for chemical dependency.

4. T F Mental health counseling does not significantly decrease the rate of recidivism.

5. T F The purpose of incarceration is to rehabilitate inmates by helping them to change maladaptive behaviors and address mental health issues.

6. T F By law, individuals diagnosed with disorders such as drug or alcohol dependency, depression, or anxiety are referred to special treatment facilities or ensured specialized counseling during their incarceration.

7. T F Inmates who are mandated by the courts to receive mental health services are often resistant in counseling.

8. T F Offering family counseling is an effective way to reduce inmates' resistance to receiving mental health services.

9. T F Correctional counselors often employ group counseling to address prisoners' uses of denial, minimization, and intellectualization of the behaviors leading to their crimes.

10. T F Most correctional institutions are not designed in a way that enables inmates to have contact with their families.

Scoring guide: **1.** T; **2.** T; **3.** T; **4.** F; **5.** F; **6.** F; **7.** T; **8.** T; **9.** T; **10.** T.

INTRODUCTION

Correctional counselors often view their clientele from the "thirds principle." According to this commonly held view among prison staff, one-third of prisoners will never learn to live successfully within a free community. They never learn to assume responsibility for their actions. Many seem to enjoy inflicting harm upon others and meet the criteria for antisocial personality disorder (ASPD). Correctional counselors frequently devote less attention to these individuals, as they appear to receive little benefit from counseling services.

Another third is viewed as having the potential, with considerable assistance, to ameliorate various personal deficits and eventually return to society. Usually assistance for this group takes the form of individual and group counseling to enhance social skills and problem solving, family counseling to decrease family stressors, and career and academic counseling. The last third of the correctional population, in this view, has the highest chance of success. In general, these individuals have experienced successful careers and interpersonal relationships but have made uncharacteristically poor decisions that lead to incarceration. Counseling for these individuals is mostly supportive, helping them to cope with the stress of incarceration.

CASE EXAMPLES

Ben

Ben sits stooped over the desk with a volunteer tutor, struggling to complete math problems. He has worked for the past three years unsuccessfully to earn the Graduate Equivalency Diploma (GED). He looks up, grins, and waves to his social worker of four years. He excitedly tells her of his recent employment in the facility laundromat. Ben is an African American male who is serving thirty years for murder in the first degree. Ben and his younger brother killed a store owner during an attempted robbery. He has served four years for this, his second offense. During his incarceration he has been a model prisoner; the staff describes him as "easygoing, helpful, and a little slow."

Ben receives little support from his family. His father is himself serving a sentence in the state penitentiary. His mother ceased contact with Ben shortly after his first offense. Ben's only brother was also sentenced for the murder and robbery, leaving only a maternal aunt to visit him occasionally. Ben's limited intelligence (his IQ is in the low 70s), makes it very difficult for him to attain an education. He appears content completing unskilled tasks and manual labor. Diagnostically, he meets the criteria for alcohol abuse. The life accomplishment Ben is most proud of is pleading guilty and accepting responsibility for the murder, thereby saving his brother from serving an adult sentence. The institutional staff has difficulty imagining how this passive, lumbering, slow-witted, teddy bear of a man killed someone with his bare hands.

Larry

Larry walked out of his cell in maximum security a free man. Having procured prestigious lawyers and solicited a congressional representative to obtain special privileges and an early release, his affluent, intact family celebrated his return to the community. This intelligent, Caucasian, nineteen-year-old male committed armed robbery, during a period in which he admits he was heavily abusing alcohol and marijuana. During his three years of incarceration, Larry committed numerous acts of aggression, drug smuggling, and theft. Larry easily passed his GED and attended a local technical college. The correctional staff described Larry as "too smart for his own good, manipulative, spoiled, and explosive." Many of the inmates regarded Larry with admiration and even looked to him for leadership when it came to the newest methods of escape, stealing, or smuggling drugs into the institution. Others regarded him with distaste, indicating that he "got away with murder" because he was White and influential. The staff, fearing political repercussions, was reluctant to confront Larry.

CURRENT ISSUES

Demographic Statistics

As of 2000, nearly 2 million persons were incarcerated in state and federal prisons, accounting for one of every 142 U.S. residents (Bureau of Justice Statistics, 2001a). The prison population has expanded considerably over the past twenty years as sentencing policies have become more severe and the public attitude increasingly favors punishment over rehabilitation (Boothby & Clements, 2000). Minorities are greatly overrepresented in the prison population, accounting for 65% of all inmates. Caucasians have only a 2.4% chance of being incarcerated at some point during their lifetime, whereas the percentage for African Americans is 16.2% and 9.4% for Latinos. Although women constitute only 5% of the prison population, their rate of incarceration is increasing faster than men's (Bureau of Justice Statistics, 2001b).

In 1991, slightly less than half of the state inmates were incarcerated for crimes against person, which are violent crimes such as armed robbery, assault, rape, and murder. One-fourth were sentenced for property crimes, such as forgery and embezzlement. Approximately one-fifth of state prison inmates were incarcerated for drug crimes. The Bureau of Justice Statistics reports that the rate of recidivism is high. A study of prisoners released from eleven state prisons in 1983 found that 62.5% were rearrested within three years (Bureau of Justice Statistics, 2001b). The case study of Ben represents a classic example of an individual returning to the system after a short parole for a more serious crime, despite extensive counseling and vocational and educational habilitation.

Statistics published by the Bureau of Justice indicate that there has been a considerable increase in the percentage of prisoners diagnosed with a mental illness. Sixteen percent of state and local jail inmates self-reported mental conditions, as did 7% of federal inmates (Bureau of Justice Statistics, 1999). However, possibly reflecting the prevailing public distaste for rehabilitation of offenders, there has not been a corresponding increase in the number of mental health workers hired to serve the mental health needs of this population (Boothby & Clements, 2000). Approximately 60% of state and federal prisoners with a mental illness received some form of mental health services. Half reported having received psychotropic medication, and 44% indicated they had received individual or group counseling (Bureau of Justice Statistics, 1999).

Counseling Needs of Prisoners

Prison psychologists report that depression, anger, psychotic symptoms, anxiety, and adjustment issues are the most prevalent problems among inmates (Boothby & Clements, 2000). Prisoners also are likely to struggle with substance abuse and addiction. Survey research reveals that 16% of inmates reported using alcohol or drugs while committing their offenses, and two-thirds of convicted inmates frequently used drugs prior to incarceration. Despite these statistics, only 43% of correctional facilities offer counseling for substance abuse (Bureau of Justice Statistics, 2000a).

SUGGESTIONS FOR ENHANCING COUNSELOR EFFECTIVENESS

A Cognitive-Behavioral Approach

The criminal justice system currently emphasizes punishment in the use of extended sentences and decreased resources devoted to rehabilitation even though research indicates that prison-based mental health programs are effective in reducing recidivism. Meta-analytic studies reveal that mental health programs significantly reduce the rate of recidivism (Andrews et al., 1990; Gendreau, Little, & Goggin, 1995; Gottschalk et al., 1987; Lipsey, 1992). For example, Lipsey's (1992) analysis of only those treatment studies that employed control group comparisons indicates that 64% of the studies reported decreases in recidivism in favor of the treatment group. The average reduction in recidivism was only 10% for all the studies combined, but the rate of reduction in recidivism for studies that met more rigorous treatment criteria ranged from 25% to 60%.

Based on his review of the literature on mental health treatment of prisoners, Gendreau (1996) drew a number of conclusions regarding effective programs and strategies. Programs that were reducing the recidivism rate utilized a cognitive-behavioral model. Such programs make use of modeling, in which prisoners have opportunities to observe more competent persons demonstrate cognitive strategies for managing stress and anxiety, and interpersonal communication skills. For modeling to be effective, the treatment program must disrupt what is referred to as the "delinquency network," meaning the typical prison environment in which antisocial values predominate and are mutually reinforced. Thus, a careful balance must be maintained in terms of providing prisoners with effective models, whether it is the mental health professionals or "model prisoners" who are striving to exemplify the expectations of the program. Prisoners who lack the intrinsic motivation for personal change are provided extrinsic motivation through the use of behavioral theory principles. These include token-economies, in which offenders receive tokens, which serve as secondary reinforcers, meaning that they can be exchanged for primary reinforcers, common examples being visitation time, leisure activities, and so on. Effective programs rely more upon positive reinforcement than punishment, with the average ratio of reward to punishment being 4:1. Programs that are based on the psychodynamic and nondirective/client-centered models are not effective in reducing recidivism, nor are "punisher smarter" programs, which rely upon negative sanctions and take the form of boot camps and shock incarceration. The cognitive-behavioral model is the primary theoretical orientation of correctional psychologists, although many also espouse an eclectic approach (Boothby & Clements, 2000).

Looking at the two case studies, Ben excelled in a token behavior-based environment. He consistently maintained the highest-privilege status during his incarceration. His difficulties occurred after he was outside the structured environment. Ben quickly volunteered for extra cleanup jobs, administrative jobs (copying, sorting, or stapling), and a myriad of landscaping jobs. He provided escort services for tours of the facilities for visiting individuals such as officials (congresspersons, senators, and governmental delegates), college classes, shock probation tours, volunteer organizations, and various interested persons. In any of these capacities, Ben always demonstrated appropriate manners.

A counselor may feel a sense of relief, optimism, partiality, and even pride when providing services to Ben in comparison to the negative feelings associated with providing services for Larry, who constantly tested the token system management. Larry engaged in fights, stealing, insubordination, and multiple rule infractions, which kept him at low-freedom status within the unit throughout his incarceration. In spite of his daily deviant behaviors, Larry earned release after a three-year commitment. In fact, he was released from a maximum-security cell.

One reason why the cognitive-behavioral model may be most effective with prisoners is that it incorporates psychoeducation. Many prisoners, due to their limited cognitive functioning, failed experience with the educational system, and lack of appropriate modeling in their family environment, lack essential skills for daily living, such as obtaining and maintaining employment and basic communication skills. Correctional counselors must learn to refer prisoners to educational and vocational training programs. Many correctional institutions attempt to be self-sufficient by relying upon prison labor. Prisoners usually have the opportunity to work in a variety of settings (e.g., laundry, sewing room, kitchen, or shoe cobbler industry, or farming and cattle production). These jobs provide prisoners with specific skills as well as general employment skills such as time management and team collaboration. Enhancing their education and vocational development increases the probability that prisoners will acquire gainful employment upon release, thus providing an alternative lifestyle to criminal activity. Furthermore, the resulting self-sufficiency inmproves prisoners' self-concepts.

Valliant, Ennis, and Raven-Brooks (1995) integrated the cognitive-behavioral model and psychoeducation in treating probationary and incarcerated offenders with excessive anger. This study is highlighted to demonstrate these theoretical models and how they can be applied to a prison population. Cognitive-behavioral psychologists such as Meichenbaum (1993) assert that anger results from an individual's interpretation of specific life experiences, affective arousal, and behavioral responses. The primary cognitive processes related to anger arousal are appraisal and expectation (Rokach, 1987). One's affective arousal and behavioral responses are determined by one's assessment of social cues, the degree to which they involve a threat, and the degree to which appraisal is subject to distortion and exaggeration. Expectation refers to one's ability to achieve realistic goals and confidence that he or she can employ behavioral responses to reduce affective arousal (Novaco, 1976).

Valliant et al. (1995) relied upon these cognitive-behavioral principles in devising a six-session anger management training program for criminal offenders delivered through a psychoeducational format. The first session of the program entailed didactic instruction on the topics of stress and anger, including examination of personal stressors and reactions to stress, and effective reduction strategies. During the course of sessions two through four, offenders were educated through the use of videotapes about the biology of anger and aggression, its causes and effects, and how anger is processed by the brain. In session five, the offenders reviewed the roles, beliefs, and attitudes that had contributed to their excessive anger. Subjects participated in role playing and discussed how they could more effectively interpret and react to common conflict situations. The last session consisted of review of the material. Results indicated that the offenders exhibited significant decreases in resentment, verbal hostility, and oppositional behavior.

Both Ben and Larry participated in a myriad of psychoeducational groups throughout their confinement. These consisted of drug and alcohol awareness; anger management training; assertiveness training; social and independent living skills development; and communication skills development. Along with these groups, both individuals, with others in the unit, participated in unstructured theme-centered groups: step work based upon Alcoholics Anonymous; relapse prevention, and a grief group. Other services included family counseling sessions, support groups, vocational training, and educational services. Both men and others in their unit participated in experiential groups such as ropes courses and art therapy. Last, Ben voluntarily participated in a group designed for those who had murdered individual(s), which addressed rationalization of their crime, and empathized with the victim(s) and their families.

Address Anti-Social Personality Disorder

Maxmen and Ward (1995) reported that up to 75% of prisoners may have ASPD. The essential feature of this disorder is "a pervasive pattern of disregard for, and violation of, the rights of others that begins in childhood or early adolescence in continues into adulthood" (DSM-IV, 1994, p. 645). Such persons tend to be amoral and irresponsible. Prisoners with this disorder tend to rationalize the crimes they commit by blaming others. Persons with ASPD tend to have a low threshold for gratification and have a high need for excitement, regardless of the potential consequences. They tend to be very mistrustful and feign a strong sense of independence, yet they frequently suffer from depression, anxiety, and substance-abuse disorders (Maxmen & Ward, 1995).

Treating inmates with ASPD is very challenging, as they are typically resistant to counseling. These persons are usually hostile toward authority figures, most likely due to their common experience with inconsistent and physical discipline during childhood. Some are superficially cooperative at first, hoping to receive some perceived gain, but then become resistant as counseling progresses (Maxmen & Ward, 1995). The correctional counselor working with the prisoner with ASPD must be genuine and display unconditional positive regard to facilitate trust (Kellner, 1982). However, the counselor must establish clear limits at the outset and use an active counseling approach, such as behavior reality therapy, to help the prisoner work toward immediate, tangible goals. Commonly, an indication of progress is that the client begins to suffer symptoms of depression as a consequence of shedding his or her image as a tough, self-reliant person. The correctional counselor should increase support and empathy, and normalize and reframe such a reaction as indication of progress (Maxmen & Ward, 1995).

A prominent characteristic of APSD is a lack of empathy. One of the authors remembers working with Mark, who was diagnosed with APSD, and was convicted for attempting to murder his mother. After years of physical, sexual, and emotional abuse by his mother, he put arsenic in her food. Correctional personnel saw a very low-functioning (IQ of 69), quiet young man with a tendency for violent, explosive behavior. During one violent outburst, he hit a correctional officer with an iron after the officer repeatedly told him to cease ironing and return to his room. Five different governmental agencies managed Mark's case, and all indicated his inability to connect or form a bond with other people, poor impulse control, and tendency toward spontaneous violent outburst. After he experienced the behavioral-token environment and participated in various groups, including a group for those individuals with below-70 IQs, he stabilized and learned self-thought stopping techniques. He successfully replaced his explosive angry outbursts with a self-imposed, quiet time-out room. Mark's connection to the unit and his social worker and his own internal locus of control surprised the clinical team.

Gagliardo's (2000) "parole-centered counseling" applies Glasser's reality therapy to the prison population. The main tenet of reality therapy (Glasser & Wubbolding, 1995) is that maladaptive behavior results from a lack of realistic goals and ability to plan and achieve one's goals. The counselor's role is to simply help the consumer identify goals and create and implement a plan to achieve them. Gagliardo devised his approach after experiencing failure in conducting counseling groups for prisoners with substance addictions. He found that the norms of the prison environment precluded group members from self-disclosing emotions. Furthermore, prisoners' motivations for receiving treatment had less to do with working toward a substance-free lifestyle and more to do with their goal of being granted parole. Gagliardo's approach starts where the prisoner is by helping the prisoner to achieve his or her goal. Prisoners are taught how to influence others, specifically their parole board, by learning about body language techniques and presentation skills. Prisoners learn how to present a calm, relaxed body position, and use speech to convey the desired effect, such as remorse and purposefulness. Having prisoners explore how their actions are likely to be interpreted by others enhances their perspective taking, a necessary component for empathy. In response to criticism that such an approach only increases prisoners' effectiveness in manipulating others, Gagliardo argues that these are the necessary skills for societal success and will transfer to the job interview and family relationships. Moreover, as prisoners learn to get their needs met in this fashion, they are less likely to resort to violence.

The unit housing Ben, Larry, and Mark utilized reality therapy in all facets of services. The clinical staff was trained in using reality therapy questioning techniques, which assisted inmates in (1) identifying what they wanted, (2) deciding if their current behavior would get them what they wanted, (3) exploring new choices and options, and (4) committing to new behavioral goals. The individuals housed in the unit learned the same theory and questioning techniques. After a short time in the unit, individuals began asking the "reality therapy questions" in their own jargon around the day rooms, groups, and in peer mediation sessions. "Man, what's up with that?" "How is that going to get you released?" "Yo, you want to stay here forever or get out?"

Encouraging prison clients to identify and seek goals may be complicated in situations in which the prisoner has a commitment order. Commitment orders refer either to a specified length of sentencing and/or treatment required, such as counseling for sexual or drug possession offenses. Prisoners with lengthy or flat sentences, where there is no opportunity for early release for good behavior, often lack motivation. They tend to avoid focusing on their present and ruminate over how past events have contributed to their current predicament, or fantasize about the future life when they are free from prison. These inmates do not connect consequences with inappropriate behavior and are often unwilling to control their impulses, leading to irrational or irresponsible behavior. When conducting coercive counseling services, the counselor looks for any means to motivate participation and natural consequences for the individual's behavior. In such cases, some counselors find it useful to adopt the perspective that the goal is to prepare the road for future change by exploring with the prisoner the advantages and disadvantages of change and helping them to assess their readiness for it (Shearer & Baletka, 1999).

These commitment orders stating a flat sentence of three or six months or ten years remain a provider's nightmare. The individual will be released on the date specified regardless of their behavior or treatment progress unless convicted of new charges. Another former client, Terry, had a commitment order that stipulated twelve months. He violated rules, engaged in fights, stole staff and peers' belongings, cursed, and assaulted the staff. He remained unresponsive to vocational and educational services and disrupted counseling groups. Terry persisted in attaining various chemical compounds to huff or drink. He never successfully completed a furlough. He assaulted a staff member, resulting in a thirty-day commitment in the county jail; still, the prosecutor would not pursue additional charges. Finally, after serving every day and hour, he walked out of the unit a free man. Unfortunately, his story concludes with his death during an attempted burglary.

Woody et al. (1985) assert that individual counseling with prisoners with ASPD is more likely to be successful within the context of a highly structured environment, such as that found in therapeutic communities (TCs). TCs make use of intense emotional catharsis-type participation sessions in which offenders are confronted about their lack of genuineness and responsibility (Lipton, 1998). TCs are authoritarian, having numerous roles and clear consequences, and rely upon peer pressure (Seligman, 1990). The general goal is to foster a more positive self-image, work habits, and increased personal responsibility and trust for others (Lipton, 1998).

Address Substance Abuse

TCs are used to treat drug offenders, as well as inmates with ASPD. Usually a prison TC is housed away from the rampant drugs and violence found in the main correctional facility (Inciardi et al., 1997). Illicit drugs are so prevalent within the regular prison population that 70% of correctional facilities drug-test inmates, and approximately 10% of drug tests conducted in 1998 were positive for one or more drugs (Bureau of Justice Statistics, 2000a). The treatment perspective is that substance abuse is a "disorder of the whole person; that the problem is the person and not the drug, that addiction is a symptom and not the essence of the disorder, and that the primary goal is to change negative patterns of behavior, thinking, and feeling that predispose drug use" (Inciardi et al., 1997, p. 263).

Self-help groups are also a common form of substance abuse treatment. Sixty-six percent of state and federal prisons have at least one twelve-step group such as Alcoholics Anonymous (AA) and Narcotics Anonymous (NA) (Bureau of Justice Statistics, 2000a). The twelve-step recovery model involves acknowledging the addiction, one's powerlessness over it, and reliance upon a Higher Power. A less spiritually oriented self-help group found in some prisons is Rational Recovery, which emphasizes self-motivated recovery and assuming responsibility for choices (Shearer & Baletka, 1999). A few prisons have in-house detoxification centers (Bureau of Justice Statistics, 2000a).

Masters (1994) advocates a tough-love approach to counseling prisoners with substance abuse problems to confront the frequent denial that accompanies the addiction. Since most prisoners are not likely to admit or be motivated to address their addiction, she encourages counselors to become aware of how to detect signs of addiction. The prisoner's arrest records should be reviewed, since frequently the inmate committed the crime while under the influence of a substance or in an attempt to get money for drugs. The correctional counselor must learn to recognize the physical manifestations of different drugs and alcohol, such as slurred speech and emotional quality of voice. The inmate's behavior is important, as offenders who are actively using may miss appointments or work, provide questionable alibis, and exhibit irritability and hostility.

Larry tested the staff's training toward the end of his commitment. Staff noticed that many of the unit's population appeared to behave bizarrely during the middle of the week. There would be no outside visitation, yet drugs appeared to be the root of the behavior. After two weeks of investigation of alibis and defenses, the staff determined that Larry had been smuggling the drugs into the unit after his on-campus landscaping job and after his off-campus vocational schooling.

Counseling students considering working within the prisons are encouraged to get training in addictions counseling. Many correctional facilities lack counselors who have substance abuse training, and as a result less than half of substance-abusing offenders receive individual counseling (Bureau of Justice Statistics, 2000a). Moreover, addictions treatment is typically seen as the purview of master's level counselors, as correctional psychologists refer out for chemical dependency (Boothby & Clements, 2000).

Correctional counselors often employ group counseling to address substance abuse and a variety of other issues. Masters (1994) identifies a number of specific advantages of group counseling with inmates. Group counseling can be effective in addressing inmates' avoidance of responsibility. Since inmates often dismiss or rationalize counselors' confrontations, a group format in which other inmates support counselors' challenges may effectively break through denial. It may provide inmates with an opportunity to release tension in more socially acceptable ways. Group members can communicate their anger with each other in a safe and supportive environment provided by the presence of the group leader and development of group norms. This may allow inmates to take the risk of addressing negative stereotypes held about each other. Inmates may work through guilt stemming from their crimes and see that others accept them despite their actions. However, a criticism of group counseling conducted with inmates is that the subcultural norms of prisoners, such as pseudo-independence and machismo, may dominate and be reinforced. Inmates tend to superficially adopt the group norms for an ulterior motive, such as a recommendation for early release. It is often difficult to encourage inmates to engage in the risk taking necessary for effective group work, as inmates bring up superficial concerns. Finally, the group may reinforce the "pecking order" that exists among prisoners, as the more powerful dominate and control issues of discussion.

Assess Depression

Depression has been identified by correctional psychologists as the most frequent problem among prisoners (Boothby & Clements, 2000). Prisoners with long-term sentences are more likely to suffer from depression, as they see little hope for the future. One approach counselors may employ to instill hope is Viktor Frankl's logotherapy (Frankl, 1984). Frankl asserts that mental illness is due to a lack of meaning in one's life. Meaning may take one of three forms. Creative meaning refers to achievements or accomplishments. Experiential meaning refers to the joy people find in experiencing interactions with others and what life has to offer, such as sunsets, food, or the fascination of momentary awareness. Finally, people may find meaning in suffering, in that they may choose their attitude toward unavoidable suffering. In other words, he or she may choose how to bear the burden by choosing his or her attitude toward it. Correctional counselors can assist inmates in exploring the meaning of their suffering, which some find in religious faith and others find in accepting responsibility for the consequences of their actions. Also, they can help the inmate to find meaning in creative pursuits, as most prisons provide opportunities for creative work, whether it is music, art, or education. This existential approach is more likely to be effective with prisoners functioning at Piaget's formal operational level, since it requires the capacity for abstract thought.

Assess Post-Traumatic Stress Disorder

Many prisoners exhibit symptoms of post-traumatic stress disorder (PTSD). These include hypersensitivity to noise, sudden movements, and smells. Insomnia and nightmares may plague sleep cycles. Other somatic illness such as ulcers, headaches, bowel disorders, high blood pressure, or skin rashes may trouble the offender . Aspects of the prison environment that contribute to these symptoms are the constant threat of violence and the prisoners' sense that they have little control over their lives. Research suggests that a number of treatment modalities are effective in treating PTSD, including psychodynamic, cognitive, and behavioral approaches, combined with supportive counseling in which the counselor emphasizes empathy and unconditional positive regard (Maxmen & Ward, 1995). Other important components of treatment include educating the prisoner about the nature of PTSD and stress management. Counselors can normalize the inmate's reaction to the trauma of prison life, including hypersensitivity, mistrust, and the heightened survival instinct. Teaching prisoners how to achieve relaxation, either through progressive muscle relaxation, meditation, or guided imagery, increases their sense of self-control. Readers who wish to learn to facilitate such relaxation techniques may refer to Benson (1973). One prisoner who found relief from PTSD symptoms through meditation remarked that she always felt that she should have control over her anxiety, and that meditation had provided her with the means for doing so.

Family Interventions

A major issue in counseling inmates is how his or her family is adjusting to the negative impact of incarceration and its disruption in the family's functioning. The inmate's contact with his or her family usually is quite frequent at first. The prison may have facilities to accommodate families, such as playgrounds, private family visiting areas, games, and food, but many prisons are not designed to be family friendly and lack such facilities for visitation (Bilchik, Seymour, & Kreisher, 2001). Over time the meetings become more sporadic. Visitation comes to be too disruptive to the daily functioning of the inmate's family to maintain for an extended period. The difficulty in maintaining regular visitation is exacerbated by the fact that many of the state and federal prisons that were built during the boom in prison construction in the 1980s were located in rural areas, usually far from the communities in which many of the inmate families lived (Bilchik et al., 2001). In fact, a majority of parents in state (62%) and federal (84%) prisons were held more than one hundred miles from their last place of residence (Bureau of Justice Statistics, 2000b). As the visits become more irregular, the inmate may experience feelings of hopelessness and abandonment, which increases their risk of depression and suicide (Couturier, 1995). Frequently, inmates' marital relationships are terminated through separation or divorce (Fishman, 1981).

Children of incarcerated parents experience a number of negative effects. The most immediate impact upon children when they learn about their parent's arrest is terror and confusion. Their confusion may be exacerbated by the common tendency of caregivers to lie to young children about their parents' incarceration (Showalter & Jones, 1980). Children have conscious or unconscious fears about their safety, wondering who will provide for them, as the incarcerated parent may have been the sole caregiver or the breadwinner. Such children are more likely to develop emotional and behavioral difficulties, such as withdrawal, aggression, and depression. They are at increased risk for alcohol and drug abuse, poor academic performance, and low self-esteem. Mental health professionals who counsel children of inmates often find that they are likely to blame themselves for their parents' imprisonment (Bilchik et al., 2001).

Correctional counselors are likely to find that using a family systems approach is advantageous for several reasons. Research indicates that there is a strong and positive relationship between the maintenance of family contact and reduction in recidivism (Holt & Miller, 1972). Prisoners typically suffer from low self-esteem as a consequence of the guilt or social rejection they experience as a result of their association with the criminal justice system. Often, the only thing left that they find meaningful in life is connection to family. While mental health services are usually a low priority for inmates, particularly for men (Bureau of Justice

Statistics, 1999), most are eager for the opportunity to have contact with their families. For example, all of the presented individuals in this chapter enthusiastically participated in family counseling. Inmates readily volunteer for and appear quite motivated when receiving family counseling, willingly exploring and disclosing painful issues that they would rarely reveal in traditional counseling groups (Couturier, 1995). Finally, research has demonstrated that much criminal behavior and mental illness is related the individual's family environment (LeFlore, 1988). Since inmates return to their families, it is essential that we modify this system that has shaped and contributed to the delinquency of the inmate (Couturier, 1995).

Although many inmates are motivated to enter family counseling, there is a tendency for them to deny problems and to have an unrealistic, idealized view of the family. Inmates often become understandably fearful that they are losing connection to their spouses. Some inmates respond aggressively to such fears, verbally criticizing and attempting to control their partner or demanding excessive demonstrations of loyalty. This typically has the unintended effect of pushing the partner away. Some inmates are particularly threatened by the partner's necessary pursuit of financial independence. These reactions exacerbate the partner's stress. This partner is most likely struggling to adjust to being more self-reliant, and meeting the demands of the family alone (Showalter & Jones, 1980).

Showalter and Jones (1980) conduct marital workshops for inmates who are soon approaching parole and their wives. The goals of the workshop include allowing the inmate and his or her partner to identify the changes they have experienced during the period of incarceration, teaching communication skills, educating the partners about how to handle stress, and most important, allowing each an opportunity to explore in a safe environment whether they want to continue the relationship and their reasons for doing so.

Transference and Countertransference

Providing counseling to incarcerated clients makes unique demands of the counselor, both professionally and personally. Personally, the counselor must learn to identify and minimize the deleterious impact of working in an environment in which crisis is the norm. The prison environment breeds hostility, mistrust, manipulation, and aggression. The responsibilities of the correctional counselor during a typical day may include intervening in a potential suicide, mediating a gang conflict, or investigating a brutal physical assault. Many correctional counselors experience increasing cynicism as they become immune to aggressive and manipulative behaviors. As one police officer remarked about his association with people who commit crimes, "you see so much that is alien to your background. You see drug use . . . violence. Your moral judgment gets kind of twisted around and you say, 'Well, this is wrong, but not very wrong'" (Baker, 1985, p. 361). In seeking a release from the constant tensions, correctional counselors often find that friends and family have difficulty being supportive as they react with horror and disgust to the daily experiences of their loved one. Consequently, correctional counselors are at a higher risk for isolation and depression.

Although research suggests that the psychodynamic model is not effective in reducing recidivism, there are aspects of the model that can be helpful in understanding the correctional counselor's relationship with inmate clients. Working with criminals typically evokes intense emotions in the correctional counselor. Counselors are likely to experience negative emotions, such as fear for their personal safety and hatred for the viciousness, lack of remorse, and manipulations of the offender. They are also likely to have such positive emotions as empathy for the prisoner, who usually has a significant history as a victim of abuse. It is not unusual for correctional counselors to feel both ends of the emotional spectrum concerning a single incident: disgust and aversion for the crimes of the prisoner as well as fascination. Some mental health professionals are deeply disturbed to find that they are curious, even titillated by descriptions of violence and sexual assault.

Weiss and Choma (1998) believe that correctional counselors are at high risk for countertransference reactions. Counselors may react to their own ambivalent feelings by projecting them onto the inmate, resulting in a punitive, judgmental stance. Other counselors deal with such disconcerting feelings by avoiding discussion or avoiding obtaining information about the prisoner's crimes. Such countertransference reactions impair the correctional counselor's objectivity. Weiss and Choma (1998) urge counselors to develop awareness of their emotional reactions to inmates as they contribute to a more genuine, therapeutic relationship and a more neutral and realistic view of the prisoner. If one accepts the notion that all behavior is purposeful, then one must attempt to understand the motivations of the criminal. What needs were being satisfied in the commission of such crimes? While it is tempting to assume a moralistic stance in deeming prisoners as simply deviant, bad, or inferior, this position precludes a more complex perspective, one that is more likely to provide answers in assisting the prisoner to meet his or her needs in more socially acceptable ways. Furthermore, we must be able to see the benefits of such behaviors for the prisoner if we are to assist him or her in evaluating the advantages and disadvantages of both the criminal and more conservative lifestyles.

Countertransference reactions also have relevancy to the correctional counselor's personal life. Correctional counselors frequently must deal with distancing from friends and family who have difficulty processing their experiences. Counselors may be reluctant to disclose their position in social contexts, having had lay persons seemingly question their integrity for wanting to associate with "perverts," "delinquents," and "low-lifes." Correctional counselors, along with prisoners, often suffer PTSD symptoms with exposure to antisocial behavior. The lead author experienced recurring nightmares for six months after having been physically assaulted by an inmate. It is crucial that the correctional counselor be committed to self-care in order to avoid burnout. Correctional counselors often find support in peer groups that enable them to analyze countertransference reactions and keep abreast of treatment, education, and research endeavors (Weiss & Choma, 1998).

CONCLUDING REMARKS

This chapter has focused on how correctional counselors provide direct services, such as individual, group, and marital counseling, and refer prisoners to vocational and educational programs. An essential role of the correctional counselor is that of advocate, which involves an understanding of how larger systems, such as society and the legal, correctional, and family systems, impact the individual and can be modified to better meet the needs of the prison population (Kiselica & Robinson, 2001). Correctional counselors must advocate politically for programs and services that benefit prisoners in the long term in order to break the cycle of recidivism. Research indicates that mental health programs can significantly reduce recidivism, and yet the criminal justice system is currently deemphasizing rehabilitation in favor of punishment in the form of longer or "flat" sentences in which there is no chance for early release. Less than half of the inmates identified with mental illness (Bureau of Justice Statistics, 1999) and chemical dependency (Bureau of Justice Statistics, 2000a) receive counseling for their condition. Research clearly indicates what types of programs are effective in reducing recidivism, and yet there currently is increasing use of punitive programs that have been shown to be ineffective. Such punitive programs include boot camps, drug testing, and shock incarceration (Gendreau, 1996). Although research and common sense support the importance of helping inmates to remain connected to their families, less than half of mothers (46%) and fathers (43%) have ever been visited by their children while incarcerated (Bureau of Justice Statistics, 2000b). One way to sell prison administrators on the need to provide family-friendly services and family counseling is to indicate that inmates who have opportunities to interact with their families are less likely to be discipline problems (Bilchik et al., 2001).

It is tempting to think of persons who commit crimes in a simplistic fashion as bad or inferior and thus requiring removal from society. What is often forgotten is how the legacy of family disconnection and the dehumanization of the correctional system perpetuate the cycle of individual and societal suffering.

EXPERIENTIAL ACTIVITIES

Outside-Class Activities

1. Arrange a tour of several types of correctional facilities, such as a county jail; prisons with various security levels, populations, parole, and probation; and/or a federal institution. Interview various individuals (e.g., the warden, mental health workers, correctional

officers, teachers, and employment supervisors), discussing your observations and reactions in class.

2. Observe a criminal proceeding at various court levels (e.g., federal, family court, criminal court, DUI court, traffic court) and discuss your reactions in class.

3. Shadow a counselor working in your local rape crisis center, spouse abuse shelter, or victim advocacy center.

4. Call and arrange to provide volunteer services to a local jail, prison, or halfway house.

5. Watch the movie *Dead Man Walking,* starring Susan Sarandon and Sean Penn. Discuss the main themes of the movie, finding meaning in the integrity, suffering, and machismo of the prisoner.

In-Class Activities

1. Have a speaker associated with the correctional system, such as a counselor, prison guard, warden, or parolee, present to the class.

2. In groups, brainstorm ways to improve the mental health services of a prison.

3. Role-play a parole board hearing, the purpose of which is to determine whether Larry, one of the inmates described in the beginning of this chapter, should be granted parole. Divide the class into several smaller groups, representing the counseling staff, parole board, local community, arresting law enforcement, family and survivors of his previous assaults, the inmate's family, and local organizations for or against a particular cause. Each group receives time to prepare their strategies and present their arguments at Larry's parole board hearing.

4. Role-play a crisis call in which it has been reported to you by a correctional officer that Ben, an inmate portrayed in the beginning of this chapter, stated that he wants to die. Select someone to role-play various individuals (correctional officer, counselor, client, significant others). Role-play various appropriate counselor interventions in preventing Ben from attempting suicide. Afterwards, discuss the ethical, moral, and legal implications of this case with the class.

REFERENCES

American Psychiatric Association. (1994). *Diagnostic and statistical manual of mental disorders* (4th Ed.). Washington, DC: American Psychiatric Association.

Andrews, D.A., Zinger, I., Hoge, R.D., Bonta, J., Gendreau, P., & Cullen, F.T. (1990). Does correctional treatment work? A psychologically informed meta-analysis. *Criminology, 28,* 369–404.

Baker, M. (1985). *Cops: Their lives in their own words.* New York: Simon and Schuster.

Benson, H. (1973). *The relaxation response.* New York: William Morrow.

Bilchik, S., Seymour, C., & Kreisher, K. (2001). Parents in prison. *Corrections Today, 63* (7), 108–113.

Boothby, J.L., & Clements, C.B. (2000). A national survey of correctional psychologists. *Criminal Justice and Behavior, 27* (6), 716–732.

Bureau of Justice Statistics. (1999, July). *Mental health treatment of inmates and probationers (NCJ 174463).* Washington, DC: Department of Justice.

Bureau of Justice Statistics. (2000a, May). *Drug use, testing, and treatment in jails (NCJ 179999).* Washington, DC: Department of Justice.

Bureau of Justice Statistics. (2000b, August). *Incarcerated parents and their children (NCJ 182335).* Washington, DC: Department of Justice.

Bureau of Justice Statistics. (2001a, March). *Prison and jail inmates at midyear 2000 (NCJ 185989).* Washington, DC: Department of Justice.

Bureau of Justice Statistics. (2001b, July). *Criminal offenders statistics.* Washington, DC: Department of Justice.

Couturier, L.C. (1995). Inmates benefit from family services programs. *Corrections Today, 57* (7), 100–105.

Fishman, (1981). Losing a loved one to incarceration: The effect of imprisonment upon family members. *Personnel and Guidance Journal, 59,* 372–375.

Frankl, V.E. (1984). *Man's search for meaning: An introduction to logotherapy* (3rd ed.). New York: Simon and Schuster.

Gagliardo, R.J. (2000). Motivating inmates by addressing their primary concerns. *Corrections Today, 62* (5), 16–24.

Gendreau, P. (1996). Offender rehabilitation: What we know and what needs to be done. *Criminal Justice and Behavior, 23* (1), 144–161.

Gendreau, P., Little, T., & Goggin, C. (1995). *A meta-analysis of the predictors of adult offender recidivism: Assessment guidelines for classification and treatment.* Ottawa: Ministry Secretariat, Solicitor General of Canada.

Glasser, W., & Wubbolding, R. (1995). Reality therapy. In R. Corsini & D. Wedding (Eds.), *Current psychotherapies* (5th ed.; pp. 293–321). Itasca, IL: F.E. Peacock.

Gottschalk, R., Davidson, W.S., II, Gensheimer, L.K., & Mayer, J.P. (1987). Community-based interventions. In H.C. (Ed.), *Handbook of juvenile delinquency* (pp. 266–289). New York: John Wiley & Sons.

Holt, N., & Miller, D. (1972). *Explorations in inmate-family relationships.* Sacramento: California Department of Corrections.

Inciardi, J.A., Martin, S.S., Butzin, C.A., Hooper, R.M., & Harrison, L.D. (1997). An effective model of prison-based treatment for drug-involved offenders. *Journal of Drug Issues, 27* (2), 261–278.

Kellner, R. (1982). Personality disorders. In J.H. Greist, J.W. Jefferson, & R.L. Spitzer (Eds.), *Treatment of mental disorders* (pp. 429–454). New York: Oxford University Press.

Kiselica, M.S., & Robinson, M. (2001). Bringing advocacy counseling to life: The history, issues, and human dramas of social justice work in counseling. *Journal of Counseling and Development, 79* (4), 387–397.

Leflore, L. (1988). Delinquent youths and family. *Adolescence, 28* (91), 629–642.

Lipsey, M.W. (1992). Juvenile delinquency treatment: A meta-analytic inquiry into the variability of effects. In T.D. Cook, H. Cooper, D.S. Cordray, H. Hartmann, L.V. Hodges, R.J. Light, T.A. Louis, & F. Mosteller (Eds.), *Meta analysis for explanation* (pp. 83–127). New York: Russell Sage.

Lipton, D.S. (1998). Therapeutic communities: History, effectiveness, and prospects. *Corrections Today, 60* (6), 106–109.

Masters, R.E. (1994). *Counseling criminal justice offenders.* Thousand Oaks, CA: Sage.

Maxmen, J.S, & Ward, N.G. (1995). *Essential psychopathology and its treatment* (2nd ed.). New York: Norton.

Meichenbaum, D. (1993). Changing conceptions of cognitive behavioral modification: Retrospect and prospect. *Journal of Consulting and Clinical Psychology, 61* (2), 202–204.

Novaco, R.W. (1976). The functions and regulations of the arousal of anger. *American Journal of Psychiatry, 133,* 1124–1128.

Rokach, A. (1987). Anger and aggression control training: Replacing attack with interaction. *Psychotherapy, 24*(3), 353–362.

Seligman, L. (1990). *Selecting effective treatments: A comprehensive, systematic guide to treating adult mental disorders.* San Francisco, CA: Jossey-Bass.

Shearer, R.A., & Baletka, D.M. (1999). Counseling substance abusing offenders: Issues and strategies. *Texas Counselor Association Journal, 27* (2), 71–77.

Showalter, D., & Jones, C.W. (1980). Marital and family counseling in prisons. *Social Work, 25* (3), 224–228.

Valliant, P.M., Ennis, L.P., & Raven-Brooks, L. (1995). A cognitive-behavior therapy model for anger management with adult offenders. *Journal of Offender Rehabilitation, 22* (3–4), 77–93.

Weiss, J.M., & Choma, M.W. (1998). Some reflections on countertransference in the treatment of criminals: Commentary. *Psychiatry, 61* (2), 172–180.

Woody, G.E., McLellan, A.T., Luborsky, L., & O'Brien, C.P. (1985). Sociopathy and psychotherapy outcome. *Archives of General Psychiatry, 42,* 1081–1086.

CHAPTER 15

Counseling the Old Order Amish: Culturally Different by Religion

Joe Wittmer

Joe Wittmer, reared in the Old Order horse-and-buggy Amish faith in Indiana until age sixteen, holds a Ph.D. from Indiana State University in psychological services. He was a teacher-counselor and guidance director in the Fort Wayne, Indiana, schools and worked in the National Teacher Corps Program in the inner-city schools of Gary, Indiana. He is currently a Distinguished Professor in the Department of Counselor Education at the University of Florida, Gainesville.

Dr. Wittmer has authored and/or coauthored fourteen books and has published more than eighty-five articles in refereed journals. His two most recent books are *Managing Your Developmental School Counseling Program* (2000) and *The Gentle People: Personal Reflections of Amish Life* (2001).

AWARENESS INDEX

Test your knowledge by marking the following statements true or false before proceeding to the text in this chapter. Compute your score from the scoring guide at the end of the Awareness Index.

1. T F Approximately 175,000 Old Order horse-and-buggy Amish live in America today.

2. T F Approximately 85% of individuals born Old Order Amish remain members for life.

3. T F The Amish are exempt from social security payments.

4. T F Tourism offers limited monetary benefits to the Amish by their own choice.

5. T F A 1972 Supreme Court decision exempted the Amish from compulsory high school education.

6. T F There are no black Old Order Amish.

7. T F The Old Order Amish are rapidly growing in number.

8. T F The Amish family organization is strictly patriarchal.

9. T F Divorce is nonexistent among the Amish.

10. T F The first language of all Amish is German.

11. T F The Amish are an offshoot of the Mennonites.

12. T F The problems with high school education caused several thousand Amish to migrate to South America during the late 1960s and early 1970s.

Scoring guide: **1.** T; **2.** T; **3.** T; **4.** T; **5.** T; **6.** F; **7.** T; **8.** T; **9.** T; **10.** T; **11.** F; **12.** T.

INTRODUCTION

The term *Amish,* in this chapter, refers to the German-speaking, horse-and-buggy-driving sect often referred to as the "plain people." Most of my knowledge is derived from growing up Old Order Amish in Daviess County, Indiana, until age sixteen. I wish to acknowledge that the Old Order Amish church rules for living vary somewhat from community to community.

It is difficult to pinpoint the exact number of Old Order Amish people living in America today. We do know, however, that at least 35,866 Amish children were enrolled (some Amish schools did not report their enrollments) in Amish schools (grades one through eight) during the 2001–2002 academic year (*Blackboard Bulletin,* 2002). Amazingly, this is a

40% increase in Amish school enrollment since 1990. Thus, I estimate that somewhere around 175,000 Old Order Amish currently live in the United States, with probably another ten or fifteen thousand more living in Canada and South America. The Old Order Amish double in number every fifteen to twenty years (Brown, 2001).

THE WRITER: A CASE EXAMPLE

I am often asked what it is like being Old Order Amish. Most Americans know the group through newspaper reports as a simple, virtuous people who live on farms and use no electricity, automobiles, trucks, tractors, radios, television, computers, or other such "necessities" of modern life. Their broad-brimmed black hats, black buggies, and tussles with educational authorities have further stereotyped them as anachronisms in the space age.

The fourth of six children, I learned the Amish way by a gradual process of kindly indoctrination. Religion on our Indiana farm was a seven-day-a-week affair. The way we dressed, the way we farmed, the language we spoke—our whole lifestyle was a daily reminder of our religion. At five I was given a corner of the garden to plant and care for as my own and a small pig and a calf to raise. All Amish live on farms, although some are quite small, and many work in related occupations such as blacksmithing, buggy making, furniture making, and local, non-government-related factories. My father had no doubt that I would someday be a God-fearing Amish farmer like himself, and my mother often added, in her German dialect, ". . . and a nice black beard like your father's you will have yet."

Because Amish parochial schools were not yet in existence, I entered the strange world of public schools at age eight. Old Order Amish children are not permitted more than eight years of formal education. My parents deliberately planned my late entry into school so that I would be sixteen, the minimum age for quitting, in the eighth grade. High school to the Amish is a "contaminating" influence that challenges the biblical admonition to be a "peculiar people."

America was at war with Germany when I entered the first grade. Without radios and newspapers or relatives fighting (all Amish are conscientious objectors), I had little opportunity at home to keep up with its progress. School was another matter. Non-Amish boys played war games and talked constantly about the war and the branch of service they someday would join. I knew that as a conscientious objector I would never go to war, but I often wished that I could help the non-Amish children gather sacks of milkweed pods, used to make life preservers for American flyers. I was taught, however, that it was sinful to engage in activities that would further the war effort. Because I did not participate, I was often the object of derision. The ordeal reached its cruel peak during the daily pledge to the flag, which my parents taught us not to salute or to pledge allegiance to. The taunts of the students and the disappointed looks of the teacher as I remained seated cut me deeply.

How could I explain that the Amish believe in praying for all governments, which, they hold, are ordained by God? How could I explain that *hate* is not in the Amish vocabulary? Explain it, moreover, in a German accent, for German is the first language of all Amish youth, required by the church to be spoken at home. In retrospect, I can understand all too well the feelings of the non-Amish students. I can understand also why the Amish have established their own schools. What was at stake was not the feelings of Amish youth but a way of life.

The average person often has difficulty understanding the pressures on a nonconformist in the public school system. Many activities are strictly off-limits to the Amish youth, not only dancing and other "worldly" entertainment, but also participation in class photos and educational movies. When it was time for these activities, we Amish children were herded into the hallways, to the chiding and laughter of our classmates.

My most vivid memories of boyhood days concern hostility and harassment endured by my parents and others in the Amish community because of our nonresistance stance to the war. Often "outsiders" attacked us when we rode in our buggies. They threw firecrackers, eggs, tomatoes, and sometimes rocks. Soldiers home on leave burned our wheat shocks, overturned our outdoor toilets, broke windows, and stole buggies. A favorite tactic was to sit in a car trunk and hold onto a buggy while the car sped down the road. The buggy was then turned loose to smash into bits against a road bank. It was not at all unusual to have swastikas painted on our farm buildings and/or houses. After witnessing many such acts of vandalism I became terrified of all adult, non-Amish people. Nonetheless, because the Bible admonished us to be "defenseless Christians," my father and the other elders of the community refused to summon law officials to our defense. By scripture they lived and by scripture they would die if necessary. They always turned the other cheek.

Although turmoil and conflict occurred outside the Amish community, peace was the watchword within its borders. We worked hard and we played hard without the competition of the outside world. We worked as a unit for the Amish community. We played together, worked together, and ate together; a meal did not begin until all members were present. There was no television to interrupt dinner. Thrashing days, barn raisings, and public auctions were a more than adequate substitute for television, radio, comic books, and organized sports. Security and love abounded.

Why, then, did I, at sixteen, make the decision to continue in school— the first step away from Amish origins? The answer is not simple. It included (1) a passion for knowledge, (2) the desire to play high school basketball, and (3) a growing resentment toward my Amish heritage, sparked by the years of derision and scorn in public schools. Somewhere on my way to earning a Ph.D. I fulfilled the passion and outgrew the resentment, leaving still some unanswered questions with which psychiatrists might wrestle.

My Amish kinsmen believe that the "outsider" community has claimed me. Indeed, the campus on which I teach is a far cry from my father's farm, and "a nice black beard" like my father's I do not have. There is no animosity, no shame, among the Amish that I have left. Though I live within mainstream society, I also served as vice-chairman of the National Committee for Amish Religious Freedom, the organization that defended the right of the Amish not to attend high school and won a unanimous decision in the U.S. Supreme Court.

A HISTORICAL OVERVIEW

The Amish sect was born out of the religious turmoil of the Anabaptist movement in sixteenth-century Europe. Points of contention included the Anabaptist refusal to bear arms and to baptize their offspring before the age of reason. The rejection of infant baptism became the most important symbol of the early Anabaptist movement, a movement the state authorities considered seditious, and that marked the unbaptized child's parents for death.

Despite much suffering and death, the Anabaptists prevailed, migrating throughout Europe in their attempts to avoid persecution. In the early 1600s, a division occurred within the Anabaptists over the practice of shunning, or *Meidung*, total physical and spiritual avoidance of an excommunicated member. In 1632, ministers from several different areas in Europe met in Holland in an attempt to heal the breach within their church. Menno Simon, a former Catholic priest, was the leader of the Anabaptists in Holland. His followers became known as Mennists and later as Mennonites. The ruling bishop of the Mennonites did not enforce shunning, but an aggressive young Swiss bishop named Jacob Amman took it upon himself to excommunicate the Mennonite bishops and ministers who did not observe the *Meidung*. Amman's followers became known as Amish.

A single historical event saved the Amish from extinction—William Penn's tour of Europe offering Pennsylvania as a haven from religious persecution. The Amish accepted the invitation to take part in Penn's religious experiment and came to America in the early 1720s to settle in Pennsylvania. As a result, no Amish live in Europe today.

The Old Order Amish strive continually to remain different from "English" or "outsiders," as non-Amish are called. They shun the use of running water, electricity, refrigerators, and most other modern conveniences. They wear home-sewn garb reminiscent of the eighteenth century. Mainstream society's emphasis on high-powered cars, computers, and contraceptive devices is conspicuously absent from the Amish world. The Amish live in isolated communities, using the scriptural admonition "Come out from among them, and be ye separate" as their basis for escaping secular influence.

The important things in life have long been tradition, and set for Amish individuals by their parents, the church, and the community. Values of peace, total nonviolence, tranquility, and humility are evident; no indigence, divorce, or unemployment exists. The Amish orient their lives toward the single goal of eternal life, and they equate their personal pursuit of this goal with work, careful stewardship, and the sweat of the brow.

Preservation of their traditional way of life has required tremendous struggle for the "defenseless" Amish, who, as a matter of Christian principle, refuse to defend themselves. Many legal battles have been fought on their behalf by interested non-Amish individuals. In 1972 the National Committee of Amish Religious Freedom won a unanimous U.S. Supreme Court decision exempting the Amish from state laws compelling their children to attend school beyond the eighth grade. In essence, the Court indicated that this practice would greatly endanger, if not destroy, free exercise of Amish religious beliefs.

In an Amish community, a man begins growing a chin beard the week before his marriage, but the upper lip and neck are kept clean. This custom is in keeping with their nonconformity to worldly values and ways, as outsiders often grow moustaches. An Amish male shaves a straight line across the back of his neck and bobs his hair in a "crockline" appearance. An Amish male does not part his hair, and it is never tapered or thinned on the sides. The men wear large broad-brimmed black hats, suspenders, home-sewn shirts without buttons (only hooks and eyes are used) or pockets, home-sewn pants without hip pockets or zippers, and home-sewn underwear without stripes.

Amish women do not wear makeup of any sort, nor do they shave any part of their bodies. They wear dresses that are full-blown and unadorned with buttons, hooks and eyes, or zippers. The only means of keeping their dresses intact is straight pins. They do not wear lacy underclothing or bras. The women's hair is never cut and is always parted in the middle and pulled tightly into a bun.

To Amish persons, the "world" begins at the last Amish farmhouse on the edge of the Amish community. The Amish farmer has not acquired the worldly need for a tractor with which to farm. He may rely on a tractor for belt power, but it will be mounted on a steel-wheeled wagon and pulled from job to job by horses. He also uses horses to plow his fields and to pull his black buggy. Work is a moral directive. Labor-saving devices are mere temptations. Something new or different is "of the Devil"; things traditional are sacred. Although these customs may seem stern from the outside looking in, the Amish are healthy and happy. They have not acquired the methods of the world to attain their happiness or to fulfill their needs. Old Order Amish men, women, and children have the same needs for love, companionship, fun, and safety as any other member of the human race. How these needs and wants are satisfied is the major difference between Amish and non-Amish. Because their lives are focused and purposeful, they know "where they are going" for the rest of their lives.

Sometimes non-Amish individuals mistakenly assume that the Amish are like them where needs are concerned, or that the Amish at least should want to be like them. For example, recently, after concluding a speech about the Amish, an individual in the audience asked, "Are you telling us that they really don't want to drive a car, that they really don't want running water, and that they really don't want to own a television set or a computer? Come on, Dr. Wittmer, this is the new millennium, the twenty-first century! Amish people surely must secretly want those things." My reply was an unequivocal, "No." Indeed, the Amish do not worry about external standards for success and are not concerned about accumulating material things for their happiness.

In addition, it is important for the reader to understand that the Amish are seldom completely comfortable around non-Amish people. Both children and adults will speak softly and shyly drop their heads and appear meek and introverted in the presence of non-Amish. Some non-Amish find this perplexing, but it is not meant as a personal affront. It is simply a matter of religious belief. By keeping their conversation with non-Amish to a minimum, the Amish avoid unnecessary mingling with worldly persons. They recognize that in order to live and trade among the outsiders, they must learn to understand and speak the language of the English, but revealing extensive knowledge or talking excessively might be considered prideful behavior and possible grounds for excommunication. Pride is a cardinal sin and is never a part of the Amish sense of achievement.

It may surprise some to learn that the Amish, when among themselves, are far from shy, meek, or introverted. As a people they have a keen sense of humor, are full of curiosity, enjoy practical jokes, and love having fun. They are not at all the sad, dull, dour, and introverted group that some writers would have us believe. Nonetheless, they are not overly talkative or boisterous at any time, regardless of who is present.

The Amish Family

The family system is the primary organizing unit that passes down dominant patterns of value orientation in the Old Order Amish culture. Older members of the family funnel the cultural heritage to the younger offspring. Within the Amish family setting, the child learns to respond to authority, to play roles in the cooperative structure, and to obey the norms of the sect. Sibling rank is based on age; the older siblings' roles include disciplining the younger children.

Kinship and religious sanction support marriage. Although varying degrees of cooperation are present between the husband and wife in the fulfillment of their roles, the Amish generally adhere to the biblical tradition that the husband is in direct charge of his wife and children (Wittmer, 2001). Male and female roles are clearly differentiated. Amish married couples do not express overt affection for one another in public. An Amish husband refers to his wife as "her" and she makes reference to "him." Out of mutual respect couples seldom argue in the presence of children.

Amish Children and Growing Up

Amish couples pray for children and do not practice birth control. Most Amish couples have several children (my Old Order Amish sister has fifteen children, seventy-one grandchildren, and thirty-three great-grandchildren), and it is indeed a happy occasion when a child is born. Neighbors come from miles around for *sees koffee* (sweet coffee), the custom of visiting and eating at the home of the proud parents. Neighbors provide the food, but there is no godparent ceremony or gift-giving.

Every Amish baby, if physically possible, is breast-fed. To outsiders, the Amish mother may appear to be hiding her infant from the eyes of the world. An Amish woman always wears a black shawl over her shoulders, and a mother carefully tucks the baby away under her shawl, often making the child unnoticeable. The Amish child is to be protected, even at an early age, from the world. The new baby sleeps with the parents for the first several months of life. Along with the security this practice affords, it also is convenient for breast-feeding and provides warmth in the poorly heated homes.

The Amish consider the child a gift from God. People marvel at the attention, the love, and the affection given to the newborn Amish infant. Even when asleep the baby will be in someone's arms. To the Amish, infants are blameless innocents. If they have adjustment problems, it is the parents and community that have erred. There is an Amish saying that clearly reveals the importance of children: "Put the swing where the children want it, as the grass will always grow back." Another adage is "Always treat children in the direction you wish them to grow."

One example of treating children in the direction you wish them to grow is teaching toddlers to fold their hands in their laps during prayers. At the silent grace before and after the meal, I have observed many small children, including infants, held in someone's lap with their little hands enclosed in the adult's larger ones. Learning to pray correctly, along with maintaining silence in church, are very important for even the youngest child to learn.

The Amish teach their young that formal education is worthwhile up to a point, but that too much is non-Christian and only for the foolish. If a fear exists among Amish parents, it is that of losing their children to the world through the process of formal education. They prefer the old-fashioned one-room school with its limited facilities, since it is more in keeping with their simple domestic lifestyle. They want to train their youth at home in the care and operation of farms. This, to them, requires no more than eight years of reading, writing, and arithmetic.

Babies grow to be corn huskers, cow milkers, and God-fearing community members. Amish parents assume that as they grow older their children will care for them and respect the wisdom the culture associates with advancing age. When the youngest son marries, he moves his bride to his parents' farm. At this time, they build a second, smaller house, usually adjacent to the original structure, called the *grossdawdy haus* (grandfather house) for the parents—older persons receive the new homes in the Amish community. The son assumes management of the farm, and the parents retire.

COUNSELING THE OLD ORDER AMISH

Many modern-day writers espouse the values and benefits that coincide with living in a slow-paced, agrarian, pacifist, nonmaterialistic communal setting such as that provided by the Old Order Amish. Living in this type of close-knit religious community provides many positive benefits to its participants. Foremost among these is a delineated, built-in social identity with a ready-made support system for every man, woman, and child. Living in a culture that provides such a social identity and support system is of great value, both psychologically and medically, for its members. For example, many who have studied the Amish believe that major depression occurs considerably less often among the Old Order Amish than elsewhere in the United States (Langin, 1994). Old Order Amish are not immune to mental disorders but are extremely reluctant to avail themselves of mental health services.

The Amish are vigilant in keeping their distance from the world, and this, for all practical purposes, includes the worldly professional counselor. To the Amish, one's mental health equates precisely with one's spiritual health. Likewise, an individual's spiritual health can only be enhanced through one's relationship to the church and the group as a whole through God, not by anything that a worldly mental health caregiver might say or do.

Any interactions involving an outsider and an Amish person should occur in the context of what is best for the entire Amish community—not what is best for the individual. Personal independence, a trait generally encouraged in American society, is considered a cardinal sin within the Amish culture (Wittmer, 2001). Members who reveal too much independence can be excommunicated from the church until they make a public confession of wrongdoing. One who becomes too independent is thought to be a lost soul, no longer dependent on God. Thus, the Amish community views anyone advocating personal responsibility or independence for an Amish man, woman, or child with extreme suspicion. The notion of counseling for personal responsibility or autonomy, as advocated in the American Counseling Association's code of ethics, can simply not be ethically or morally applied when working with the Old Order Amish.

Mental health service caregivers have made few inroads into this pious, austere community. I am happy to report, however, that some Amish communities are now requesting individual assessments through vocational rehabilitation. With an increasing number of Amish working in factories and shops, more personal injuries occur. Since work is a moral directive in the Amish culture, some Amish bishops have permitted certain vocational assessments to help Amish persons get back to work. This came as a surprise to me, since the Amish must gain consensus where any changes in their "rules for living" are concerned, but in at least one case the assessment included the administration of an intelligence test to a young Amish woman with limited intellectual skills so that she might be placed in a sheltered workshop. This is progress indeed.

Nonetheless, Amish bishops are the final authority on what may or may not be permitted for members, and they are likely to be quite cautious, even suspicious, in overseeing the results of an assessment. A bishop can quickly change his mind, and the administration of vocational assessments will come to a halt on that very day without explanation. Counselors and other mental health service providers should not be shocked, therefore, if their Amish clients simply do not show. If, however, a genuine and empathic professional outsider counselor continues to make clear that assessments are conducted with the sole purpose of assisting the individual to return to work, the church and the bishops will, most likely, cooperate.

I have been personally involved in several situations in which Old Order Amish families have, with consensus from the church elders and with the bishop's permission, successfully requested mental health assistance for family members exhibiting serious mental illness. In each case, however, they sought assistance from a physician, not a mental health service provider. The physicians prescribed medications for stress, anxiety, or depression and, in two situations of which I am aware, psychotropic drugs for bipolar disorder. Unfortunately, the Amish in general have a reputation among medical practitioners as "doctor changers." They may abandon their medications for no apparent reason; cease making appointments with their current doctor and seek the assistance of an Amish faith healer instead; or flock to a doctor who the bishop, or some other church elder, believes has found a cure for a particular illness. Sadly, unscrupulous, self-proclaimed medical specialists often take advantage of the Amish.

Mental health service providers, school counselors, and public school teachers should realize that Amish parents are extremely leery of any outsider dispensing mental health advice for them or their children. They will quietly listen to suggestions but not incorporate them until after they have sought council with at least three Amish adults. Using three adults to solve problems and/or make decisions is an Amish practice that seems to work for them. For example, if a dispute develops between two Amish farmers, three men are selected to arbitrate and find the solution. Their decision is final.

I realize that I have presented a perplexing and confusing description of the Amish as it concerns their mental health. They are, in general, suspicious and secretive where mental health is concerned. Some Amish will see the counselor as interfering with "God's way" and view counseling as leading their members "astray" into the world. Careful explanation of the counselor's role may result in acceptance. My father used to say that "God let man make modern medications for a good reason" and that it was okay, up to a point, to go to the English doctor when necessary and, with permission, to take some of these medications. Amish leaders may eventually be convinced that a "talking cure" is of value to their members, but for the present the elementary schools provide the most probable setting in which professional counselors will engage Amish clients, as a limited number of Amish children still attend public schools (Wittmer, 2001).

SUGGESTIONS FOR ENHANCING COUNSELOR EFFECTIVENESS

The counselor who is effective with Amish children (and with Amish adults) will be genuine and empathic, but also will respect the following guidelines.

Deemphasize the concept of self. The Amish child is taught to be cooperative rather than competitive, innovative, or aggressive. To the Amish, a child is not a unique individual. He or she is simply one member of a God-fearing group and should be treated as such.

Recognize the limitations of standardized assessment. To my knowledge, there are no assessment instruments available today normed using Amish children, youth, or adults. Can you imagine the frustration of taking a test that requires you to take part in a vocabulary subtest (written in English) when you barely speak the language? In addition, Amish children will not have the same points of reference; they will not recognize a popular cartoon character, electrical appliance, or automobile.

Similarly, speed is rarely stressed in the Amish culture. Parents and church elders admonish children to do careful, accurate work. Children are expected to work steadily, never skip anything they do not understand, and attend to detail. They are to ponder the problem, to work at it until they have mastered it, rather than do work too quickly and make careless mistakes. Thus, a teacher or counselor who administers a timed test to an

Amish child could cause unnecessary psychological stress and fail to gain a true picture of the child's skill.

Due to differences in motivation, Amish children are at a disadvantage when taking any standardized test. Performing well on a test in order to gain a better job or enter college has no meaning to the Amish and is useless as a motivational scheme. Furthermore, testing of any sort is viewed as competition, a taboo in most Amish communities. Educators will find that Amish parents are not interested in knowing their children's achievement test scores as compared to those of other children in the United States, or, for that matter, in the classroom. A counselor should seek the consent of Amish parents before administering any test.

Understand the Amish world of work. Neither children nor parents are interested in career exploration. The vocational preferences of Amish children tend toward service occupations and manual work. Children emulate the work roles of Amish adults, and their vocational aspirations and dreams are realistic and attainable within the limits of Amish culture. One should also note that the feminist movement has not brought about any changes in the Amish lifestyle.

Respect the social distance that Amish children maintain with non-Amish children. A very real concern among Amish parents today is the possibility that their children will form close, personal friendships with non-Amish children and become too comfortable with the ways of the outside world before they totally understand their own Amishness. Any attempt on the counselor's part to have Amish children form friendships with non-Amish children (such as in mixed-group counseling) will be contrary to the wishes of their parents.

Avoid probing into home or Amish community problems. Because institutions such as the home and the church are held in high esteem, Amish children enjoy participation in these institutions. The possibility of bringing shame on their family will inhibit children from talking about family or cultural problems. For example, even though an Amish child may be overwrought concerning an excommunicated family member, it would be even more shameful to discuss it with a non-Amish person.

Realize that a caring relationship is not enough. Affective understanding alone is not sufficient when counseling Amish children. The effective counselor also will be knowledgeable of the customs, traditions, and the values existing in the Amish child's unique environment. The acute disparities in culture will most certainly be compounded if a counselor lacks knowledge and then interacts with a confused and bewildered Amish student.

Accept the fact that parents may have asked their children to avoid counselors. Amish parents are responsible for training their children and consider themselves accountable to God for doing it correctly, especially where their spiritual well-being is concerned: mental and spiritual well-being are one and the same. Thus, your counseling a child about values or morals may appear disrespectful. If the home is responsible and obligated for moral and religious training, then you may appear to be a meddler.

Keep your own cultural biases in check. Work at not being guilty of assumed similarity. They are not like you and really don't want to be like you! Be genuine and empathic but gain accurate, cognitive knowledge of their cultural standards, principles, and rules for living prior to counseling any Amish person.

CURRENT ISSUES

Although the Amish wish to remain unchanged, the Amish farmers face many issues and problems in the twenty-first century. As believers in primitive farming methods, the Amish reject as counter to the Bible and ecologically irresponsible the use of artificial insemination for breeding animals and the genetic modification of crops. For example, new laws and demands of milk inspectors have made it difficult for Amish farmers to sell their milk to dairies. In addition, the Amish cannot afford today's high land prices, especially if they live in an established Amish community where tourism is flourishing. It is common for ten to fifteen Amish families to move from an established Amish settlement such as Lancaster County, Pennsylvania, to a new area of the United States or Mexico in search of less expensive farmland. Thousands have emigrated to South America to escape the influence of technology and the demands of the increasingly complex North American society.

Another issue is the recent development of home-based cottage industries among the Amish. Home enterprises generally require compliance with employee and government regulations and thus more exposure to the outside world. Any business involving commerce outside the Amish community is fraught with potential hazards for the Amish and their way of life.

I anticipate many more battles between the Amish and the modern world. It is extremely difficult for them to stay the same in twenty-first century America. As our secular society becomes even faster paced and computer driven, it will be even more difficult for the Older Order Amish to maintain their slow-paced, closed society.

CONCLUDING REMARKS

I have presented a few basic principles, concepts, and skills that the culturally skilled professional counselor should know prior to interacting with Amish children and adults. The Amish are not immune from many of the problems and concerns that other non-Amish Americans face on a day-to-day basis. Most certainly, the problems facing their youth, for example, are similar to those facing all youth in the fast-paced world of the twenty-first century.

The Amish are a tenacious people and are intent on maintaining their way of life. Family and closeness to one another are everything to the peaceful Amish. With those ties they have survived in America for well over two hundred years. Now, in the new millennium, the land offered to them by William Penn is cluttered and costly, and offers little accommodation for their way of life.

I hold a continuing affection for the Amish culture I left behind and believe strongly that they will do whatever is necessary to preserve their faith and sustain the family. They will continue to grow in number in America, and I sincerely believe that my Amish heritage will continue to be a source of satisfaction and enjoyment to your descendents and mine for years to come.

EXPERIENTIAL ACTIVITIES

1. Some non-Amish individuals known by the Amish as "seekers" attempt to become Amish. Although always accepted, few have remained in the community. Assume you have decided to join the Amish church, and role-play the initial steps you would take to ensure your success.

2. Construct an artificial environment in which no one has electricity or telephones for a day and observe what it is like. Write a brief essay on your feelings concerning the experience and share it with colleagues.
3. Debate the ACA ethical principle of "autonomy" where Amish clients are concerned. How can a counselor adhere to this important principal and yet uphold the Amish value of dependency on others?
4. Select three Amish characteristics given in this chapter that contrast most with your own. How would these differences affect communication between you and an Amish person? How would they affect your ability to effectively counsel an Amish person?
5. Review the guidelines given in this chapter for counseling Amish people. Ask a friend to assist you in making a videotape of a counseling session in which the two of you alternate playing the role of an Amish client and non-Amish counselor.
6. Assume the role of an Old Order Amish person of your age and write a short essay entitled "Living in Modern-Day America."
7. Read the following poem, written by a sixteen-year-old Amish female. What insights about the Amish culture did you gain from this reading?

A Buggy Ride

Who'd want to drive a motor car
    when he could have a horse?
There may be many others who
    would take a car, of course.
They do not know the joy of it,
    a horse and buggy ride.
The feel of wind upon your face,
    no stuffy seat inside.
Along the road we hear birds sing,
    and watch a squirrel dash,
    and just enjoy the scenery
    instead of rushing past.
The sound of horses' trotting feet
    is music to the ear.

No car is ever half as nice
at any time of year.
True, winter's snows are very cold
and rain makes me quite wet.
The wind can be uncomfortable
and our fingers freeze, and yet,
I still would choose a buggy ride.
In spite of cold or heat
I shall insist that it is true,
a buggy can't be beat!

(Reprinted with permission.)

REFERENCES

Brown, J. (2001, May 26). Keeping the kids in the fold: Some religious colonies are thriving. *Gainesville Sun,* pp. B6.

Blackboard Bulletin. (2002, January). Amish schools today. (p. 23). Aylmer, Ontario: Pathway Publishers.

Langin, G. (1994). *Plain and Amish: An alternative to modern pessimism.* Scottsdale, PA: Herald Press.

Wittmer, J. (2001). *The gentle people: Personal reflections of Amish life* (Expanded ed.). Minneapolis, MN: Educational Media Corporation.

CHAPTER 16

Preparation for Helping Professionals Working with Diverse Populations

Larry C. Loesch
Kelly M. Burch-Ragan

Larry C. Loesch, Ph.D., NCC, is a professor in the Department of Counselor Education at the University of Florida. He has been president of the Florida and National Associations for Measurement and Evaluation in Guidance, FCA, Chi Sigma Iota, and SACES, and a CACREP board member. He has been an evaluation consultant for the NBCC since 1980. He was a corecipient of the ACA's 1983 Research Award and of its 1992 Hitchcock Distinguished Professional Service Award. He is a charter member of Chi Sigma Iota's Academy of Leaders and received the 1998 CSI Sweeney Professional Leadership Award. He received a 1998 Professorial Excellence Award from the University of Florida. Recently, Dr. Loesch was a Fulbright Scholar in Slovakia.

Kelly M. Burch-Ragan, LMFT, LMHC, NCC, is a doctoral candidate and alumni doctoral fellowship recipient in the Department of Counselor Education at the University of Florida. She is responsible for counseling services at two facilities operated by Family Medical and Dental Centers of Florida. She serves as treasurer for the International Association of Addiction and Offender Counselors. Kelly is a member of the ACA, ACES, and Chi Sigma Iota. She is serving as a member of the NBCC Examination Committee, was a recipient of a 2001 SACES Emerging Leaders grant, and received a 2000 grant/award from the Commission on Colleges of the Southern Association of Colleges and Schools.

AWARENESS INDEX

Please test your knowledge by marking the following statements true or false before proceeding to the text in this chapter. Compute your score from the scoring guide at the end of the Awareness Index.

1. T F The perspective that "counseling is counseling is counseling" suggests that counselors do not need specialized knowledge or skills to provide effective help to members of diverse populations.

2. T F Experiential, interactive experiences with members of a special population assist professional counselors to improve their knowledge, attitude awareness, and interpersonal skills in regard to working with members of diverse populations.

3. T F In working with members of diverse populations, counselors use a special set of counseling or helping functions.

4. T F Cost-effectiveness is not an important consideration in determining the best way to counsel members of a diverse population.

5. T F Effective counselor preparation programs include having trainees engage in supervised, *actual* helping processes with members of a diverse population.

6. T F A counselor's attitude toward the diverse population is the strongest influence on the effectiveness of the helping services the counselor can provide for members of that population.

7. T F A well-defined, structured method of professional preparation for counselors to work with members of diverse populations has been developed.

8. T F A counselor's consultation function for work with members of diverse populations is complicated by the fact that the counselor may assume any of several roles in the process.

9. T F By definition of their status, members of diverse populations are subject to bias in assessment procedures applied to them.

10. T F The specialized continuing professional development of a counselor who works with members of diverse populations should include further training in all areas of counselor functioning.

Scoring guide: **1.** T; **2.** T; **3.** F; **4.** F; **5.** T; **6.** T; **7.** F; **8.** T; **9.** F; **10.** T.

INTRODUCTION

The importance of counselors being able to provide help in different ways, and in particular, in ways individualized for persons who differ (i.e., are diverse) from them, is well recognized. The effectiveness of helping in such contexts is to a large extent contingent upon the skills and attitudes of the helper. Egan (1994) described the situation succinctly: "Helpers differ from their clients in any number of ways—gender, sexual orientation, social status, economic status, religion, politics, ethnicity, work experience, age/life stage, type of problem, and so forth. Therefore, as many researchers and practitioners have pointed out . . . understanding and valuing diversity is critical to effective helping" (p. 52). The significant question is, how do helpers come to have the "appropriate" understandings and attitudes necessary for effective helping for persons from diverse populations?

Historically, two broad positions have been advocated about the nature of helping services for persons from diverse populations. One position, grounded primarily in person-centered approaches, essentially holds that "helping is helping is helping." In other words, so-called fundamental counseling skills, such as provision of accurate empathy, congruence, unconditional positive regard, and genuineness, are applicable to and effective with *any* person needing help, *if* they are applied correctly (see, e.g., Patterson, 1996). From this perspective, a helper who has sound and well-developed fundamental counseling skills *and* is highly sensitive to the uniqueness of each individual should be able to help *any* person effectively. This perspective has found favor with many helpers in part because of its apparent simplicity and in part because it implies that to be an effective helper one has only to continue to fine-tune basic helping skills (Patterson, 1996). For example, often this is the attitude of students in our counselor preparation program as they begin their course in multicultural counseling; they think they are just going learn how to be "more sensitive." At a theoretical level, it is difficult to argue with this perspective. Certainly a helper with exceptionally well-developed sensitivity should be able to understand fully the nature of a person's reality (i.e., affective and behavioral factors in the person's environment with which the person must contend), and then act within that reality to help the person. A nagging question remains, however. How many helpers can actually achieve this exceptional level of sensitivity?

A second perspective holds that each person needing help has unique characteristics and circumstances that can be addressed effectively only through application of specific helping skills derived from thorough knowledge of the person's cultural characteristics (D'Andrea, Daniels, & Heck, 1991). In other words, a helper must have substantive knowledge of the cultural characteristics (i.e., traditional and unique personal and familial attributes) of the person to be helped and of the helping skills presumed to be effective for persons with such characteristics. This is the attitude frequently held by students in our multicultural counseling course as they near its completion. Again, at a theoretical level, it is difficult to argue with this perspective. Certainly a helper who clearly and fully understands the characteristics of a client should be able to use that knowledge, and the skills based on it, to provide effective help. But here the nagging question is, can any individual helper ever achieve all the knowledge and skills necessary to be effective with all the many different types of people with whom the helper is likely to work?

These two perspectives have generated considerable debate in the helping professions about what knowledge and skills helping professionals should have in order to help members of diverse populations effectively, as well as about how aspiring helping professionals should be prepared to provide help (e.g., Das, 1995; Dinsmore & England, 1996; Locke & Kiselica, 1999; McFadden, 1996; Midgette & Meggert, 1991; Nwachuku & Ivey, 1991; Pedersen, 1996, 2000; Weinrach & Thomas, 1996; Williams, 1999). Two recent developments have influenced current emphases and practices in professional preparation for working with members of diverse populations. The first was the development of multicultural counseling competencies (Arrendondo et al., 1996). Although counselor educators had long advocated training in multicultural competency (Atkinson, 1994; D'Andrea et al., 1991; McRae & Johnson, 1991; Ponterotto, Alexander, & Greiger, 1995; Sue, Arrendondo, & McDavis, 1992), only recently has a set of such competencies been available. These multicultural counseling competencies were developed through the collaborative efforts of various members and member organizations of the American Counseling Association (Arrendondo et al., 1996) to identify the knowledge and skills counselors should have in order to avoid being culturally inappropriate, provide effective helping services, and reduce prejudices or biases in working with persons from diverse populations (Arrendondo, 1999; Sue, 1996). Although education and training in these competencies are given in many counselor preparation programs and some evidence that training in the multicultural counseling competencies increases counselor effectiveness with persons from diverse populations has been found (e.g., Holcomb-McCoy & Myers, 1999), such preparation is not as widespread as many professional educators believe is necessary and appropriate (e.g., Arrendondo, 1999). Nonetheless, introduction of the multicultural counseling competencies has done much to clarify the knowledge and skills needed for effective helping for persons from different cultural populations.

A second development is the allegation that counselors who are not sufficiently knowledgeable and skilled in their work with members of diverse populations are not only ineffective, but also unethical (Casas, Ponterotto, & Gutierrez, 1986; Cayleff, 1986; Ibrahim & Arrendondo, 1986). Presentation of this allegation always sparks lively debate in the professional ethics course our students take. Yet while this allegation is debatable, it nonetheless ensures that appropriate professional multicultural behavior and preparation are of concern to *all* current and future helpers.

Even in light of these advancements, there remains no clearly preferred method of preparation for helpers working specifically with persons from cultures different from theirs. There are only preferences. Our preference is to focus upon the functions (i.e., individual and group counseling, vocational counseling, assessment, consultation, research, special types of counseling and teaching) that most helpers use in their work. The multicultural competencies alluded to earlier can be integrated across these functions relatively easily. Thus, many of the methods currently used to train helpers for work with typical populations can be adapted successfully to train helpers for work with persons from diverse populations.

Our discussion should not be construed to mean that innovative preparation methods are not needed or do not exist. Innovative training methods always are an excellent complement to established methods, and indeed some supplemental creative training practices already exist (see, e.g., Leong & Kim, 1991; Pedersen & Ivey, 1993; Vontress, 1988). The preparation methods suggested here fall into the "established" category because space does not permit allusion to all possible methods.

POTENTIAL COUNSELING FUNCTIONS

The professional preparation of helping professionals who intend to work with persons from diverse populations must necessarily take into account what these helper trainees will actually be *doing* in the future (Arrendondo et al., 1996; Das, 1995; Ridley, Mendoza, & Kanitz, 1994; Steenbarger, 1993; Whitfield, 1994). For our purposes, a convenient categorization of functions is provided in the CACREP (2001) professional preparation standards. These standards identify six major counselor functions: individual counseling, group counseling, vocational counseling, assessment, consultation, and research. However, to be as comprehensive as possible, two additional functions will be addressed: special types of helping (e.g., marriage and family or lifestyle) and teaching.

Individual Counseling

The helping professional's functioning in individual counseling is typically dictated by a preferred helping orientation. When helping persons from diverse populations, the question is not whether individual counseling is appropriate, but rather which approach is potentially most effective. For example, there have been numerous suggestions in the professional literature about how much structure and/or directiveness is needed in helping persons from particular groups. However, selection of the one, "right" counseling approach is a tenuous proposition at best. This lack of specificity often gives rise to consternation among our newer counselor trainees because they want to know the "best" way to counsel. Regardless of the approach taken, however, consideration of the client's cultural context is essential (Ibrahim, 1991). For example, what are the typical levels of self-disclosure and/or sharing of difficulties to strangers in the cultural group of which the client is a member?

Group Counseling

The helping professional's functioning in the group context also is dictated by individual preferences for various possible helping orientations, and thus the helper's personal orientation preferences also are an issue here. Additionally, the group context requires focus on the interactions among group members. Persons from some diverse populations are much more willing to interact in a group counseling circumstance than are others. Accordingly, the social interaction characteristics of a diverse group are an important issue in the group counseling process (Sodowsky & Plake, 1992). For example, what is each group member's cultural norm for eye contact in verbal communication?

Vocational Counseling

The key issues in vocational counseling with persons from diverse populations center on their unique characteristics (Campbell & Hadley, 1992). To what extent do these unique characteristics (e.g., values, history, education, or family configuration) affect their vocational development? What are their abilities and/or desires to capitalize on vocational opportunities? What can the counselor expect in regard to career maturity, previous career exploration, or employment discrimination in a special group? What part will counseling for self-esteem play in their vocational guidance? Understanding and capitalizing on their unique characteristics and circumstances is essential to effective vocational counseling for special populations (Sharf, 1997).

Assessment

More than any other function, assessment is at the center of controversy within the helping professions (Loesch & Vacc, 2000). The controversy exists because, regardless of the procedures employed, some *evaluation* is made based on the results of the assessments. Evaluation involves judgments, and judgments are almost always controversial.

Bias is the term applied when the comparison (i.e., evaluation) process is deemed unfair. Typically, debate about bias in assessments with persons from diverse populations centers on sociolinguistic differences, which in some cases may invalidate the assessments. Unfortunately, many students in counselor preparation programs believe (initially) that this means that assessments automatically should not be made with persons from diverse populations. However, it is more appropriate to suggest that assessments (and subsequent evaluations) should be made especially carefully. For example, a respondent's cultural group should be well represented in the assessment's normative group, the respondent should have sufficiency in the language of the assessment, and the assessment procedure should be investigated for biases against specific groups of persons.

Consultation

Perhaps more than any other function, consultation activities allow helping professionals to influence very large numbers of persons (Conley & Conley, 1991). Briefly, consultation is a process in which a person (i.e., the consultant) provides assistance to another person (i.e., the consultee) so that the second person can provide more effective services to others (e.g., clients). A major concern about the consultation function is that the helping professional is "one step removed" from the people to be affected by the consultation. This distance between source and impact raises significant questions about which consultation strategies and activities have the greatest potential for success. Should the consultant assume an educative, counseling, advice-giving, change-agent, or source-of-information role for the consultees? The unique characteristics of the diverse population, as well as those of the intermediary, further compound the difficulty. Because any consultation intervention may very well have broad social or political ramifications, careful examination of all facets of the situation is essential. For example, are there substantive cultural differences between the consultant and the consultee, and, if so, can they be overcome to allow the consultation process to be effective? A related question is, to what extent do cultural differences between the consultant and consultee influence the ways the consultee will carry out the actions recommended by the consultant?

Research

The research function in the helping professions is another source of controversy in regard to diverse populations (Ponterotto & Casas, 1991). The need for research in counseling is generally acknowledged and widely espoused; however, only a small proportion of helping professionals actually engage in research projects. Moreover, only a small portion of the research is specifically concerned with applications or implications for diverse populations.

A major issue in research on helping members of diverse populations is lack of significant numbers of persons from which to derive data. Often, relatively large samples from various groups are difficult to obtain, and some diverse population groups resist participation in research activity out of concerns for fairness of representation, biased interpretations of findings, or overemphasis on unimportant cultural characteristics. These situations necessitate great sensitivity from helping professionals engaging in research activities.

Special Types of Counseling

The rapid growth of the helping professions and increasing recognition of their value to society have allowed for the development of many specialized types of helping. Recent innovations include culturally sensitive marriage and/or family, bereavement, lifestyle, leisure, midlife and preretirement, and health and wellness counseling, and assertiveness and stress management training. While such services have expanded greatly, their use with persons from diverse populations has lagged (D'Andrea et al., 1991). For example, what are the unique considerations faced by a family composed from different racial backgrounds (e.g., in an interracial marriage) or social levels (Fontes & Thomas, 1996)? There exists a great need to expand the delivery of specialized helping services, but this expansion should take into account the unique characteristics and situations of persons from diverse populations.

Teaching

The teaching function is not typically considered a part of "regular" helping functions. Helpers, however, teach through techniques such as modeling, interpretation, demonstration, and bibliotherapy. In concert with the reasoning throughout this chapter, teaching methods used with diverse populations must be uniquely adapted to them. Some "teaching-in-counseling" activities that can be readily adapted include use of literature (e.g., bibliotherapy), role-playing, visual media (e.g., discussion of current films), and experiential activities. Our students particularly enjoy developing these types of activities because they believe that such activities "liven up" the counseling process. Of course, teaching persons how to gain and evaluate cultural knowledge, investigate diversity literature, and use specific behaviors to increase sensitivity also are applicable to direct service work with persons from diverse populations.

EVALUATING FUNCTIONS FOR USE

These eight functions are all *potentially* useful for helping persons from diverse populations. The word *potential* must be emphasized because a particular function will not necessarily be appropriate or helpful for all people. Indeed, some of the preceding chapters have provided specific examples of functions that would have little or no utilitarian value for persons from some diverse populations. The appropriateness, and therefore potential for success, of any of these functions for a given population may be evaluated relatively easily by considering some fundamental questions:

1. Is the counseling function *feasible* for use with the person(s) in question? Our students often think, at least initially, that they can or

will be able to perform any counseling function. But the important question is, *can* the function be implemented? If not, the evaluation process stops here. An affirmative response, however, raises another question.

2. Is the counseling function *necessary*? Feasibility alone is insufficient justification for application of an intervention. Definable need(s) and goal(s) must be established. Again, a negative response stops the evaluation process while an affirmative response raises another question.

3. Is the counseling function *cost-effective*? A particular function may be feasible, desirable, and necessary, but its implementation cost(s) may far exceed its potential benefits. This often is a difficult concept for counselor trainees to grasp because they have so little experience with the financial aspects of the provision of counseling services. Nonetheless, it is an important point to consider. A negative response to this question implies either termination of the helping process or reevaluation of the second question. Of course, an affirmative response suggests that the function should be implemented.

Other questions that must be considered if a function is to be implemented include: Is the function desirable? Is it potentially harmful? Is it the best strategy in the context of the overall approach? These are difficult questions and ones that require extremely careful consideration before final answers are determined. Effective preparation programs provide helping professionals with the skills and knowledge necessary to come to effective answers to these questions.

COMPONENTS OF A TRAINING PROGRAM

Preservice and in-service training programs for helping professionals who intend to work with persons from diverse populations must encompass a multitude of dimensions and experiences. There are, of course, complex interactions among these dimensions and experiences; however, it is more convenient to describe a desirable training program in terms of its major components: knowledge acquisition, attitude awareness, experiential interaction, and skill development. These components are related integrally in actual practice, but they are separated here for discussion clarity.

Knowledge Acquisition

A strong cognitive base is an acknowledged foundation for the helping professions (Vacc & Loesch, 2000). Indeed, a helping professional must be well grounded in the cultural and/or sociological characteristics of diverse populations (Arrendondo et al., 1996; Arrendondo & D'Andrea, 1995; D'Andrea et al., 1991; Holcomb-McCoy & Myers, 1999). What are their unique personal and situational characteristics and attitudes? What are their identifying characteristics? What are their lifestyles? Are there common personality traits? What are the within-group similarities and differences? A helping professional needs to be informed of the group's normative and idiosyncratic behaviors. Do they have unique speech patterns or specific vocabulary? What are their common gestures, facial expressions, or body movements?

If effective interaction with persons from diverse populations is to be achieved, helping professionals also must be familiar with the sociopolitical functioning within each population. Who are the leaders? Which persons are held in the greatest respect? More important, *how* and *why* are these persons influential? With regard to direct contact helping functions (e.g., individual or group counseling), helping professionals must be knowledgeable of preferred modes of interaction (Arrendondo et al., 1996; Pedersen, 1996). What helping techniques have proven effective? Which have been ineffective? Which are yet untried or unevaluated?

Finally, the helping professional needs a thorough knowledge of professional ethics as well as the informal ethics (i.e., moral guidelines for behavior unique to a group) within the diverse population (Casas et al., 1986). In what ways are they similar? In what contexts would they come into conflict? This type of knowledge will largely enable helping professionals to avoid situations that are both personally and professionally compromising.

Attitude Awareness

Attitude awareness is especially important for working with persons from diverse populations (Arrendondo, 1999; Ibrahim, 1991; Steenbarger, 1993). Such awareness includes personal as well as general attitude awareness about a diverse population and its members. Our students find these discussions intriguing, particularly as they explore and become aware of their own perspectives. Emphasis is typically based on an assumption of attitudinal differences between helping professionals and clients in cross-cultural situations. If such differences exist, they may interfere with the helping process. Given the need for professional preparation in terms of attitude awareness, the question then becomes of which attitudes should the helping professional be aware? For our purposes, five types of attitudes are most important.

The helping professional's attitude about self. The importance of effective knowledge of this attitude is based on a fundamentally simple premise. Helping professionals who are able to assess and evaluate themselves accurately generally are more effective in helping others because they are aware of how their attitudes affect their helping activities (Arrendondo, 1999; Nwachuku & Ivey, 1991; Weinrach & Thomas, 1996). If a helping professional is aware that she or he holds a particular prejudice about a particular group, he or she may be able to avoid situations in which that prejudice will influence the helping process.

The helping professional's attitude about the diverse population. Helping professionals must be aware of their potential biases if they are to be able to work effectively with persons from diverse populations (Weinrach & Thomas, 1996). Such awareness enables the helping professional to be authentic, a characteristic generally understood to be necessary for competent helping in any context. Further, it enables helping professionals to compare their attitudes about the diverse population with their attitudes about themselves. This comparison then provides a framework from which to approach their helping activities or, if the differences are too great, to move toward client referral.

The population group's attitudes about helping professionals. Perceptions of the worth and value of the helping process (as typically conceived) vary greatly across diverse populations. Some people readily enter into the helping process, while others do so only if forced. Development of awareness of such attitudes is essential for the helper, particularly in the initial stages of the helping process.

Society's attitude about the special population. Particularly important in this regard are stereotypes. Which characteristics of the diverse population are typically stereotyped? What validity, if any, is present in the stereotypes? How do such stereotypes relate to, or affect, peoples' behaviors? Which of society's attitudes about the population are evolving or changing? What characteristics of the population seem to be the basis of stereotypes? Answers to questions such as these give helping professionals a clearer perspective on the society in which a particular population exists. This perspective should, in turn, enable helping professionals to understand some of the "realities" of the people within the group, thus facilitating the helping process.

The diverse population members' attitudes about themselves. What do members of the diverse population perceive as their positive and negative characteristics—their self-perceived strengths, weaknesses, assets, and liabilities? What is the nature of their collective self-concept? How do these attitudes interact with those identified previously? Finding answers to questions such as these also enables the helper to better understand the nature of a particular group's "real" world.

The establishment of a comprehensive knowledge base and the development of valid attitude awareness are essential for effective preparation of helping professionals who intend to work with diverse populations. Thus, they serve as the basis for the third preparation component, experiential activities.

Experiential Activities

An effective preparation program will provide helping professionals with a broad set of experiences with diverse populations (Arrendondo et al., 1996; Dinsmore & England, 1996; Whitfield, 1994). These experiences are important because they allow trainees to validate their own knowledge and attitudes. They also promote appreciation for diverse lifestyles and have the subtle benefit of allowing people from diverse populations to interact with potential helping professionals. Thus, experiential activities play a significant role in the preparation process by benefiting both trainees and persons from diverse populations.

The most obvious experiential activity to be incorporated into a training program is direct interaction with a particular population, including both formal and informal interaction. Formal interactions might include attending meetings or other "structured" social events such as a worship service, public or private ceremony, or workplace where there are likely to be large collections of members of a particular group. Informal interactions might include visiting typical homes and social gathering places or engaging in casual conversations, leisure activities, or social events. Trainees should note the environment, social and familial atmospheres, and behaviors present in order to supplement their impressions of the lifestyles of the particular diverse population.

Another important set of experiences is for trainees to interact with other groups that have reason to interact with persons from a particular population. For example, one way for a trainee to understand group A better is to interact with members of group B (e.g., another diverse population group) known to interact frequently with members of group A. Dynamics similar to those investigated through direct contact should be investigated and again in both formal and informal ways. Observation of how the diverse population is perceived and received by members of other groups enables trainees to gain further appreciation and understanding of the life circumstances of the population of particular interest.

While these experiences add significantly to the preparation of helping professionals, in any preparation program only a relatively limited number of experiences is possible. Accordingly, these experiences should be selected carefully and developed so that maximum benefit is achieved (Arrendondo et al., 1996; Sue et al., 1992). At the same time, helping trainees should be cautioned against overgeneralization from very small samples and encouraged to continue such activities throughout their careers.

A strong knowledge base, attitude awareness, and experience assist helping professionals in their professional interactions with persons from diverse populations, but even they are not enough. A professional must have specific, identifiable skills.

Skill Development

A major portion of the professional literature in the helping professions is devoted to the theoretical development, practical application, and subsequent evaluation of a variety of helping skills. Indeed, this is the heart of counselor preparation. These processes have led to the identification of a large number of such skills; however, they also have fostered considerable debate concerning what constitutes basic helping skills, particularly for use with persons from diverse populations (Arrendondo, 1999; D'Andrea et al., 1991; Nwachuku & Ivey, 1991). At best, the resolution of these debates seems to be that the basic skills are what any particular author believes them to be. The ones presented here are no exception. It also is important to remember that the skills themselves are not unique. Rather, the ways they are used with particular individuals are unique. Accordingly, the following skills should be evaluated carefully for their use with persons from various diverse populations.

Active listening. Numerous authors hold that active listening skills, sometimes known as facilitative responding, are at the heart of helping. Included in this category are verbal interaction skills such paraphrasing, reflecting feelings, summarizing, questioning, and clarifying.

Helping professionals also should receive training in "helping approach discrimination" (i.e., deciding which skills to use in any particular circumstance) so that they will be able to use an appropriate approach with a given individual. For example, counselors (at least) need to know when to ask a question, when to make a statement, and when to be silent.

Individual and group appraisal. Individual and group measurement and evaluation skills also are among the commonly cited basic helping skills. The considerable debate surrounding the validity of appraisals made on persons from diverse populations suggests that helping professionals should receive preparation in the selection, administration, and interpretation of standardized tests, including cognitive ability, interest, and personality measures. In addition, they should receive preparation in the use of unobtrusive measures, behavioral observations, self-reports, and structured interviews. For many diverse populations, these latter types of appraisal may be more appropriate. Failure to provide thorough training in both types could seriously limit helping trainees' eventual professional effectiveness.

Vocabulary adjustment. A third basic skill in which helping professionals should be trained is vocabulary adjustment. A societal group will have elements of speech and/or dialectics best interpreted in the context of the group. Effective helping professionals learn this specialized vocabulary and associated dialectical patterns, and use this knowledge to alleviate communication difficulties. Similarly, nonverbal communication behaviors and their associated interpretations often differ dramatically across societal subgroups. Effective helping professionals learn of the idiosyncrasies of a group's nonverbal communications and use the information to improve communications with members of the societal group. Because nonverbal communication constitutes a great proportion of human communication, our students find learning new aspects of nonverbal communication to be both fun and exciting, particularly in regard to how their nonverbal behaviors are understood (or not understood) by others.

Confrontation. As a counseling skill, confrontation may be defined as the act of pointing out discrepancies between a client's thoughts and behaviors or as the inherent contradictions in the client's reasoning. Use of confrontation is potentially dangerous in any helping relationship, and in particular with persons from diverse populations, because of the great possibility for misinterpretation. Using confrontation skills effectively is difficult for several reasons. First, it at least temporarily places the counselor and client in an adversarial position. Second, it often raises a client's feelings of defensiveness and withdrawal. Third, some helping professionals interpret confrontation as license to be aggressive and punitive. For these reasons, confrontation is a common cause of premature termination of a helping relationship. At the same time, confrontation is an extremely powerful method of bringing about change within a helping relationship. Accordingly, helping professionals should have careful and thorough training in the use of confrontation, in particular for its use with persons from diverse populations.

Effective training in these basic skills should allow helping professionals to be at least minimally competent in their helping efforts with persons from different backgrounds. These are, however, only *basic* skills. Other skills specific to particular diverse populations, such as use of titles in addressing people or touching, also should be included in the preparation process. Space does not permit discussion of all these other skills, save acknowledgment of their importance to effective training of helping professionals. Suffice it to say that professional preparation is a lifelong process, although it need not be a difficult one.

EXPERIENTIAL ACTIVITIES

Acquiring Knowledge about Diverse Populations

A careful reading of this book is a first step toward establishing such a knowledge base. Use of computer-based technologies is another good tactic. Following are activities that might be used to facilitate learning about diverse populations.

1. Select a diverse population of interest. Do an Internet search using the name of the diverse population as the key word. Follow links of interest to find what is available for knowledge enhancement. Next, do an Internet search to learn about the "country of origin" for the diverse population selected. Look specifically for information about the social, cultural, and political heritage of the diverse population selected. Many of our students subsequently enjoy doing a similar investigation of their own heritage, thus considering themselves as members of a diverse population.

2. Assume that you have the opportunity to interview representatives of a diverse population of interest to you. Develop a set of ten interview questions.

3. Assume that you have been asked to describe a given diverse population to a class of fifth-grade students. Prepare a ten-minute presentation to fulfill this request.

4. Identify a particular diverse population. Write a paper, complete with references, defending the use of a particular helping orientation with persons from that group.

5. Assign each person in a group to be representative of a different population group. Conduct a mock United Nations activity by having the representatives create a plan for the worldwide enrichment of the human condition. Identify the major problems and concerns to be considered and formulate a document of resolution.

6. Select any two diverse populations and interview three or more persons from each group about their attitudes about the other population. Develop a set of at least four questions about how their attitudes affect intergroup behaviors to ask the representatives of each population.

7. Select any diverse population group and interview three or more persons from it about their attitudes about helping professionals and/or counseling processes.

8. Create a *self-attitude awareness* activity that you think would be effective for use with members of a particular diverse population group.

9. Contact a faculty member at a college or university in another country and ask that person for assistance in establishing electronic communication with an E-mail pen pal in that country.

10. Interview a helping professional who is a member of a particular diverse population group. Inquire about the professional problems and issues the professional most frequently encounters in helping activities.

Supervised Practice as Preparation

The latter portion of the preparation process is supervised practice in helping relationships with persons from diverse populations. Note that these activities should be used only after participants have successfully achieved a good knowledge base and basic interaction skills for work with members of diverse populations.

1. Read the article by Kiselica (1991). Discuss the points made in the article. How could the experience be improved?

2. Have one person role-play the part of a helping professional and another person the part of a person from a diverse population. Have

a third person serve as an observer. Role-play for approximately five minutes a situation in which the diverse-population member is experiencing verbal abuse (taunting, derogatory comments, etc.) from a member of another population group and is seeking help for how to cope with the verbal abuse. Afterward, critique the activity. Change roles in the triad and repeat two more times. Our students particularly enjoy talking about which was the "most effective" approach exemplified in these triadic role-plays.

3. Have one person role-play the part of a helping professional and several other persons role-play the parts of people from a given diverse population. Simulate a group helping session for approximately twenty minutes in which the group members are angry about apparent discrimination by a college or university professor toward members of their population group. Critique the simulation. Change roles (i.e., of the helping professional) and repeat as time allows.

4. Prepare a review of a book focused on multicultural counseling, such as Pedersen's (2000) *Handbook for Developing Multicultural Awareness,* McFadden's (1999) *Transcultural Counseling,* or Lee's (2002) *Multicultural Issues in Counseling: New Approaches to Diversity.*

5. Solicit volunteers from various diverse populations. Role-play the part of a helping professional working with them.

These culminating activities should allow helping professionals to put into practice all that they have learned from their previous learning experiences. However, they are not the endpoint of preparation for a helping professional truly intending to be highly effective in helping persons from diverse populations.

CONTINUOUS PREPARATION

Successful completion of a fully developed and effectively implemented preparation program should result in a helping professional with adequate competencies to undertake unsupervised professional interactions. For many professionals, however, preservice or in-service training terminates the preparation process. On the other hand, fully competent, highly dedicated helping professionals continue the preparation process across their professional life spans through additional training. Additional training should provide for extension and improvement in all the preparation areas: knowledge acquisition, attitude awareness, experiential interaction, and skill development.

CONCLUSION

Regardless of whether a helping professional believes that *any* carefully and skillfully used counseling approach or that *only* specialized and individually tailored counseling approaches are necessary to effectively provide help to members of diverse populations, a strong knowledge base about special populations and well-developed counseling skills are crucial. In particular, effective helpers must be knowledgeable and skilled in individual, group, and vocational counseling, assessment, consultation, research, and specialized activities such as teaching. Helpers effective in working with members of diverse populations receive foundational training in counselor preparation programs that provide a substantive knowledge base, foster self- and other attitude awareness, include educational experiential activities, and promote skill development. They also continue to develop their knowledge and skills after initial preparation. Effective helpers know their clients well, know which skills to use and when to use them, and get better in working with members of special populations throughout their professional careers.

REFERENCES

Arrendondo, P. (1999). Multicultural counseling: Competencies as tools to address oppression and racism. *Journal of Counseling and Development, 77,* 102–108.

Arrendondo, P., & D'Andrea, M. (1995, September). AMCD approves multicultural counseling competency standards. *Counseling Today,* pp. 28, 32.

Arrendondo, P., Toporek, R., Brown, S., Jones, J., Locke, D.C., Sanchez, J., & Stadler, H. (1996). *Operationalization of the multicultural counseling competencies.* Alexandria, VA: American Counseling Association.

Atkinson, D.R. (1994). Multicultural training: A call for standards. *Counseling Psychologist, 22* (2), 300–307.

Campbell, N.K., & Hadley, G.B. (1992). Creating options: A career development program for minorities. *Journal of Counseling and Development, 70,* 645–647.

Casas, J.M., Ponterotto, J.G., & Gutierrez, J.M. (1986). An ethical indictment of counseling research and training: The cross-cultural perspective. *Journal of Counseling and Development, 64,* 347–349.

Cayleff, S.E. (1986). Ethical issues in counseling gender, race, and culturally distinct groups. *Journal of Counseling and Development, 64,* 345–347.

Conley, J.C., & Conley, C.W. (1991). *Consultation: A guide to practice* (2nd ed.). New York: Pergamon.

Council for the Accreditation of Counseling and Related Educational Programs (CACREP). (2001). *Accreditation procedures manual and application.* Alexandria, VA: CACREP.

D'Andrea, M., Daniels, J., & Heck, R. (1991). Evaluating the impact of multicultural counseling training. *Journal of Counseling and Development, 70,* 143–150.

Das, A.K. (1995). Rethinking multicultural counseling: Implications for counselor education. *Journal of Counseling and Development, 74,* 45–52.

Dinsmore, J.A., & England, J.T. (1996). A study of multicultural counseling training at CACREP-accredited counselor education programs. *Journal of Counseling and Development, 36* (1), 58–76.

Egan, G. (1994). *The skilled helper: A problem-management approach to helping* (5th ed.). Pacific Grove, CA: Brooks/Cole.

Fontes, L., & Thomas, V. (1996). Cultural issues in family therapy. In F. Piercy, D. Sprenkle, J. Wetchler, and associates (Eds.), *Family therapy sourcebook* (2nd ed.; pp 256–281). New York: Guilford.

Holcomb-McCoy, C.C., & Myers, J.E. (1999). Multicultural competence and counselor training: A national survey. *Journal of Counseling and Development, 77,* 294–302.

Ibrahim, F.A. (1991). Contribution of a cultural worldview to generic counseling and development. *Journal of Counseling and Development, 70,* 13–19.

Ibrahim, F., & Arrendondo, P.M. (1986). Ethical standards for cross-cultural counseling: Counselor preparation, practice, assessment, and research. *Journal of Counseling and Development, 64,* 349–351.

Kiselica, M.S. (1991). Reflections on a multicultural internship experience. *Journal of Counseling and Development, 70,* 126–130.

Lee, C.C. (2002). *Multicultural issues in counseling: New approaches to diversity* (3rd ed.). Alexandria, VA: American Counseling Association.

Leong, F.T.L., & Kim, H.H.W. (1991). Going beyond cultural sensitivity on the road to multiculturalism: Using the intercultural sensitizer as a counseling training tool. *Journal of Counseling and Development, 70,* 112–118.

Locke, D.C., & Kiselica, M.S. (1999). Pedagogy of possibilities: Teaching about racism in multicultural counseling courses. *Journal of Counseling and Development, 77,* 80–86.

Loesch, L.C., & Vacc, N.A. (2000). Testing and counseling. In D. Capuzzi and D. Gross (Eds.), *Introduction to counseling* (3rd ed.; pp. 215–234). Boston: Allyn and Bacon.

McFadden, J. (1996). A transcultural perspective: Reaction to C.H. Patterson's "Multicultural counseling: From diversity to universality." *Journal of Counseling and Development, 74,* 232–235.

McFadden, J. (1999). *Transcultural counseling* (2nd ed.). Alexandria, VA: American Counseling Association.

McRae, M.B., & Johnson, S.D., Jr. (1991). Toward training for competence in multicultural counselor education. *Journal of Counseling and Development, 70,* 131–135.

Midgette, T.E., & Meggert, S.S. (1991). Multicultural counseling instruction: A challenge for faculties in the 21st century. *Journal of Counseling and Development, 70,* 136–141.

Nwachuku, U., & Ivey, A.E. (1991). Culture specific counseling: An alternative approach. *Journal of Counseling and Development, 70,* 106–111.

Patterson, C.H. (1996). Multicultural counseling: From diversity to universality. *Journal of Counseling and Development, 74,* 227–231.

Pedersen, P. (1996). The importance of both similarities and differences in multicultural counseling: Reaction to C.H. Patterson. *Journal of Counseling and Development, 74,* 236–237.

Pedersen, P. (2000). *A handbook for developing multicultural awareness* (3rd Ed.). Alexandria, VA: American Counseling Association.

Pedersen, P.B., & Ivey, A.E. (1993). *Culture-centered counseling and interviewing skills: A practical guide.* Westport, CT: Praeger.

Ponterotto, J.G., Alexander, C.M., & Grieger, I. (1995). A multicultural competency checklist for counseling training programs. *Journal of Multicultural Counseling and Development, 23* (1), 11–20.

Ponterotto, J.G., & Casas, J.M. (1991). *Handbook of racial/ethnic minority counseling research.* Springfield, IL: Thomas.

Ridley, C.R., Mendoza, D.W., & Kanitz, B.E. (1994). Multicultural training: Re-examination, operationalization, and integration. *Counseling Psychologist, 22* (2), 227–289.

Sharf, R.S. (1997). *Applying career development theory* (2nd ed.). Pacific Grove, CA: Brooks/Cole.

Sodowsky, G.R., & Plake, B.S. (1992). A study of acculturation differences among international people and suggestions for sensitivity to within-group differences. *Journal of Counseling and Development, 71,* 53–59.

Steenbarger, B.N. (1993). A multicontextual model of counseling: Bridging brevity and diversity. *Journal of Counseling and Development, 72,* 8–15.

Sue, D.W. (1996, Winter). ACES endorsement of the multicultural counseling competencies: Do we have the courage? *ACES Spectrum,* pp. 9–10.

Sue, D.W., Arredondo, P., & McDavis, R.J. (1992). Multicultural counseling competencies and standards: A call to the profession. *Journal of Multicultural Counseling and Development, 20,* 64–68.

Vacc, N.A., & Loesch, L.C. (2000). *A professional orientation to counseling* (3rd ed.). Philadelphia, PA: Taylor & Francis.

Vontress, C. (1988). An existential approach to cross-cultural counseling. *Journal of Multicultural Counseling and Development, 16,* 73–83.

Weinrach, S.G., & Thomas, K.R. (1996). The counseling profession's commitment to diversity-sensitive counseling: A critical reassessment. *Journal of Counseling and Development, 74,* 472–477.

Williams, C.B. (1999). The color of fear and blue-eyed: Tools for multicultural counselor training. *Counselor Education and Supervision, 39* (1), 76–79.

Whitfield, D. (1994). Toward an integrated approach to improving multicultural counselor education. *Journal of Multicultural Counseling and Development, 22,* 239–252.

Index